BEYOND
— *the* —
SHADOW

MW01030933

To: SPENCER
5/16/14

Thank you!,
Blessings!.
Please enjoy!

Sam

SAM LIEN LE

BEYOND

the

SHADOW

A journey of a young boy to find life meaning through his own sufferings

TATE PUBLISHING
AND ENTERPRISES, LLC

Published by Tate Publishing & Enterprises, LLC
127 E. Trade Center Terrace | Mustang, Oklahoma 73064 USA
1.888.361.9473 | www.tatepublishing.com

Tate Publishing is committed to excellence in the publishing industry. The company reflects the philosophy established by the founders, based on Psalm 68:11,
"The Lord gave the word and great was the company of those who published it."

Book design copyright © 2014 by Tate Publishing, LLC. All rights reserved.
Cover design by Nikolai Purpura
Interior design by Gram Telen

Published in the United States of America

ISBN: 978-1-62994-452-4
1. Biography & Autobiography / Cultural Heritage
2. Family & Relationships / Death, Grief, Bereavement
14.02.06

Dedication

To my children and grandchildren for whom this life story is written with love and hope that they all will see their blessings in all circumstances and the rainbow beyond the shadow of their lives.

Acknowledgments

Poet Kikakou once wrote:

> "A blind child,
> guided by his mother,
> admires the cherry blossoms."

These three lines sum up my gratitude to the following beings whose love and support have made this work possible.

My dear wife, Tammy Le, who encourages and allows me time to work on this story.

Dr. Ray Striler, my former commander at the US Special Forces camp A-232, Tan-Rai, Lam Dong, Vietnam, who makes sure I am on the right track by, once a week, checking on my writing with a caring-commanding voice, "How many pages for this week, my little brother?"

My promise to him is to have the book done and laced with a bow for his birth day, December 21, and I did it. I could not have done it without his nudging and support.

Dirk Edmiston, my Toastmasters buddy and walk-mate, whose encouraging words are endless and effective.

Contents

Introduction

Once again, Lien Le will win the hearts of readers. First, in *Spirit Stills the Storm*, he invited us into his courageous journey to freedom in the memoir of his family's dramatic escape from Vietnam.

Now, in *Beyond the Shadow*, he immerses us into the life of Lin, a young boy coming of age in the turbulent years of war in North and South Vietnam of the 1940s and 1950s.

Historical background punctuates the drama surrounding his childhood years. *External* circumstances shape Lin's fate from the moment of his birth in a sam pan to a North Vietnamese fisherman's family who are hiding from French air-raids. Later the family flees as refugees to South Vietnam, and then lives under the constant shadow and inhumanity of war as the communist rebels and government soldiers increasingly clash.

However, *Beyond the Shadow* draws us into the *interior* story of a grieving young boy. After losing his beloved mother at seven, Lin endures years of terrible cruelty and severe beatings from a raging stepmother. He also feels such betrayal from his once kind father that he contemplates suicide in a longing to reunite with his mother's spirit. But knowing his little stepbrother needs his care prevents him from such action. "It's a simple thing that when one loves, one will not and cannot hurt the ones one loves."

This is also a story of hunger and longing. Many times, it's gnawing physical hunger from a stepmother who denies basic food. Even more, we vividly see a child's hunger for any signs of kindness, recognition, or scraps of love. Fortunately, little Lin absorbs such moments from others. Whether a kindly aunt who saves his life during a brutal bamboo beating, a caring couple who feed a famished Lin some fresh-caught fish and support his dreams of a high school education, or teachers and staff families at a poly technical institute who see his exceptional commitment to learn, his heart stays encouraged. Even brave. Such stories remind us how daily encounters with children offers important chances to extend love.

Lin also grows in hope, finding restoration in the transformative power of forgiveness. Beyond this, he eventually chooses to be thankful for earlier suffering because it forged his strong spirit and determination to give kindness to others. Lin exemplifies the Biblical idea "Let no root of bitterness spring up." For any reader who lived a troubled childhood, Lien Le's story offers gems of insight. For all readers, Lin's capacity to turn heartache into confidence provides a harbinger of hope in hard times. Despite hardship, he lives with a growing belief that with heaven's help, "good will emerge," and that "all things happen for a reason." When he is suddenly homeless at school because a house burns down, it opens the door to staying with a teacher who tutors him in English. This proves to be an enormous gift in his future life.

Along the way, we also gain glimpses into Lin's awakened spirit that finds simple beauty in moments of wonder. We see a land abundant with Eucalyptus and giant banyan trees, fresh mango, papaya and jack fruit, the universal fun of starring in a school play, the soothing cup of fresh green tea, the festivity and feasting during New Year village celebrations, and daily comfort when one lives with safe familial love and friendship.

To capture such a story, written in Lien's fluent second language, is truly remarkable. Enjoy this treasure!

—Linda Lawrence Hunt,
author of *Bold Spirit* and *Pilgrimage through Loss.*

Prologue

If you ever heard someone say "Things happen for a reason," or, perhaps at some time in your life, you have whispered these magic words to yourself, then this book, which happens to be in your hands right at this very moment, is for you.

You are wondering, *Who is he to make such a bold statement?* Fair enough a question that deserves a fair answer. I do say that with all sincerity and conviction from my heart, for it took me a long while—*yes, a long while, and I hope you know what it means a long while*—to understand it as I was awakened to find the light and the beauty beyond the pains, hurt, and the turmoil I had endured.

It all seems that one must go through the paradox of life to grasp the meaning why things happen the way they happened.

It is hard to imagine that at the age of seven, Lin lost his mother to an infection after giving birth to his sister. He had to endure the hunger, the hatred and the abusiveness from his ignoble stepmother to the point that his pain, his hurt was so intense and so unbearable that he had, at times, wanted to end his miserable life in the river behind his house so that he could be with his mother. However, Lin, through the wisdom of his elderly teacher Mr. Nguyen, found the reason for this suffering, reason for this brokenness, beyond which he saw the light, the beauty, and the meaning for his life.

Lin, at last, discovered that like an alloy of metal that must travel through the heat of an oven, it must go through the forging, hammering, and the molding from the hands of a blacksmith to become a useful tool. He, too, had to go through the hatred, the wickedness, and unkindness of his stepmother, who came into his life at a tender age so that he could find the meaning of his life.

All the tears, all the heartaches, all the darkness he experienced in the early years of his life have now transformed into crystal-clear light of blessings in which not only is he able to appreciate the life he is given but also capable to look at the one who caused his life so miserable and say, "Thank you for showing up in my life and made me who I am, a better person, a better human being, and that was the reason you came into my family to become my stepmother."

> I saw grief drinking a cup of sorrow and called out, "it tastes sweet, does it not?"
>
> "You have caught me," grief answered, "and you have ruined my business. How can I sell sorrow when you know it is a blessing?
>
> —Jalaluddin Rumi (1207–1273)

December 21, 1946

On the flat-surface water of the Black River, fifty-five miles north of Hanoi, Vietnam, under the shade of a broad canopy of an aged sycamore tree that leans outward from the bank of the river moored a small-curve roofed fishing sampan, nervously hiding from the French air raids under the clear-blue sky.

It was 4:15 p.m.

Lin was born. He cried his first cry, greeting the world right on the boat. No hospital. No doctor. No nurse. His father, a young fisherman, delivered him from his mother's womb and cut his cord. His father, a midwife, must be a good one, for he was in good shape. Later on in life, his father told him that it would be much safer for him to be born on the water than to risk everyone's life, exposing themselves to the air raids had he chosen to row his boat back to the village to get help. His life, as it happens, began on the murky water of one of the biggest rivers in North Vietnam that runs off from Mainland China. He was born at the time in which the Viet Minh (communist-nationalist revolunationaries) was at war with the colonial French.

May 7, 1954

The French was defeated at Battle of Dien Bien Phu, ending her colonialism, first in Vietnam, then throughout the French Indochina. As a result, Geneva conference stipulated the dividing of Vietnam in two parts, north and south, at the seventeenth parallel, with the north given the control to Viet-Minh as Democratic Republic of Vietnam and the south becoming the state of Vietnam under the governing of emperor Bao Dai.

While waiting for the general election to take place for the country, as postulated by to the Geneva conference, hundreds of thousand north Vietnamese fled to South by small boats, sea vessels, and a smaller number via French aviation, creating the biggest exodus of men, women, and children in the history of Vietnam. Lin and his family were among them.

February 10, 1955

After leaving the temporary transit camp in Saigon, his family along with many other refugees was transported to a woodsy area, a part of Tay-ninh province to settle, to build houses and to make everything into becoming a village. However, not too long of the new life here in the village came the death of his mother due to an infection. His dad pioneered another move, along with a few of his friends, to a village by the Krong Ana River in the central highland, hundreds of kilometers away, to start a new life for his family. After all, he is a fisherman; he must go where there is a river and where there is fish.

Then his father remarried; his stepmother, a farmer who had never been married, had turned his childhood life into a broken and painful one.

Brutal Beating

"Dad, oh, Dad, don't hit me, Dad!"

"You worthless, you rotten rascal, I'm going to beat you to death; I will kill you," screamed his father from the top of his lungs as he hit the son.

"Dad, oh, Dad, please have mercy on me. Oh, God, help me," Lin, the boy's name, cried out loud every time the flat-shaped bamboo stick pounded on his skinny back, which curved at each stroke of the hitting from his father's rage.

The boy's trembled, broken words now soaked with tears as he was sobbing, pleading to his father. His crying words were lost to the cold, senseless power of the bamboo stick, gripped in his father's hands, which now swung high and low to his back, hitting his front and to his sides. The boy tried to shield, to cover his fragile, skinny, skeleton-like body with his short, tiny hands only to feel hurt and became numb at the striking of the bamboo. His aunt, who was standing from the side of her house, watching and seeing the whole drama from the side of her house, could not take it anymore. And from the top of her lungs, she screamed at his father, "Brother, stop your madness. You are insane! You are killing your son for no reason."

The beating finally stopped. But the pain, the hurt, the anguish inside the boy had climbed to the peak of numbness. He wanted to die, which he had thought of at times.

It all began in the evening when the sun was setting, gradually hiding behind the mountain at the west side of the village, casting the last rays of daylight onto the valley where the fisherman, the farmers have built their homes along both sides of the river that runs across the village. This was the time when the farmers would be coming home from their farming, the fishermen from their fishing on the river, and also it was at this time his father was coming home from his two-day fishing trip. The river was only a walking distance behind his house. He wanted to tell his father how much he had missed him while he was away fishing. He wanted to let him know how bad he had been abused and mistreated at home by his stepmother. He wanted to empty all of his horrible feelings to his father. But he was not fast enough to utter the words of his distressful feelings. He was outrun by his stepmother—a five-foot-nine, 179-pound, dark-tanned skin woman, who, prior to marrying his father, had won a sport competition in the village by carrying rice bags of 100 kilograms (210 pounds) each on her shoulders and to walk from a bus station to the warehouse's one-mile distance. She could walk five times faster than he could even run.

Whatever lies she told his father, whatever untrue the story she made up against him to cover up the inhumane things she had done on him while his father was away now worked very well for her because his father, without checking, without giving him a chance to tell his side of story, flared up his wrath, his madness, grabbed the bamboo pole, which was leaning against the dirt wall of his house, pounded repeatedly on his back, his side, creating the scene in the neighborhood.

His crying and his father's screaming rage along with the hollering from his aunt, his father's sister-in-law, brought about the commotion in the whole neighborhood of the fisherman's.

The adults and their children, some of them his friends, came over to satisfy their curiosity, to pity him, or to make sure his father would not commit a crime by killing his son. Maybe all.

Now that the beating was over, some of the adults were now asking among themselves: "what had happened?"

Some came to comfort the boy, who was sobbing uncontrollably for the pains and anguish he had suffered by saying, "My poor skinny child, I am so sorry for you. I wish I could do something, but I wish your mother were alive so that you would not have to go through this hell on earth." Were these the comforting words, or were they invisible spears and knives that twisted through his heart and brought more pains to his soul? He was not sure which, but it surely made him feel terribly miserable. He swallowed his tears that kept oozing out of his swollen eyes for he has lost his voice to cry. And if he did have his voice, he wouldn't. He couldn't cry because he was afraid that if he did, he might upset his father more, then the more beating would be coming on him.

Some elders came over to see his father, who now went inside the house, to express their concerns over his madness, his unreasonable judgment over his poor young son, a motherless boy.

One of the elders, whose voice revealed that of Mr. Bang, the father of his friend, said, "We know you are mad. But why? Did you ask your son whats and whys and if he had done anything wrong? Even though he did, don't you think you should not beat him almost to death as you did? Remember, he has lost his mother not too long ago. Do not make him feel like he has lost his father too. The old saying, '*May doi...banh duc co xuong, may doi di ghe co thuong con chong*' Unless one finds bones in a plain rice flan, one will never find love from his stepmother is now so true, Have mercy on your poor son, my friend."

He overheard this one-way conversation from the adults to his father inside the house. He did not hear anything from his father, which made his anguish climb to its peak. *Oh, Mother, why did you leave me? Why did you have to go? Why did you have to die? I want to go wherever you are. I missed your holding me, your caring for me, your love for me. Oh, how terribly do I miss you! Where can I find you, Mom?* He has asked these question millions of times ever since his mother died from an illness, an infection after giving birth to his sister.

It was early in the afternoon in a small village in Tay-Ninh province, a couple of days' travel from here. The sun was high on the cloudless, blue sky. The mango, the papaya, the jackfruit trees were standing still, bearing the hot sun, giving shade to a few lazy birds chirping inside the canopy of thick, green leaves. The sandy-grayish-colored ground was flat and lifeless; not even an animal roaming on the empty streets. He remembers now it was siesta time, and he was with his friends raking through piles of leaves, of dried grass, digging up holes in the field to catch crickets at the end of east side of the village. Cricket fights were his childhood thrills. He could let his energy, his attention, and his emotion spent on the fighting between the two male crickets. It does not matter what color the crickets are—black, yellow amber, or gray—as long as they are male. Boys, they fight! The winning fighting cricket sings his triumphant songs by rubbing his rugged wings to his victorious melodies while chasing his defeated opponent off the ring, a large, round bottom of a metal can. While his attention was on the raking and digging, a friend of his family came rushing to tell him that his mother had died. Stunned with the shocking news, he left the crickets; he left everything running home as fast as his skinny, little legs could possibly help him. Upon arriving home amid a throng of neighbors—men and women, elders and youngsters—what he heard were prayers in the air, very fervent, very intensive for the soul of his mother whose skeleton-like body was half-covered with a patched, moss-green blanket, lying motionless on the straw mat atop a bamboo bed. Little did he know that it was the beginning of his miserable life. Little did he know that his mother had left him for good to eternity.

The next day, he remembered the elders helped tie a band of the beige-white, coarse cloth on top of his head. It was a mourning sign of the death in the family. He wore that wherever he went, to the burial ground where the body of his mom lay in a wooden casket lowered in the ground. He wore it to the church where the mass was said on her behalf. He wore it to the school. He wore it faithfully from dawn to dusk, every day. Not to be funny, but he somehow liked it. It was different. It set him apart from the rest of the kids in the village, for he did not feel the impact of the loss of his mother, forever. Maybe he was too young to feel it; maybe because his mother was sick and being confined in bed for too long. The infection had taken the toll on her. No antibiotic was available anywhere in the region for her illness. She was losing her weight to her bones. He remembered lying in bed was her long, slim, and thin—like a magnified bamboo leaf taking a shape of a skeleton, motionless and sustained by a small bowl of cream of rice soup every day until the day she lost her battle for life. Her tiny body was wrapped in a piece of white linen cloth, placed into a plain, unstained wooden coffin, securely rested on the two carrying poles, one at each end of the coffin, and the four adult men helped carry her body to the burial ground. He was in full white coarse mourning garment, slowly walking behind the casket along with his dad and other relatives who were reciting prayers to God to have her soul rest with him in paradise and to say a final good-bye to her at her tomb. A white-painted wooden cross was erected at the end of the mound of the fresh, dark-gray dirt. It was the last time he saw his mom. A dark cloud hovering over the clear sky, he felt the raindrops, and his eyes welled up.

He had not completely felt the loss, the emptiness, the feeling of life without a mother until his father decided to move, along with many of his friends, to this village hundreds of kilometers away to start a new life as fisherman. He instinctively knew that he could no longer visit his mom at her grave site, which he had been doing regularly to pray for her, to talk with her spirit, and to pull the fresh green grass and other weeds off the grave.

Now, at this late hour into the night, he was sitting on the dirt floor against the wall in front of the house, his chin on his chest, hidden between his knees, like a lifeless stump, a decor item placed in front of some rich people's houses. The mosquitoes were all over his bare skin, sinking their needles in for his blood, but he was too tired to care, too hurt to fight them off. He wanted to be with his mom, and maybe, just maybe, this is a better way, shorter way for him to get to her. God could witness this miserably missing of his mother. He missed her so terribly! The crickets were now crying in every corner of the front yard of his house as if they were sympathizing his circumstance. A few bats were swooping up and down, wheezing over his head for mosquitoes, and he could feel their wings almost touching his ears, his face. He thought about the river behind his house. Maybe the current, the swelling water could help him quickly.

All he has to do is to go to the bridge, walks on the wooden plank by the edge of the bridge at the middle of the river where he knows is the deepest and the strongest stream of water whirling, churning underneath of the metal frame crossing the river. He would take a deep breath, and off he jumps deep into the water, and the current would take his skinny body, his soul to his mother, who is, he thinks, waiting for him somewhere in heaven.

He had thought about this bridge, this river, this jumping off into the water a lot lately. But he would miss his little brother, half brother, whom he loves so much that he would take him to school with him in the morning, in the afternoon. Who is going to play with him if he dies and gone? He loves his baby brother so much that he feels he should not die, should not leave him. In his young mind, the mind of a eleven, going to be twelve years old boy, he simply knows the simple thing that when one loves, one will not and cannot hurt the ones one loves. And besides all else, he is a good swimmer. He would ask himself a question such as, how can a swimmer die from jumping off the bridge? It is impossible. It could only happen for those who do not know how to swim. And for him, someone needs to tie a rope around his body, his hands and feet in one bundle, and roll him off like a boulder, and then he will die. But this is going to be too much work, and everyone will know his plan. Besides, as long as his legs and hands are free, he will swim and will not die.

It was quiet inside his house. The oil lamp on the table by the door cast a faint weak light into the room and to the front entrance, which was wide open. He wanted to go inside, but he was not sure if his parents were asleep. He did not want to make any noise that would get him into trouble. He was dead tired and felt hungry but decided not to go into the kitchen, for he was still hurt and distressed. He still could not figure out why his father was mad at him, beat him as if he wanted to kill him. What did his stepmother tell him to trigger his rage? Would he ever find out? Now he felt hopeless. He felt miserably abandoned. He was hoping that his father would come out and hold him and take him inside. But it was just a plain far-reaching hope. He now really missed those good old days, going fishing with his dad, just the two of them on the boat, an oared boat. His dad would cuddle him inside his strong naked dark-skin, weather-baked smelly arms at the end of the day into the night when his boat moored anywhere along the river, be it at a sandy beach or tied to the end of a tree branch that was grown out from the bank of the river. The simple meals of home-grown jasmine rice and freshly caught fish cooked right on the back of his boat brought their unforgettable delicious time together. He had never heard his father say that he loved him. But his arms said it more and louder than any words. An incident on the fishing trip on the same boat at the beginning of last year proved it even more. The three of them, father and son and his stepmother, were on a three-day-fishing trip. The boat was moored at a shallow beach at the end of the fishing day. He was inside the boat, which was covered with a curve bamboo-framed roof, and fell asleep. Somewhere in the middle of the night, he was awakened and wide awake at a very strange thing that was happening. His dad held him tight to his warm chest; a firm squeeze in his father's arms he felt. His father's chin rested on his head, and he could feel the soft normal inhale, the exhale warming his forehead from his dad's nostrils. But his stepmother was not on the boat. Instead, to his shock, he could not believe his eyes because, through the opening at the end of the roof, under the faint, fuzzy light of the crescent-shaped moon, he saw her outside, tall-figured, standing knee-deep in the slow-running water, crying her heart out, bellowing and sobbing. God only knows what had happened on the boat that night. He was too little, too young, to understand and to find out. Was there enough space for the three of them on the flat wooden surface, cushioned with a straw mat under the roof? Of course, there was! Were his dad's arms big enough to hold more than he could? Perhaps not. Lin was just simply confused, innocently confused. His young mind could never comprehend the situation that night on that boat. Was there a fight, an argument, a tug-of-war? If there was, he must have slept like a baby. All he knew was the knowing that his father was protecting him, and he felt the love that his father had for him. But now those feelings were gone, evaporated in the heat of the summer night. The beating, the rage, the abandoning are the reality. He resigned to his fate, the fate that goes with the saying from the mouth of everyone in the village: "*May doi...*unless one finds a bone." He, like a rejected hungry dog, cautiously, quietly dragged his aching body over the threshold of the front door, which was wide open, to the corner of the house by the wall. He then gingerly rolled himself inside a battered, beaten-up straw mat on the dirt floor. It was quiet and very late into the night. The opposite side was a large bed, where his parents and his little brother were sleeping. He could hear their snoring echoing in the empty quiet space of the night. He closed his eyes; his mind was too thick and tired to think. He quickly fell asleep.

He woke up the next morning to the cry of his little brother, Manh, who was next to him. He opened his eyes trying to pull himself up. But his body was aching, and his hands were stiff all bruised up. He noticed that his parents had gone to work in the field, and the front doors were shut close. He now realized that he had his work cut out for him too. That is to take care of his little brother and takes him to school with him. His teacher at the village did not mind having a baby student in his classroom. He, like many in the village, has compassion for Lin. The teacher understands the boy's situation and goes out his ways helping him out. He remembers one incident recently: his little brother made a stinky mess right inside the classroom. The air was fouled. The classroom became quiet. From the corner of his eyes, he noticed all the eyes of his friends were on him. They all felt sorry for him. He excused himself and took his baby brother out to the bank of the river where he, like a well-trained babysitter, washed, cleaned, and dried his little brother up. They both returned to the classroom afterward. Thanks to his teacher's kind heart that, despite all conventional rules, he tolerated and expressed his love in his own way, extending his hand to lift him out of intellectual poverty so that he could have a chance to continue his education in his village.

He held his brother to calm and to comfort him, knowing that his baby brother was hungry. He himself wasn't in the best shape of the world but pulled himself altogether to take care of his little brother. He looked at him and asked, "Hey, little bro, are you hungry?" He rubbed Manh's tummy with his fingers, tickling him.

"Yeah, yea." Manh smiled, made some funny sounds, as he looked at his older brother, begging. Lin was hungry too. He had nothing in his belly since the day before. He now let himself totally absorbed in loving and caring for his brother; he didn't have time to think about all the miserable things that had happened yesterday.

"Let's go, my little pet." That is what he called his brother. He sounded more like an adult, and he was not even twelve yet.

"I will cook you some soup and feed you." He grabbed his little brother's hand, and to the kitchen they went.

The charcoals began to glow as the boy scrapped out the ashes underneath the three-legged metal cooking stand with a bamboo stick. He rushed outside of the kitchen to a pile of dry branches, firewood, and dry leaves and quickly grabbed a handful of everything his hands could dig into and brought them inside, setting atop the amber glowing charcoal. Within minutes, the smoke began to float up into the air from the leaves. He bent his head down close to the charcoal and the leaves, gathered a deep breath, rounded his lips, his mouth, and gently blew into the pile of smoldering leaves. It took a few blows from his breath to the glowing charcoal, the leaves now turned into flames. Tears had started rolling down as the smoke got into his eyes, and the water began running from his nose. He looked pretty miserable but satisfied with the branches now caught on fire, and up was the flame. He quickly dried his face with the sleeve of his shirt on his arm. He stood up, reaching for a small cooking pot sitting on the smoke-blackened bamboo rack, which, with one end mounted on the bamboo wall, and the other hung by two bamboo strings, one at each corner off the ceiling. He filled half of the pot with water from a dark-brown, weathered ceramic water container sitting by the kitchen door, using a coconut-shelled ladle, which was hung on a pole by the water container. He set the pot on the three-legged stand, which now almost covered with more glowing flame than smoke. He added about ten large table spoonfuls of rice flour from the brown paper bag that his stepmother had bought from a grocery store on the other side of the river. He never measures anything in his cooking. He always guesses and then adjusts the amount of water and the amount of ingredients. He added a little salt into the pot and stirred the white, creamy floured liquid until it boiled and thickened. He removed the pot and set it on a bamboo stand adjunct to the outside wall of the kitchen so that it could be cool down faster, for he knew that his brother was very hungry and impatiently waiting to be fed.

The aroma of the thickened soup made his hunger crawled up to the roof, but he needed to tender his baby brother. While his brother was enjoying the food, he also helped himself some leftover food of white rice and boiled green mustard, sprinkled with grains of coarse salt, which were left in the pot inside the smoke-blackened wire cage inside the kitchen.

He is resigned and used to leftovers and not-full meals except whenever he was alone on a fishing trip with his dad, or when dad was at home. A meal at home without Dad would mean he was not supposed to eat more than he was allowed to. A glance, a gaze full of threat is enough to tell him to stop even thought he wanted more. But on the boat with his father, he could eat as much as he wanted, nice fresh-off-the-water fish, all kinds, from dark-skin mud trout to white big-mouth perches, full pot of rice for the two of them, and best of all, he cooked them too. His father, a simple man but a picky and almost-hard-to-please eater, is a lover of new-crop rice, the one just harvested from the field not too far from his house. His rice has to be cooked perfectly right, not too dry and not too pasty. He had to learn a hard way to become the right cook for his dad. One time on a fishing trip, it was time to prepare lunch. The boat was tied to a leafy yellowish-colored bamboo branch, cascading down from the bank of the river. The sky turned gray with dark cloud hanging low, and it started drizzling then turned heavier. The sounds of the raindrops falling on the roof of the boat, like music of the nature, always make him feel at ease and peaceful. He is addicted to this sound of music and is in love with watching the raindrops falling on the water of the river, splashed sometimes, but most of the times, gently became a part of the river. His dad was sitting in the middle of the boat mending his nylon fishing net while he was doing the cooking in the back the boat. Underneath of the roof was the cooking area, which consists of a rectangular metal tray, twenty by thirty, sinking down into a wooden box almost to the bottom of the boat. On the tray sets a metal tripod on which the cooking is done. While the boiling rice was at its final phase, he used a pair of chopsticks to stir up the rice, which was thickening, to make sure that the rice wouldn't get a chance to get burned at the bottom of the pot and to give the grains an equal amount of thickened cream before it got moved off from the tripod down to the front of the metal tray. It is where now the hot glowing charcoal and ashes are kept to give the rice pot the right amount of heat to bring it to its perfection before it gets served. He then placed the other pot with the fresh-cleaned cut-up perch they had caught earlier. He seasoned it, added water, and brought it to boil for fish soup. Never did he know that his father was watching every step, every move he made. His father must have noticed that he had a little too much water into the soup according to his standard and his taste. However, instead of telling him "Hey, son, you have too much water in the soup," he told him the opposite, sort of a trick, a trap, sarcasm perhaps. In his normal tone of voice, he said, "Why, so little water?" Was it a question? Was it a short cooking tip? An advice? Nonetheless, he immediately, obediently, innocently grabbed a white ceramic bowl by his side, reached over the side of the boat to fetch the water from the river only to feel his dad's right palm, slapping the side of his head. *Bang!* He could see millions stars in his head. He could feel the burning on the skin and the ringing inside his right ear. Child abuse? No, it is tough love from his dad!

"Dumb! You are so dumb," said his father, short but not sweet, and went back to his mending business as if nothing had happened.

His philosophy "Spare the rod, then spoil the child" is really in action here. He let his tears roll down on his cheeks, not from the smoke, which was floating up, trapped inside the roof, but from the love and hate for his dad. He knew in his heart that his father loved him but expressed in an anomalous, peculiar way.

The cry for more food from his little brother brought him back to reality. He emptied everything in the bowl for him, scraping clean from the pot, and his brother happily finished it. The sun has climbed up high in the clear-blue sky, shortening, narrowing the shadow of the tall, lush, green mango tree by the kitchen and the house. It was too late for the morning session of his school. He asked the little Manh, "Hey, little bro, we are late for school. We stay home today, okay?"

The little one smiled as if saying, "You deserve to stay home to take care of me, big bro."

Oh, how I love this kid. He is the reason for him to live and stay alive despite all odds against him. He looked at little Manh with loving eyes, full of care.

He remembered now the incident that had just happened in this very spot, in this very kitchen, which might have something to do with what happened yesterday evening. He is dead sure about it. His stepmother outraced him because she did not want him to have a chance to tell his father what had happened in this kitchen while his father was away on the fishing trip. Yes, he wanted to tell him the whole thing, the terrible thing that had killed his spirit, crushed his hope to continue his life.

It was noontime on a warm day. He got home from school, hungry. The roosters, the hens, and their baby chicks were enjoying, raking the soil for worms, for foods under the shade of the mango tree. A few birds were chirping, wheezing from branch to branch, flying in and out from the canopy of the long, slender, sun-glazing mango-leaves. He set his brother down to stand on the ground, went inside to get some food for himself and his brother. While standing outside of the kitchen, enjoying the first few bites of his food, charbroiled dried fish and white rice, then, out of the blue, maybe out from the blue sky on that cloudless day, or from nowhere appeared his stepmother, who must have come home from the field, unexpectedly. Her face was bright red like a ripened pomegranate in the hot summer sun, or from her angers, masked with beads of sweat. The front of her brown work shirt was partially wet from perspiration. She took off her conical hat, threw it on the ground, looked at him with the angry, gazing, popping eyes, like those of a wild beast hypnotizing, paralyzing her prey—like those of a big cat to her little helpless mouse. And in her high-pitched voice, full of hatred, she said, "You worthless monkey, what are you doing in my kitchen, eating my food? You know what? You don't' deserve to eat my food."

The boy was frozen in fear, motionless. He wanted to tell her that he hadn't eaten since the day before, and that he was hungry, but all he could utter the words, "Stepmother, child was—"

"Shut your stinky mouth." She cut him off, like a razor blade to his throat, letting no more words to come out of his mouth, and knocked him out with a final blow.

"Eat my shit! Drink my blood."

At that, he was terrified! He was petrified! The bowl escaped his trembling, shaking hands to fall to the ground. *Clang!* It shattered into pieces along with the white rice scattered on the dirt floor. His twelve-year-old tender mind could not comprehend such a language from a mother to a child. He could have run away to tell his father, his aunt, but didn't. He was knocked out, beaten dead emotionally. The hunger for food, the hunger for love—all went far away, beyond his reach. He broke down sobbing. He was afraid she might harm him, kill him, choke him to death, and throw his dead body into the river, and three days later, his body would float up somewhere down the stream like many half-rotten bodies found floating by the banks of the river throughout the year. She is physically giant and strong and shouldn't have any problems bringing his life to an end. As a matter of fact, a thought came to his mind that it would be better for him if she did just that to end this miserable life of his. But she took off. She left. She disappeared; as a ghost she came, as ghost she vanished, after bringing a quick but destructive, devastating storm into his life. Was it another type of torture? Another form of punishment she has just invented? But for what reason? He knows the size of his cot. He knows his circumstance and has behaved accordingly. He had never asked for anything other than an ounce of love from her. He had never disobeyed her orders nor had he ever argued, ever talked back to her. Couldn't she figure out the chores he did for the family, such as cooking, hauling water home from the river by having two tin cylinder-shaped containers, ten gallons each, dangling by a twine, on each end of a bamboo pole on his shoulder? Could she not understand that he had to go to school with on his back was her son, his half brother, whom he pours his heart out to love him? Could she ever understand that, besides all of his work, he had to do his home work at home, do study at school, and kept his grade high? He could not ever figure it out. He never felt from day 1 since she became his stepmother a touch of her love. He instinctively knew from the beginning that any gesture of love from her was not authentic, not genuine. Children do have natural ability, sensitivity to diagnose that. A child will know, will sense, will pick the love of an adult if it is genuine, and he, too, never felt that she loved him at all.

One night recently, he found himself plopped on the dirt floor in the bedroom, thinking maybe he had been walking in his dream, a walking dream, and somehow got off the bed, landed on the floor in the middle of the night. He did not pay one bit attention to that incident more than any misfortune, any unfortunate incidents in his young life. Like any typical family of the countryside in Vietnam, there are no individual family rooms; parents and children are on the same bed except married ones.

He was no exception. Children can be moved around, from one spot to another, while they are in their sleep as their parents wish, or as needed.

The second night after that incident, he was awakened by a push from her foot, and then one more harder merciless push; off the bed, he was falling onto the ground. It reinforces the feeling from him that she hates him. It brought him a naked, true realization, like a clear daylight, that she hated him from the get-go, from the beginning of her coming into his life, by her choice, to fulfill the prophecy to the life of a motherless child: "Until one finds."

There is a girl about his age in the village. Her name is Ve (pronounced: vae), whose mother had also passed away. Her father, Mr. Bao, had also been remarried. (He took the name of his first son, Bao, for no one knows of his real first name. It is customary in Vietnam that once a married couple has their firstborn child, their own first names given away to their first blossom of their love, by taking their child's first name and everyone calls them by that name.) Her situation was not any better than his. She was very short, skinny, and perpetually hungry, for her stepmother allowed her little or no food. She would go around the houses in the village, sneak into their kitchens (most of the houses do not lock their doors) for leftovers to cub her hunger.

A few times she was caught red-handed inside someone's kitchens, eating their foods, the leftovers, but no one wanted to bring charges against her. If the outsiders, the neighbors, the unrelated ones could extend such a kindness, a loving compassion to her, the one from the heart of one human being to another, then what was wrong with the one inside the household, namely, the mothers, the stepmothers?

Occasionally, the home owners, the hosts would let her have a meal with them, or they would say, "Oh, my poor child, eat some more, eat some more, for you will be hungry again." They understood what it meant to be a child without mother.

Now that his atrocious, ruthless stepmother had left, the quiet siesta time of the sunny afternoon returned to his surroundings. The chickens under the shade of the trees did not notice the human storm, the man-made conflict he had just gone through. They seemed careless about what went wrong with the human world, but to enjoy the chicken world of their own, the mother hen and her chicks. If one could notice, one would see the mother hen, with her feet, busily raking up the soil, the dirt, finding worms, bugs, and other chicken foods in the soil, and in her very hen-chicken voice, she lovingly called her babies to come for their meal. What a caring, loving gesture practice in a pet family! Lin couldn't help feeling envious even with the chickens! The mango tree could care less about the human turmoil, standing tall and straight under the hot sun, extending its hands and arms of green-purple leaves, forming a huge canopy and giving a cool shade to the others. He could not help wishing that his mother were alive so that he could enjoy the cool of her love and the shade of her protection. He just wanted to stand here, feeling in awe and letting himself absorbed in the kindness of the nature around him. He experienced firsthand that nature is love, is beauty and gentle, and he was deeply grateful.

Lin was now thinking about the national examination, which was coming up in about two months. If he could pass this crucial one, his future would be a world brighter. He could have a better chance to go to school in the city where public high school classes are offered, and they are available only in the city. Therefore, he would have a better chance to get out of his stepmother's grip. However, he is facing his world of reality, which makes him unsure and nervous. He now is thinking about his situation, his dilemma in which his family is too poor to fund for this once-in-his-lifetime experience in the city where the national examination will be taking place. It is the exam held in every major city around the country. Those who passed this exam will be proudly and joyfully advancing to the next level, namely, high school, and furthering their education.

He has no idea how much it is going to cost him for this event, from the bus ride with other kids in his class to and from the city to lodging and food for the three days of the exam. He prays and hopes that his father loves him enough that not only he is determined to foot the bill, even he has to borrow money to help him, but also keeps his wife out of this affair, keep her influence off the chart of his future. It is his only chance for him to have a better education and, ultimately, a better life. He understands his fate as well as the fate of all students who will be taking the exam that when they go for the exam, they take with them the pride of their family; they take with them the very hope from every member of their families. One can see the pressure being put on the students. It does not matter how good, how smart a student is; if he fails, it is a disgrace to him and to the family. There is no second chance until the following year, another exam, and no one could advance, could move to next grade until he has passed the examination. The national school system is set up that way for hundreds if not thousands of years. It is quite brutal and harsh in such a way that the ones who failed would not only have no chances until the following years, but also feel the pains of being a loser, carry the disgrace, and sometimes, out of shamefulness, commit a suicide. The suicidal rate is far more eminent involving students at the higher level of exams, such as those of high school and college students than those at his level. He is not concerned about that possibility, which is far off in the horizon. However, he felt the pressure, the weight on him.

Ba Thong, The Mother's Love

He decided to take his little brother to go down to the river to visit Mr. and Mrs. Thong who live on their boat and do their fishing on the river for living. They both deeply understand his circumstance and pour their hearts out onto him. Every now and then, he would come to see them at their boathouse and felt the love, the care, the tenderness they gave him and the warmth on their boat. It is not a big boat; in fact, it is rather long and narrow, twenty-feet-by-eight-feet wide, with a bamboo roof curving across the middle part of the boat, like a caterpillar on its back after a big meal, making it a living space for the two elderly soul mates. Mrs. Thong, her husband's first name, that's how everyone calls her for no one knows their last name, is an excellent cook. Her cooking is entirely different from anyone's in the village; simply, she is not from here. Her caramelized, simmered-cooked catfish is top of the world. The way she does it is different from his family and everyone else; she fries the fish lightly first, not to let the fish thoroughly cooked, then she would season it with her own ingredients, which includes salt, black pepper, fish sauce, and then add caramelized juice for color before cooking. Knowing that he is always hungry, she never fails to feed him, and he thoroughly enjoys her food. Mrs. Thong, in her late forties, and her husband, Mr. Thong, about ten years older, both came from somewhere he never knew, and he never heard anyone commented on the whereabouts before they came to live and fish on this river. They have an air of being an educated couple and rarely seen on the ground. But their boat is always moored at the sandy beach behind the village when they are home from their fishing trip. The rumors are such that they both practice martial arts, like the ones you see in the martial arts movie, and during one of their routine trainings, she had an upper hand and accidentally touched his jaw, busted his teeth. As a result, he is missing a few upper teeth, which make him older and funnier when he smiles. Rumor has its own life, no one could tell if it were true, and he never bothers to ask. They both love him like their own kid, and as a matter of fact, he does not know if they had any children, and he truly enjoys and embraces their loving care for him. Not only do they feed him with their food, but also their wisdom, their kindness, their words full of encouragement. They would always say to him, "We know and understand your circumstance, your situation. The only way to get yourself out of this is you get your education. You will pass your examination, and high school in the city is where you will go and begin your new life."

"Da, Ba Thong, chau cam on Ba," he would softly say to her, like a son to his mother. (Yes, Mrs. Thong, I will and thank you.) Yes, in fact, he felt the motherly love from this woman more than anyone else in his life in this village.

He saw their boat tied to a tall bamboo pole by the light-brown-colored sand beach as he was descending from the road. He ran on the sand with his brother on his back, wanting to get to the water as fast as he could for he felt the burning underneath his bare feet. He was running and jumping on the glaring, baking sand under the hot sun. He was not sure he was running that fast because of his wanting to get to the cool running water of the river, or to see his own mother in Mrs. Thong's loving care so that he could swim in her love. Maybe both. He thought of his own confusion. He finally got to the water and felt the refreshing coolness running up from the bottom of his feet. He loves this sand beach; he loves this river that brings life to his family and many others in this village. Water, rivers, and his life are inseparable, he thought. This river, K'rong Ana, named by the indigenous tribal people, runs from the mountains, from the hills very far away; he can't tell how far, but beyond his eyes could see. It passes through his village and downs through valleys beyond his imagination. Every year, he remembers, when it rains for nights and days, or the monsoon as they call it, the water rises and rises, and overflows the banks of the river, flooding all rice fields in the areas, flooding the farming hills, the cemetery. One year, the river grew into a sea, the sea of maroon, foamy, murky water floated his house and many houses in the village away to who knows where. All he knew it was the house his father had built with thick and big bamboo trunks, which had been soaked in the grayish-dark, thick mud by the river for months before turning them into poles for the house. It was such a painstaking process to treat the poles for months in mud for two reasons: one is to keep the bugs from eating, destroying it, and the other is to bring about the ebony look on the poles.

Yes, this river holds much of his childhood memories, most of which happy, some teary, and some painful.

Yes, on this river, an incident happened that he will never forget as long as he is alive. It brought the naughtiness of a young boy in him out into the day light on this water. It was an early morning; everything was quiet. There was a thin fog spreading, floating here and there atop the surface of the water. The sun was creeping up on the horizon, casting shadows of the trees along the bank of the river onto the still water like a mirror reflecting the fuzzy images of the trees. On his little wooden fishing boat, shaped like that of a canoe, with a single oar, he rowed it smoothly and quietly across to the other side of the river, where he had his fishing poles stuck deeply into the ground at the bank of the river the previous night. Actually they are bamboo sticks, about three feet long, slandered, tapered at the end, sunk deeply into the claylike soil at the bank of the river. At the end of the pole, where a twenty-four inches clear nylon line with a hook, baited with a worm, submerged its full length into the water—waiting.

When he was about ten yards to the poles, he could see the end of one of the poles being pulled down and then up, and then the side way, and then a splash, a mud trout fighting for his life, trying to get off the hook, jumping off the water into the air. Obviously, the trout was startled by the sound of a coming boat and tried to get away. After bringing his first catch on board, he went on to check the rest of his poles, and by doing so, he saw some poles that don't belong to him got fish too. A temptation! An invitation! He was debating, contemplating. It is a sin! He knew it, but he also wanted to impress his family, he father, and his stepmother. Not on a second thought, not to think any further, he looked around, making sure no one on the river was watching him, a young thief. He yanked the poles with the fish off the bank, off the water, and onto the middle of his boat. The fish jumped, glided, and made all kinds of noises audibly on the wooden planks while he was rowing his boat back home, thinking his parents would be very proud of him. Yes, indeed, his father, with a proud smile on his face, said, "Ca ngon qua, gioi that, con." (Oh, good-looking fish, good job, son.) Little did he know that his pride, his happiness was a very short one. A young man, the owner of those poles came to the bank of the river right after he had left and did not see his poles and must have seen him carry the fish home. He came to his house and caught him red-handed. His poles, his two catfish on the lines with the hooks were still on their mouths. One can imagine the punishment he got from his father, very severely. The shame, the guilt compounded, made a lifetime lesson for him: "Thou shall not steal," one of the commandments, and he violated the first time in his life.

As always, whenever Mrs. Thong sees him, she shows her joy and welcomes him with her smiles, as if she were waiting for him, as if she wanted to express the bond between a mother and her own child. This time was no difference. In fact, she got out from her roof when she heard him calling her name from a distance. "Ba oi, chau den them ba." (Mrs. Thong, I come to visit you.)

She stood up at the back of her boat, waiting for him to come. As soon as he let Mrs. Thong have his little brother, he quickly lifted himself up on the boat and joined her inside the roof. Once they were all inside, she looked at him very strange, staring at him for a long while, a minute or so; then she, in her soft, caring, loving voice, she told him that she had heard about the beating at his house last evening and felt sorry for him. His eyes were now welled up, and he let his tears roll on his cheeks. In his young mind, he wished that she would come forward, hold him, and told him, "Son, my dear son, I will protect you. Stay with me, I am your mother."

"Ba Thong," he told her, "I am deeply distressed, what should I do? My stepmother hated me to her guts. I don't think she wanted me to be around her in the family." He continued.

"I want you to hold yourself up, no more crying. Boys are not to be soft with tears." Those are exact words his own mother had told him when they, at moment of desperation, out of hope, were ecstatically united at the Gia Lam Airport, not too far from Hanoi, and together, catching the last flight to South Vietnam in 1954.

"Listen." Her voice was soft but firm full of gravity. "I want you to be strong and get ready for the exam. I will have a talk with your dad in a day or two. My husband and I have a small saving. He and I did talk about your circumstance, and you must, by all means, go for the test. The money will help you with the expenses on the road to your examination in the city. It isn't much, but every little bit helps. You will pass the national exam; your life will be different, and a better future awaits you outside of this village, son."

"Da, chau nghe loi ba." (Yes, I listen to you.)

He spent a little time with her on the boat, and of course, she fed him and his little brother too. He inquired about her husband, for he was not with her at the moment. She told him that he had gone to the city to do his personal business and that he would be back later in the evening. He left the boat after thanking Mrs. (Ba) Thong for feeding him and his brother. He then went home to get his books and off to school for the afternoon session.

While he was walking, he felt the joy inside him, which he had not felt that way before. He knew in his heart that if Mrs. Thong helps, his life shall be a whole lot better. It is just as simple as that. He trusted that feeling for it was so very real. She and her husband are educated people (he learned this when he heard people talk highly about them), and everyone in the village respected them; besides that, not many people in this village could read and write. He felt very comfortable and assured about his chance of going to the city for the exam, which he had been worried about. And God knows he had every reason to be concerned and to be worried because of the fact that if his stepmother would not let him have one bowl of rice, would not let him eat a full meal, how could she allow him go to the city on her money? How could she spend her money to buy his uniforms when she did not allow him wear a single pair of pants and shirt made from the coarse material, dyed from soaking in the dark-marooned liquid from the smashed tree barks? He is the one to go into the woods with a machete-like knife along with other adults to get the bark from a tree. He has no clues as to what the name of the tree whose sap is red like blood. All he knows the tree is very tall with a very large trunk. He could put his arms around it, press his chest against it, stretch his arms around it, but their fingers would never touch each other. He would swing his machete high in the air and, with all of his might, sink it down into the tree at an angle about forty-five degrees. He then repeats it at about five to six inches above the first chop, pries it really hard, and voila! He has his prizes, a basket load of barks to take home. He would smash it and let it sit in a large pot with water. He learns how to dye the fabric, the material for clothing by watching the adult do it. He did it for the whole family, and then one day, he soaked that yellowish yardage of coarse fabric his parents had bought to make the clothes for him. After many times, he put the material into the dark bloody-colored liquid and hung it out in the sun. It was a long process, but at the end, he had a hard sun-baked, stiffed-feeling piece of fabric that he would take to a tailor in the village, who would then turn it into a set of pajama-like clothes for him. What he did not know was a profound lesson he had learned, absorbed from the dyeing of his own fabric. It is the patience, a virtue that would help his life later on. One evening not too long ago, he put the new clothes on after the tailor had made it; he wanted to go to church, which he loves to do twice a day, morning mass, and evening rosary, with a new set of clothes only to be yelled at, screamed at by his stepmother. She told him to take it off. She told him he could only wear it on New Year's days. In tears, sobbing, he had to gingerly, slowly taking it off from his skinny body, as if savoring the sound of the stiffened material, as if lingering on the smell of the sun-baked, tree-bark-dyed clothes.

He's dreaming, day dreaming and imagining. He is, no kidding, asking for an impossibility, definitely. She is going to block it; she is going to fight it, and his chance will not happen. She is going to tell his father, regardless how much he cares for him, regardless how much he loves him, regardless how much he pushes for his education; her answer is going be a big no, but that will be changed. Ba Thong will help, and he will not disappoint her and his dad. His imagination stretches far to the city where he will be in high school; he will be studying under the light of an electric lightbulb, which gives light just like that of the daylight. How cool, he thought, for he has never had one in his life. He would have to wear uniform to school. But then, where is he going to stay? With whom? Life in the city is completely different than here. He went to the city with dad only once and felt alienated. People talked, dressed, behaved differently. He somehow felt intimidated. What about his little brother? Oh no! Who is going to play with him? Who is going to take care of him when he is not around? He is going to miss him. He now is vacillating. Maybe he should not go to the city. Maybe he should not take the exam at all so that he could have him any time, carry him, swimming with him, and taking him to school with him all the time. But the reality is that his stepmother would not leave him alone; she would find every chance she gets to make his life more miserable. He had made up his mind about the exam, about the city when his friends greeted him at entrance of the school. He had forgotten all the troubles the day before. He loves school and his friends. Thank god that he does not let the pains stay with him for a long time.

The day that would change his life was approaching. There were fifteen students from his school, the primary school of Giang-Son village to take the national examination, to be awarded the primary school diploma. All of his friends, boys and girls, dressed very nicely. New clothes, navy-blue pants, and white shirts. Each had some short of a suitcase to bring the belongings, the notebooks, the pens, the ink pot, and the list goes on. Perhaps, best of all, the money their parents gave them to buy food, drinks, and school supplies if needed.

He did not have much to carry on a five-day trip, of which three days of test, ranging from calligraphy to drawing, from mathematics to science, from literature to music. He did not have nice clothes, the money his dad gave him, mostly from Ba Thong, was barely enough for food, which was prepared right inside the school compound. He brought with him a notebook, a pen, an ink pot, and a ruler. That was all he had to go into the test. Everything else was inside him, and he was very content that he had that very chance for his life.

National Exam

The day he climbed on that bus along with his friends was a big day for him. His dad, his little brother on his arms, Mr. and Mrs. Thong, his aunt, and uncle were all out to see him off to the city to the grueling test, even for the kids. They wished him luck.

When the open-window, dark-yellow-colored bus rolled off on the dusty road, it left a cloud of dust whirling into the air behind. It bounced. It shook at each pothole. The bumpiness that made both of his hands grab tight to the rusted-metal hand bar in front of him until it got onto the main street, which was paved mostly with gravels and little asphalt. The air filled with burned gasoline made him sick and nauseated. He had forgotten how he felt the last time he went to the city with his dad. He wasn't sick for sure, as he reminded himself. Was he nervous? Yes, he had to admit. He felt like a fish from his river, long, wide, all freedom, moving, swimming, now being put in a little container, suffocated! He began to pray. It is his habit to call on God to help him with anything. His pastor, his teacher, his dad taught him that, and he loves to pray. He even asked his mom, in her spirit, to guide him in this special journey.

The bus now moved faster and smoother once it was on the main road to the city. The cold morning wind blew right through the windows, caressed his face, making him feel much better, no more nauseating, thank goodness. Every now and then the engine howled when the driver—a gray-haired, weathered, dark-skin middle-aged man—shifted the gear to climb the slopes, the hills, and there are a few of them before he got to the city. When the bus was passing the rubber tree plantation, he was amazed at row after row of the straight-lined, dull-beige-colored rubber trees leaving behind. It doesn't matter how slow, how fast the bus moves; it does not matter which side of the bus he cast his eyes, the lines are always straight, and the space between the lines is narrowing, tapering to the end, far away, one after another, as the bus continued to roll pass them.

At last, about an hour on the road, the bus reduced its speed, as it was entering the city of Banmethuot, one of the cities in the central highland of Vietnam. It is about one-day drive from Saigon, the capital of South Vietnam. One of the characteristics of this city is its color. The color of the soil, the dirt, the ground of this region is perpetually red, a maroon, dark-red-colored type of the soil. It is also a good soil, fertile soil. Is it because of its color? He doesn't know for sure. But it shows on the healthy-looking, broad green leaves of the banana trees around the houses. It shows on the tall mango trees with huge canopy of slandered-green leaves. It also displays on sizable green and light-yellow mangoes, in cluster of two, three or four, dangling on the vines in the air under the shade of the trees, making one's mouth salivated. The tall hedge of colorful hibiscus, the tall rose bushes, especially the red ones, they have to compete very hard to show their color off in this windy, dusty city. The half bottom of the walls of the houses here covered with red dust and red dirt makes one wonder how often the owners of these houses have to paint their houses. It would be a tough job to keep them nice and clean.

The driver, guided by a uniform guard, pulled his bus in front of a large building inside of the barbed-wire fence. It must be for a security reason that the examination is held here to protect the integrity of the test. Imagine a national test whose questions and topics were leaked out into the public? That would be a disaster. There were hundreds of kids on the ground, looking puzzled, perhaps intimidated, fidgeted, roaming in the open area inside the fence.

As he was descending from the steps of the bus, he could not help feeling nervous, sort of an anxiety, one might say. Now, he really felt like a fish being out of water! He tried to control this sort of feeling of intimidation in this strange place, of which a line of coiled barbed-wire fence, like that seen at a military compound, is closing in on hundreds of kids from different schools in the region. Where does he go from here? Which one of the rooms in this giant tin-roofed, brick-walled, one-story building he is going to stay? Where else and how far does he have to go for taking the exam? Question after question were rushing through his little mind, which he had no answers. The voices from his friends, talking, laughing, got him out of his own contemplating world:

"Let's go, Lin, you are as slow as a snail," one of his classmates said half-jokingly.

"Why so hurry?" he wanted to say it, but before he could utter the words, as kids would do, they pushed him off the last step onto the ground, which threw him off the balance. It took him a few seconds to gain his control and kept him from falling on his face.

As he was going to say something like "Rascals, behave or you are going to get yourselves into lots of troubles," the whirl of wind, full of red dust, blowing, whirling, covered everyone on the parking lot. It happened so quick that no one could get a decent cover, nowhere to run to, and when it was over, when the whirl of dust took off, passing over the fence, rushing to the housing area nearby, everyone was uniformly dusty red, as if they just came out of a giant powder machine that sprays color powder on them for decoration. Not to be funny, but they all, like monkeys, dusted their hair, their clothes with their hands. They jumped up and down to shake off the dust. The ones who suffered the most are those who wore white shirts. What a way to welcome them to the city! He thought.

After a roll call by one of the teachers (he assumes that because everyone addressed him "teacher"), he was assigned to a room with three other boys, none of them from his school, which made him feel sort of bummed out. What was reason for this, he was not sure. Maybe this was arranged by an alphabetical order of students' name. Maybe his fate, he thought.

There were a set of two bunk beds, made out of bamboo, one stacks on top of another. Each sets against a wooden wall in a room of twelve-by-twelve feet on a cement floor. In between the bed, sits a small, dark-stained wooden desk against the wall. The whole room was lit by a one hundred watts lightbulb, which was dangling on a two-feet electrical wire off the ceiling, casting a warm-amber light on the four souls, who now crossed their paths in this very room. Kids do not take long time to get to know one another, and it happens here. He got to know their names and from what school they came. By looking at their luggage, their clothes, he could tell he was not near close to their social class, but content that he was here to do what he needed to do for his tomorrows. Before the dinner, he pulled out his money to give to a man who was in charge to collect money for their lodging, food, and beverage. He was grateful that the money he had was just enough, thanks to Ba Thong and his dad. He did not plan to go anywhere outside of the facility for any reason, even shopping, for sure.

The evening came, and before going to bed while his friends were out looking for their friends, or hung around with them, Lin gathered his belongings and sorted out his notebook, pens, and pencils. He decided to work on his calligraphy before climbing on his bed, the one in the bottom, as he had told his new friends. His teacher at home told him that he should get very high marks for his nice and neat calligraphy, and he wanted to get the highest possible marks on this alone. He went through every subject, mentally and physically, and then, after prayers, he slipped on his bed and passed out before his friends got in.

The following day, bright and early, was breakfast for all students. Scrambled eggs and warm sugar-powdered mini french rolls were served. It was very different to him for he had never had it in his lifetime, and, of course, it was very tasty, he must admit. At 9:00 a.m. all students were inside the examination hall filled with tables and benches. Hundreds of them lined up neatly. Four students for each table, plenty of room in between each of them to make sure the test is done with utmost integrity and uncompromising. The PA system is announcing the rules and regulation for doing the tests. On top of that, one teacher, or supervisor, is assigned to watch the students sitting at four tables to make sure they do their work honestly; once they are done, the teacher is there to pick up and sign their tests. It was one day full of tests, one subject after another, beginning with mathematics, science, civics, literature, essay, music, drawing, and calligraphy. He felt he did the tests very well and finished within allowed time or earlier. He did exactly what his teacher had told him: "Do not turn in your test early even you have finished it. Take your time; go over it to make sure you have everything right before you turn it in."

At last, the two grueling, nerve-wracking days of examination came to an end, all students breathed with relief and retreated to their quarters, rested overnight after dinner, and the following morning, they would be transported back to their schools. Of course, there were many students whose parents were outside the gate to pick them up for sight-seeing, relative visiting, or even shopping.

At his home in the village, there was not much to talk about his exam. The sun was high up in the bluish sky. It was one of those hot days of summertime. He could feel the heat coming down from the sun; he could see the steam rising up from the ground. A few clumps of lazy clouds were hardly moving in the vast sky. The birds on the mango trees seemed careless about his absence, his taking test in the city, still chirping, flying in and out of the dense canopy of the green leaves. The river still quietly runs under the bridge. Here and there along the river, a few boats moving about, doing fishing. He did not see Ba Thong's boat. She and her husband must have left on their fishing trip. Nothing has changed. No one had asked him how he did it except that he had to get on the boat to go fishing with his dad the evening after he got home. It was very much of his affairs, lonely to himself. He had forgotten everything about the test, the examination a few days ago and now back to his real world, his life to become a fisherman. He began to get a quick bite of leftover in the kitchen and scooped rice from a large wooden container nearby into a small bag, making sure it is enough for a four-day trip for two persons, him and his dad, as his dad had told him earlier. His stepmother and his little brother were not around, but he thinks they went to her parents who live across the river, at the end of west side of village by the hillside. He was told to call them Grandpa and Grandma, which he did not mind at all. They were at the age of his own grandparents anyway. The only thing that bothers him is he could not understand these folks when they talked. Their accent was so heavy that 90 percent of their conversation went off from one of his ears to another, like the one who listens to a foreign language and has not a clue the meaning of what being said. He just dutifully said yes and yea and smiled and nodded his head most of the times when seeing them at their house, or his house. They were nice folks, and he liked them. He had a hard time understanding his stepmother's speech when she first became a member of his household. She could never pronounce his name correctly. The letter *L* becomes *N*, and his name Lin becomes Nin. It does not bother him one bit; besides, it amuses him at the sound of his name, which makes him think of a pill, yes, the round-shaped, bitter taste of malaria pill called "quinine." And it is the same in her family. The letter *L* has become dysfunctional. Sometimes he wanted to ask his father how he got through that language barrier when he first got introduced to meet her. But he never got a chance, and it is too late now. He wanted to make sure that he had everything for the fishing trip, from cooking pots to rice and salt, the coarse grain salts, and a not-allow-to-forget fish sauce in a small bottle. Most of these items stay in the boat, except rice, after each trip. But his responsibility is to make sure they are there, and in sufficient amount, or else, the troubles await for him on the water.

His father would carry to the boat the fishing net, the casting net that weights a ton, he guesses. At this age of his life, he has learned how to and not to get in troubles, especially with his dad and his stepmother. Undoubtedly, he has learned a hard way and still learning every day.

He untied the rope to the bamboo pole at the mooring dock, pushed the boat out and quickly brought the boat out into the current. His dad had mentioned to him that this fishing trip would be at the Daklac Lake, one of the famous lakes that the king Bao Dai had his royal vacation facilities built right on the lake, about thirty miles on the road from his house. But it would take half day to bring his boat there with the two oars, one on each side, almost to the back of the boat, and he is the one to do that with his feet.

He had learned this skill of using his feet to maneuver, to push the oars at the time he was as little as seven years old when he started going on fishing with his dad prior moving to this river. Since this technique of rowing the boat would require a solid back support on a firm seat, the two oars would be strung on a rope tied to two short wooden posts, each held by two wooden brackets, about five inches apart, vertically attached to the inside walls of the boat. The end of each oar is interlocked with a piece of wood, five inches long, to make it a tee-shaped joint. This is point where his foot rests and controls the pedal of the oar to push the water. With this unique technique, the boat moves a lot faster than that using hand and less tiring.

While he was foot-pedaling the boat, and his dad mending the net in the middle of the boat, he always mends his nets, whether a floating net or a casting one, to make sure no fish could escape the holes. His dad, with unusual caring voice, started asking him questions about the exam.

"How did you do on your exam, son?"

"Everything went well, Dad. I finished all tests within time and answered all questions adequately." He wanted to add that he wished he had a little extra money to visit the market in the city to buy a gift for his dad and Ba Thong, but he was afraid it might cause him trouble.

"You passed? Do you think?" his dad continued without looking up.

"I really don't know, Dad. Hoc tai thi phan. But, I do hope I have passed so that you will be proud of me, and that I could go to high school in the city." (It is fate, not how smart .)

"Will see," his dad said without much of enthusiasm. Perhaps, he did not want to promise and not able to deliver; perhaps, he wanted to negotiate with his wife about his going away for high school. Who knows what was in his father's mind; what was he planning?

The conversation between them came to an end. It has always been short between his and his father's. It is as if they communicated more through their language of silence, through their eyes, their facial expression, their hand gestures than verbal words. A glance, a gaze of his father's eyes could mean a lot of things, and sometimes, or most of the times, for that matter, he has to guess. It could mean "Don't you dare" or it could shout out loud in his mind, "You are worthless boy" when he was comparing him to other boys in the village. He just has to always guess what to do or how to respond. He just hopes that the adults were not that complicate. Just say it, then he will do it; just give an example, he will follow, just as simple as kids are and do. No sarcasm, no tricks, no nonverbal language, which would sure make his life better. He knows in his heart his father loves him, as a father would do, but does not express it verbally. He had never, up to this point in his life, heard his father say, "Son, I love you." Those simple three words, three magic words would make him "die and go to heaven"; that would make him scream inside, "I am very happy," and because of that, he was afraid to express himself in return. He is afraid to say, "I love you, Dad, not once, but thousands and millions times." This wanting, this longing, this desire to say it was now, like a loudspeaker, screaming in his head, but could never come out.

Each had different thinking in mind. His dad might be thinking about how to support him in the city while he had enough trouble making a living for the whole family. He, on the other hand, was thinking about the school in the city. He doesn't even have a clue of what school he would be going to, or accepted. He does not have any ideas whereabouts he is going to stay in, and whom he is going to be staying with. All he knows in his mind, in his heart, is that it is going to be better for his life. The amount of hatred, of meanness, of abusiveness his stepmother has had on him is the very same amount of desire, of wanting, and willingness that he has to get out of the house, out of the village, and out to school faraway.

Now as his feet were busily pedaling, pushing the water behind his boat, his mind went back to the examination hall where each of the tests came back in his mind, one at a time. The math test he did very well with all the numbers written neatly and nicely on the test papers. He used the draft paper to work on it first and then carefully transferred the results to the test papers without a scratch, without a trace of erasers (a tip from his beloved teacher). The essay, a composition, about "your cat" at home was a perfect topic for him to do simply because he has a black cat that loves to sit lazily in his kitchen, especially in the cold winter months, and he is like a professional killer, doing what cats are supposed to do: catch mice! He knew he did well on that too. He felt very confident that he would earn the highest marks possible and the certificate honoring his achievement would be delivered to his school any time any day, soon. He felt particularly good about the comment that one of the teachers gave him when he received the papers, the calligraphy one. The teacher looked at him and proudly said, "Lin, what a beautiful hand writing you have, son. Very impressive, I must say. Keep up with the good work, and I wish you luck."

"Thank you, teacher," he said softly and felt the joy that ran through his veins.

Despite all the things he had done for the test, which he knew he did very well, the word "luck" from the teacher somehow interconnected with the word "fate," which faintly took him to another level of awareness, another level of thinking. What if his fate were predestined? What if his name were not on the list among the chosen ones? His fate would be that of forever staying in this village; his father would feel disgraced for having him, a failure in the family. He knew what he needed to do. He needed to pray.

His boat now entered a part of the river where it is flanked by trees and hillside that quickly cut the light off from the sky. He guided his boat to stay in the middle of the river where there is a little light left for him to see. It was all quiet except the sounds of the oars, pushed by his feet, monotonously chopping the flat water. Every now and then he could hear the cry of the monkeys echoed from the hillsides. Birds were flying over his head from one side of the river to the other, chirping, talking, as if they were calling their babies to their nests.

At last, his dad, with his silver flint lighter, lit up the oil hurricane lamp, which hung to the side of the roof of the boat, sending a faint smoke and smell of burned kerosene oil into the air and floated to his nostrils in the back of the boat. After hours of mending his nets, he finally broke the silence of the night.

"Let's take a break here, and we will start early in the morning. Fishing should be good by then."

"Dad, my feet are killing me. My knees are tired and disjointing."

"Really? Are you sure? Just only a couple of hours?" was his dad's usual sarcastic comment.

"Oh yes, Dad, I am tired and sleepy." As he said that, he veered his boat to a sandy beach on the left hand side where his dad grabbed one of the largest pointed bamboo poles off the Y-shaped wooden brackets, which stood straight up on the sides of the boat. He then sunk the pole into the sand at the bottom of the river and tied the boat to it with the rope. Lin hung up the oars off the water and carefully inserted each of the oars, at its tee, to a braided nylon ring at the side of the boat to secure them. He does not want to be in a situation in which, when he woke up in the morning, he would discover that the oars had somehow slipped off and floated away, and the boat would have become an oarless one, like a car whose wheels got disappeared overnight. He would be in serious trouble, no, make it dead meat! He would never hear the end of it. Finally he got inside the roof, crawled on the straw mat to the side of the boat, leaving the other to his dad whenever he wanted to come in. He just wanted to rest for it has been a long day. Flat on his back, straightened his legs on the straw mat, even though he's tired and sleepy, he could not shake off a story in his brain, the story of a tiger that came on the boat told by his dad sometimes in the past.

His dad did not actually tell him the story directly, but he listened to it while he was telling it to his friends.

"Years and years ago," his dad began his story. When he was in his early twenties, he went fishing, all by himself, on the

Red River in North Vietnam. It was late in the evening, and he decided to quit after a long day fishing, dead tired. He moored his boat by the beach about ten yards from the edge of the water. Beyond it was an open field, full of tall grass. It was a covered boat with a curve bamboo-framed roof, like the one on his boat now. Once he was inside, making sure that both ends of the roof were all covered with a piece of beaten dark-green tarp, just in case it rained, and he quickly fell asleep.

Somewhere late into the night, he did not know what time, or exact time, he awoke to the sounds and the swaying of the boat, and then he felt his boat tilted to the front as if there were a heavy load, or someone just sat on it. There was a foul smell in the air and heaving breathing. He was scared; he was startled and frozen to make any move. Is there someone trying to steal his boat? He was thinking. Nonsense! Impossible! There are no houses here along the river from where he lives. There is not a single soul living in this remote woodsy, grassy area, and besides, there had never been an incident, as long as he could remember, in which a boat was stolen. Everything was still and quiet and tense. He was scared to even breathe, for he was afraid that might give out the spot, the whereabouts he was hiding. He finally pulled up his courage to slowly, gently peek through the fabric tarp, and holy cow! He could not believe what he saw under the starry night. The animal sitting only a yard and half away from him was none other than a tiger, and not just tiger, but a big tiger. It was as big as he was, facing him behind the tarp, around hundred and fifty pounds, or more, he guessed. What was the tiger doing on his boat? To catch a fish? He had been told by the elders that tigers could catch fish by exhale his stinky, foul breath to lure the fish in and catch it with his paws. He did not think this is the case. The tiger was here for meat, his meat! He must have smelled the meat inside the boat and taken his time to make a move on him. He must think fast how to get away from this hungry tiger, the king of jungle. The one choice was to quickly dash off to the back of the boat, into the water and dive away like dolphin. But the tiger, with one giant tiger leap, could catch him, grip him in his paws. Not a sound option, he thought. Another would be, as it had been told by the elders, using two aged-skin bamboo poles, rubbing against each other to produce a skin-slashing sound, which will cause the tiger to run away as fast as his legs could let him. That is why tigers do not stay or hang around an area where bamboo trees are grown. He was inclined to the second choice because, as he was thinking, if this did not work, he could always go back to the first option, jumping off into the water. He slowly, gingerly, in the dark, reached his hand to the side of the boat, grabbed one piece of the bamboo splits with his right hand, and then the next with his left. He gently put them one against the other and, with all of his strength, his might, in the darkness, in the still of air, rubbed them as fast as his hands could move. He could feel the bouncing of his boat as the tiger, scared of the sudden sounds of bamboo rubbing, leaped off the boat and disappeared into the grassy field.

The picture of a tiger came into his mind, and his imagination had got hold of him. He was dreadful of the idea, of the possibility in which, at the middle of the night, a tiger, a big tiger would come on his boat, prey on him and his dad. He wanted to tell his dad to come inside so that he could be next to him, so that he could feel safe in his strong arms, but reluctantly decided against it and fell asleep.

The next day, very early in the morning, even before dawn, it was still dark; his dad woke him up to begin a fishing day. He was used to this kind of boot camp. He was sleepy, very sleepy, but he needed to get up to do as fishermen do, that is, to catch fish. He knew very well that the best time to catch fish is either early in the morning, or at sunset, and he wanted to catch lots of fish. It would make him happy and his dad as well. He leaned over the side of the boat, curved his right palm, scooped up the running water from the river to wash his face and to stay awake.

He was now in the back, moving his boat out into stronger, faster current water.

His dad told him to paddle faster so that he could get to the best fishing spot he had known from many previous trips. He started to put more strength, more push on his moving legs, and the current was on his side, his favor, making his boat glide on the morning water. Since his dad decided to use casting net, he needed to be double, triple extra careful with his maneuvering the boat, which, with any wrong move, could send his dad and his casting net, altogether, into the water. Yes, it did happen a long time ago, when he was younger, learning all aspects of becoming a fisherman. It was a big and heavy net with fifty pounds of lead clipped to the bottom twine of the net. It would cover an area of twelve feet in diameter. His father is one of a few in the whole village who could swing and make it a perfect cast on top of the water every time. It bloomed out nicely in the air like a round chute, descending, splashing on the surface of the water and quickly sank into the bottom of the river.

His dad asked him, "Turn right," which means his left because his dad was standing, facing him with a small portion of the net on his right shoulder and a raised arm, ready to cast. As he did what he thought "right," his dad gave him a scornful look and a stern voice.

"Stupid, I told you to turn right. Is it right to you?" He tried to make a quick correction, veering the boat too fast that threw his dad off the balance.

Oh, my Lord, my God, save me, he silently cried as his dad and the net, altogether, tumbled into the water, making a huge splash right at the front of the boat.

It took his father less than a minute to free himself from the tangled net, and then, with both of his hands gripping on the side of the boat, he lifted himself out of the water onto the boat. Sat in front the boat now was his father, a soaking wet man, his faded, thin, brown-colored shirt pasted to his skin, showing his disguised muscles, panting. His dad was more a madman than tired; he could kill the boy.

While his dad was standing, pulling up his net from the water, Lin was mentally prepared for a storm of rage, a thunder of punishment from his father. But it did not happen. Perhaps he saved for the next time when he goofed; perhaps the water had cooled him down. Whatever it was, the whipping did not happen, and he was so relieved.

Here it was again. It could be the day if he were not careful, if he were not listening and not paying attention.

The bright-pink light of the new day began emerging in the horizon, allowing him to see and observe his surrounding better. The morning breezes ruffled the surface of the water and cooled his face, his neck, as his legs were moving, picking up their speed on the paddling. The giant trees, the tall bamboo bushes with trunks shot straight up into sky, greeting the morning with their leaves moving, gently swaying in the breeze. Birds started flying about, dashing from trees to trees and across the sky, singing, chirping like a heavenly choir in the wilderness. A whole family of monkeys scattered on the limps of a giant brown-skin mahogany tree right at the bank of the river. They were hanging, moving, swinging, on the branches like agile, lean, slim athletes, training on their morning gymnastic exercises. It seems quite amusing that they know how to tease, to make fun of, and to scare their human counterparts. They would sometimes sit on the limps, on the branches of the trees, in the dark of early morning or early in the evening hours, patiently watching, like well-trained guerillas on their ambush, quietly waiting for you to get closer, closer, and closer. And all of a sudden, they would, in unison, vigorously shake the limps the branches, as they all laugh their monkey laughs at the same time, like the sounds of a stuttered engine of a motorcycle, in the quiet air. They know how to get you. They know how to scare you, and you wish you could splash the water from the river on them.

He kept the boat moving, and not before long, the first circle of the net casting was perfectly coming down on the water. As the net was sinking, getting to the bottom of the river, the dark-brown line, the twine, to the top of the net in his dad 's hand, started moving as it got straightened. He watched the line, from the back of the boat, with all excitement. His adrenaline climbed up as the line moved, from one direction to the next. Sometimes, it pulled too. It has to be a good size of fish to make the rope wiggled in his dad's hand.

"It's a big one, don't lose it, Dad," he told his dad, full of excitement in his voice.

"Move the boat backward a little more," said his dad with a big smile on his face. He wanted to close the gap at the bottom of the net to trap all the fish inside.

"Yes, Daddy," he said as he was excitedly moving the boat slowly backward with his oars.

"Come over here, son." His dad whispered from the front of the boat as if he were afraid that his voice would frighten the fish inside the net, and then lose it.

As soon as he got to the front of the boat after crawling through the roof of the boat, his dad handed him the rope and quickly slipped himself off from the side of the boat and into the water after telling him, "Hold on to this."

His dad quietly sank down, disappeared deep into the water to make sure that the fish, whatever kind of fish it is, would not get to the bottom of the net and gone. That would be disappointing if it happened. He wanted to wrap the fish with a chunk of the net by using his hands at both ends of the fish, and up, he hauled it onto the boat.

After what seemed an hour, he saw his dad surfacing with both of his hands and arms wrapping around a white fish under layers of net against his chest. He quickly pulled the net up to give his dad some room to lift the fish onto the boat.

Once on the boat, the man was wet and exhausted, and the fish fought for his life, jumping, trying to break loose from the net. He helped his dad to slowly and carefully remove the net from the fish, a fat gray-black top and white belly carp, at least thirty-five pounds. The fish lay flat on its side, big wide eye open as if looking at the boy, begging, "Let me go."

There is no way the fish will fit inside bamboo cage, shaped like a bomb, pointed at both ends, on an air fighter, attached to the side of the boat to keep the fish alive for days in the water. His dad quickly ran a fishing line through its lower lip behind the bone, and both his dad and him, four hands, lifted the carp up and gently let him into the water after carefully tying the line to the boat. The fish was now obediently swimming along in the back of the boat to wherever it went. It does not happen often to catch that size of the fish with the casting net. It was just a beginning of a lucky day for him and his dad, he felt.

By noon, after hauling off the water a few dozens of variety of fish, keeping them in the cage, his dad decided he had had enough of the net casting for the day. The net has to be dried before it can be stored away inside the boat. Lin, like a pro, found a perfect spot to do that. A beach, a sandy beach along the river, was waiting for him at distance. He finally pulled his boat over and jumped ashore. He felt so good touching the sand, walking along the edge of the water. After a long day, confined in the narrow space of the boat, Lin found this moment quite exhilarating. Dad had a wide, sandy field under the hot sun for him to dry his net by casting it on the sand. Such a simple, convenient, and efficient way to dry a non-nylon fishing net right on the hot toasty grains of sand! He was able to cook lunch right on the boat for both of them.

Later in the afternoon, after the lunch break, he had his boat inside a lake after paddling through a shortcut, merging with the water of the lake, as his dad had planned earlier. It is at least two to three miles from one side of the lake to the other, and the water was clear but full of sage-green algae. Water lily flowers with light-pink-yellow buds cubed in the center of white petals on their green stalks, which were swaying in the gentle breezes of the evening as if greeting, acknowledging, and welcoming their guests. Here and there fish were jumping up in the air in their pretwilight shows, promising a good fishing night.

The net used in the lake is different. It is about four feet high, from the lead sinkers to the floaters, and the length, one hundred yards each section. It is medium-sized mesh, three inches, a perfect type of net for the lake fishing, as his dad told him.

It took him and his dad a long while, a good half an hour, to find a stretch of water clear of algae, barely the width of the boat, so that he could lower his net without getting tangled in the algae. While waiting for the sun setting to get the net going, the wind suddenly, out of the blue, came and picked up its speed as minutes ticked by. It was blowing side way against the left side of his boat, which makes it impossible for him to move his boat backward with his oars. He could foresee the problems he was facing if the wind did not let up. He prayed in silence for the wind gone and for the good fishing night started so that his family could have money to buy foods and clothes, and, perhaps, money for his school in the city, which he had completely forgotten.

Unfortunately, what he was concerned and worried now became a reality. The wind kept blowing, and his oars were stuck in the algae, in the lily pads that he could not move either way, not forward, not backward. His dad sat at the front of the boat, the net in his hand, anxiously to get his net in the water. But the boat could not move. The oars were tangled up with the seaweeds and other aquatic plants in the water. His tears were coming down as his dad started yelling at him, calling him names. His dad was mad, and he himself had become incapacitated, utterly helpless.

Boop, boop, boop! The sounds of the bamboo rod, like muffled gunshots, curving in the air, landed repeatedly on the roof from the hands of his father who'd run out of patience, went into his rage, lost his control, and blew up on him. Terrified, he dove under the roof, taking the cover from the angry rod and angry man. " You are such a loser, a worthless and stupid boy," said his father as he hit the boy.

He finally removed the oars from their posts to free them from the tangles and kept the boat moving by using the pole to push the boat backward.

At last, the net was in the water, despite the wind, despite being late, despite the rage from his dad, and despite the odds against him. In his corner at the back of the boat, in his loneliness and darkness of the evening, he was trying to make some senses out his situation and his life. He felt that the adults were not fair in dealing with and treating their kids. He wondered if they ever put themselves in their kids' shoes to see if they could do things differently, better perhaps. Can they feel the pains their kids have to bear? Any moments of remorse they might have for being too rough on their children? He doubted, for if they did, he would not have to suffer this much. Is it the ways kids learn in life? Is it the way to becoming an adult? It is absolutely unfair! He needs to break this cycle of nonsense, and he was determined. He wanted to tell his dad what he was thinking, what he had in his little brain, but did not have courage to do that. Someday when he is older, he will tell him that. Someday when he has kids of his own, he would not be treating them this way. He would be more understanding and, definitely, be kinder, gentler.

He pulled himself together, dried off his tears on his face with his palm, with the sleeve of his shirt. No more tears, he was determined. No more crying, he decided to become a man even at an age of nearly thirteen.

The next morning, very early, the wind had died down, completely subsided; after the net was pulled on the boat, the fish were gathered and sorted, and he headed home. Besides the fiasco with the wind, the tangled, the heartache, the tears, the catch was good. The bamboo cage by the side of the boat was almost full. It needed to be lowered, deeper in the water so that the fish can stay alive until they got home with him.

It would be a long day to paddle home for not only he had to go against the current, but also the cage now lowered in the water, fully emerged becoming a drag along the big fish on the line. But he did not mind the hard work. He had to do what the fisherman had to do: be glad and thankful that the catch was good.

It was late in the evening; after numerous times of taking turns between him and his dad to keep the boat moving on the water, he got his boat to the usual mooring spot at the bank of the river. His dad, after telling him to stay and sleep in the boat and to watch the fish, gathered his belongings—a beaten, elbow-tattered faded-green fatigue jacket, and his inseparable bazooka-shaped bamboo tobacco pipe with its companion, a tiny tin can of shredded dark-brown glazed tobacco leaves—stepped off the boat and went home.

Scattered along the beach area, along the river, were boats with their oil lamps on, blinking in the grayish-dark evening. It was all quiet, a normal quiet at this part of the river at this hour for everyone was ready for a good-night sleep after a hardworking day. He was looking for a particular boat, Ba Thong's boat, which was moored at her usual spot. He moved his boat out into the deeper water and quietly pushed it up next to hers with the bamboo pole. The lamp, a hurricane oil lamp, was hung in the back of her boat on a pole, flooding the whole back of her boat with an amber light as if she had been waiting for him.

As his boat approaching next to hers, from inside her boat, Ba Thong, with her motherly voice, greeted him. "Is it Lin?" she asked him softly.

"Yes, it is me, Ba Thong, and how are you?" he answered her with his tender voice as if to his own mother.

"How was the fishing? Did you catch a lot?" asked Ba Thong as she gently flipped the edge of her chocolate-brown mosquito net over her head and crawled out to the back to see him. As if to answer her question for him, the fish inside the cage made some audible noises, splashing, jumping inside the cage, and perhaps trying to get out.

"Yes, Ba Thong, it was a good trip. There is a big one on a separate line in the back of my boat, and the cage is almost full."

"Good for you, lucky boy." She then continued to ask him a question that has nothing to do with the fish, the trip, or anything that he could have anticipated or related to.

"Lin, my dear," she said, "what kind of beans would you prefer? Black bean? Mung bean? Red kidney bean?"

Startled for a long moment in the quiet night, he did not know what she was talking about, where she was leading to, or, in this case, alluding to. Was she talking about the sweet-soupy bean desert that every Vietnamese loves? But she did not mention anything about the soup of any kind in particular.

He was puzzled at the question; he was racking his brain, trying to find the answer to this very simple question. What does the color of beans have to do with him? What difference does it make whether he likes the red or the black bean? It was too simple, and yet he could not jump into the answer—black, green, or red. Finally, he gave up at what seems to be a trick, a riddle.

Like a little child begging, talking to his mother, he said, "My dear Ba thong, I don't understand why you asked me such a question? Does the color of bean have anything to do with me? As you know, I do not have much choice in my life when it comes to food, hardly a full meal, much less the choice of the color. Would you please help me, tell me more?"

"You have passed your national exam," short and sweet was her answer.

"Ba Thong!" Joyous, he almost screamed aloud in the quiet night. Now he understood the riddle she had challenged him. A bean in the Vietnamese language is *dau*, used by southerners, or *do*, the northerners; it doesn't matter what color the beans bear or have, they all are beans. They both mean "pass." He, however, wanted to know it is a sure thing that he had passed.

"Ba Thong," he asked, half-assuredly, "is it true that I passed?"

"It is solid true, my dear Lin." She continued in her loving and happy voice.

"They sent the paper to your school, my child, and guess what?" She continued with her softened tone of voice but carried some degrees of seriousness. "Do you know that you are the only one who passed the exam out of all students in the village?"

What quickly flashed off his innocent mind was, *How could that be? It is impossible! There must be a mistake; something was wrong.* He was in denial to this fact that he began to have questions.

"Ba Thong, did the letter say why? What happened to all of my friends? They were all smart students."

"The fate, son," she went on to say. "It doesn't matter how smart one is; it is the fate that decides." He noticed a subtle change in the language she used on him. He was deeply touched. Yes, in his heart, he would love to be her son, and her, his mother.

The sky was full of stars, twinkling in the dark vast sky. A few of them dashed across the domelike sky as he looked up, thanking God for his good fortune; which one of the billions up there is his lucky one? He wondered. A brief moment of silence between Ba Thong and him seemed to deepen the notion of fate upon him, the blessing that would allow him to break the cycle of life on the water as a fisherman, the life in this village as a farmer, and most of all, he knows it, and Ba Thong knows it, as well that his life would be better when he was out of his stepmother's grip. It has now just begun with this joyous news of his passing the exam and of his receiving the award, the certificate of achievement, namely a diploma.

"Are you going to celebrate, son?" she broke the silence.

"I don't know, Ba Thong," he told her, for he did not know what to do to celebrate this little but big accomplishment of his. He knows that his dad would be happy to hear the news. He is not sure about his stepmother whom he does not know if she would appreciate or even like it. He wished that his dad had not gone home in such a rush so that he could also learn about the result of the exam firsthand with him. He could not wait to see him in the morning to tell him this great news.

"Child, are you hungry?" she asked at last, knowing it was late. She would cook him something before he went to bed if he were hungry. That is what a mother would do to be sure her child is full before going to bed.

"No, Ba Thong, I am fine. I am just too happy to be hungry," he said to her with a happy, thankful tone of voice. He wanted to say more, a lot more to her, like a child to his mother, to express his love and appreciation for her, but the words escaped him, letting the silence convey his feeling to her, instead. They exchanged good-night wishes as he went inside his boat after tying the rope of his boat to the back of hers. The news of his fortune stretched his imagination far beyond the village, far beyond the city to faraway lands that took him a long while before he could fall asleep.

He woke up to the sound of merchants, the peddlers, who came to buy fish, turtles, and any types of seafood the fishermen were offering to sell. The voices became louder as the merchants came closer to the beach. It is the place where the sellers, the buyers, gather to do their business. The sounds of their portable metal scales, the chains rubbing, clanking against the metal bars and the metal trays, along with voices, high and low, fast and slow, bargaining on prices let him know that his dad or his stepmother would be down to the beach very soon to take care of this selling business of the fish for him.

With this size of the catch, which his father would have already told her, she would take it to the market to sell it herself. She would make more money that way, for she has bypassed all middle persons at the riverside. She is physically a strong person who loves to do that; besides, she gets to keep the money.

"Nin, bring the boat over here," his stepmother's high-pitched voice was calling, ordering him while he was untying the rope from Ba Thong's boat. He handed over the whole catch to her, the big carp, the cage full of fish just as soon as he got to the beach. He got out of the boat on his short, barefooted on the cool water and sand, pulled the boat aground, at least almost half of it; he then tied the boat to a bamboo pole and, not wasting a second, galloped home to see his little brother and his dad. He wanted to save the good news as a present to his dad.

Upon arriving, panting, out of breath from running, he saw his dad sitting on a wooden stool, carved out of a tree stump, with his little brother on his laps, waiting for him, grinning. Obviously, the way it appeared, he had been told by his wife about his *do*, his bean, his passing the exam.

"Very well, son, you have passed," his dad told him with some reserved pride and satisfaction in his voice as he came over to hold his brother, who was eagerly waiting for him with both of his arms up in the air ready to jump over to him. He knew his little brother missed him, and he, too, a lot.

The news, his dad said, had traveled around the village while he was on the water, fishing. He loved the way it turned out. Somehow it fits his life pattern, his fate, the way it has happened. The give and the take. The dark and the bright. The heartbreaking fiasco on the water while fishing is now giving birth to the joyous, heart-warming news, waiting for him at home.

"Dad, we should go to the city to check out my school, my high school," he impatiently asked his father for the next venture of his life.

"We need to find the school that would accept me, Dad," he continued with an almost-one-way conversation. The choice would be either a private or a semiprivate high school, which he had heard about from Ba Thong, and they both located right inside the city limit. *This certainly is not an option, for it will cost lots of money*, he thought and immediately pushed that idea completely out of his head. The only hope, not choice, he had was a public school, and he prayed that would happen for him.

"And, by the way, Dad, where am I going to stay?" he asked the last question.

His dad reluctantly said, "Wait and see."

For what dad? Please help me, please do not change your mind on me, he almost blurted out but held it to himself for he did not want to make his dad upset. He knew his dad had to negotiate with his wife for there would be money involved, money to be spending on his behalf at school, buying books, food, and rent. His mind was totally in for going to school in the city.

Later in the evening, on his boat, his dad and Mr. and Mrs. Thong, all together, had a little celebration for him. Why not on his house? he asked himself that question, but he immediately had the answer to it. His dad wanted to share the joy and pride with them since he knew Ba Thong had special care and love for Lin, his son. He wanted to make sure they know how much he, as a father, on behalf of the family, appreciated the loving care the couple had poured out for his boy, and without their love, their support, financially, the boy would not have made to the city for the exam.

The four of them, the two men sitting on the straw mat inside the boat, Ba Thong and he were on their seats in the open-air space, next to the men, in the back of the boat. The oil lamp hung from the edge at the top of the roof, sending warm-amber light on the four of them, who were in good spirit, in the mood for celebration, a very simple and undecorated one. On the mat were two large-sized bottles of Tiger beers, a Vietnam-brewed product. Two tall, clear, thick glasses were half full of ice cubes, melting, standing on the mat, one in front of each man; a dozen of duck eggs, the hatched ones, hot boiled, stacked up against one another inside a round bamboo basket. A large basket full of a variety of fresh, lush green veggie—including mints, basil, and rings of sliced off-white-and-purple banana heart—was sitting next to a tiny white ceramic bowl of salt and black pepper. The music was from the crickets singing from the bushes or from their hideouts at the bank of the river. The summer sky, like a dark dome, sprinkled with stars. The water on the river was quietly running underneath of the boat. Some small fish were making their show, audibly splashing and playing by the sides of the boat.

Very formally, his dad, as he always does, thanked his friends, Mr. and Ba Thong, for their love and help with the money so that, the fruit of their labor was this little celebration for his achievement. His dad filled the glasses; the foam of the Tiger beers began rising, climbing over the brim and slowly spilled over down to the side of the glasses. The two men gave toast to him and congratulated him on his accomplishment, which made him shy, and he awkwardly leaned against Ba Thong, whose arms were over his shoulders, holding him, and a squeeze from her arms, he felt. He had never dreamed for this moment in his life of loving and caring from a woman other than his own mother. In his mind, surrounding with love, he felt heaven has descended right on this boat.

While the men enjoying their drinks, talking about the places they grew up and came from, the things that they had experienced in life, Lin and Ba Thong started cracking the eggs at their rounded ends and enjoyed the delicious distinctive juice at their tongues. Broad-leaf mint and sweet basil and a variety of veggies helped to bring out the best of the half-hatched eggs. When did he acquire the taste of this type of the boiled eggs? He did not know. It must have been a slow process that turned him into this culture; it is probably the circumstance of him growing up poor, in which almost everything can be turned into food, and ultimately, nothing is to be wasted. Leftover cooked rice can be dried in the sun and roasted, stored away for future use. Aged mustard greens can be pickled for long-term usage. The unhatched chicken eggs—usually one, two, or three, after an incubating period, after the mother hen taking her baby chicks out of the nest, left lonely among broken shells—can be boiled and then food. But for the boiled hatched duck eggs, it is something else; it is quite a different taste, a better taste than that of the chicken one. You will be starting with the white, which now has become hardened, solid more like clay, not much of a taste, but it gives the fill to your tummy. You then come to the best part, the yolk, which has now transformed into a full-shaped baby chick with everything, the head with eyes, the tiny, teeny bill, the wings and the thin layer of gray feather on the skin.

When he looked at it the first time he got introduced to it, he was not inclined or excited to have it in his mouth. But admittedly, he loved it for its taste is entirely different. No wonder it has become a delicacy and the luxury of the haves. It turned out that Ba Thong was the one who threw the party at her own expense. She had gone to the store, a minimarket, by the dirt road across the river, to buy the beers and the rest. He was, again and again, touched by her kindness, her love for him. The two women—one is not related, no relationship, none whatsoever—came out from nowhere into his life, poured out her love on him, showered him with her caring for, did everything for him as a loving mother would. The other, whom he calls mother, stepmother, a part of his family, hated him, tortured him, wanted him gone out of her sight, dead, perhaps. God, he thinks, is compensating him for what he had gone through, for what he had been deprived from, and he is very grateful.

The two men continued their life stories; they both left their birth places in 1954 after the whole country was physically, politically, cut in halves at the seventeenth parallel where a small river divides the north and the south, stipulated by the Geneva conference. His dad told his friend about an incident in which he became a hero on the air by reaching out to pull down the door, which was accidentally flipped open while the plane was airborne, losing its balance.

"Were you scared?" Mr. Thong asked as he emptied his glass to the last drop of beer, leaving a few chips of ice at the bottom of the glass as he sat it down on the mat.

"Not at all, I forgot to be scared. I did not think of me, but rather of my family and others on that flight. They were all I was concerned of and all I cared for," his dad told his friend. It was a part of the story he had witnessed himself on that last flight by the French aviation from north to south, fleeing from the communists. In his mind and heart, dad was his hero, a superhero!

"You were a brave man, my friend," the old man continued, admiring his dad's bravery and heroic act on the air. He never knew the age of Mr. Thong, but he looked a lot older than his dad, perhaps ten or more years on his life chart.

The life stories about life of the two souls continued into the night while Ba Thong nurtured him with the importance of education. She told him that she had a cousin who became a professor at a very young age and now lived in the city, teaching in one of the schools in the region. She hinted that she would ask her cousin to help him, perhaps a place to stay, perhaps a hand, an advice, a direction on the road of education.

"Never, never, ever, give up, you hear me?" She made him promise her, like a solemn request from a mother to her son, on the back of his boat, in the dark night.

"Child, promise Ba Thong that child will never, ever." He gave his childhood promise to her, as if it were a solemn vow to his own mother. She could see the rough road ahead of him. The life in the city isn't as easy, rosy as one would have imagined. The instinct, the intuition, and perhaps, the experience of a mother could tell the temptation, awaiting in every corner of the city, ready to ruin his life, his future, especially, when love, care, and guidance for him are far from reach. Ba Thong has every reason to be concerned, but he did give her his promise.

He and his dad thanked Ba Thong and her husband for their loving kindness as they were leaving their home boat. He wished he could stay next to her much longer, perhaps, forever for he felt safe and loved when sitting next to her.

His dad left for home after reminding him to go to bed early and to make sure the boat was securely tied to the pole.

It must have been very late, passed midnight; the crescent-shaped moon crept up on the horizon. The early morning mist in the air made him chilled and shivered. He could not help, however, feeling the warmth in his heart, for he had been touched by the magic of love.

He immediately fell asleep after covering both ends of the curved roof and curled himself inside an old sage-green blanket that has more than a dozen of holes of different shapes and sizes

Somewhere in his sleep, he had a dream—no, no, make it a nightmare—in which he was in a middle of an argument, escalating to a fight, a bloody fight between his father and his stepmother.

It all started late one evening just before dinner when the whole neighborhood was quiet. He told his wife that he wanted to send his son away to school and that he was going to take a week off go to the city to explore, to check on the school for him. Upon hearing that, she went into a storm, yelling, screaming, pounding her feet on the dirt floor, telling him that she did not have money to send his son to school, any schools for that matter. His son should be like the rest of the boys in the village, work in the farm, on the river, be a farmer, and be a fisherman like all men and women around here.

"What makes your son different from the rest of us around here?" his wife challenged him.

"I want my son to be educated, to be a teacher, to be different than me. His life will be better," his dad told her. His voice was solid; his stance was firm.

"Get your own money and do what you want. Besides, he is as dump as a donkey. He is not going to pass the exam. You will see."

His wife did not budge. Her words matched her tall, muscular physique and her face was grim.

The heated conversation tapered down like wind losing its momentum momentarily in the storm. In the corner of the house, sat a small rectangular table, on which an old, round, thin brass tray, spottily oxidized, was placed, and in the middle of the tray, there was a sizable serving bowl of hot mung bean soup along with three small bowls for rice. His stepmother sat on one end of the table, his dad the other. He was sitting next to his dad by the side of the table. The air at the table was so thick and hostile that he felt so uncomfortable, so scared that he could not dare to look at either one of his parents, particularly, his stepmother who he knew was watching him with hawkish eyes. He kept starring at his bowl and wished that he could run away or vanish into the thin air. He knows that he was the sole topic of their heated argument, and God only knows what is going to happen next.

"Eat your rice." His dad broke the ice, the thick silence, in his loud voice.

"I am not hungry, Dad," softly, teary voice, he told his dad.

"Eat!" his dad told him.

"Yes, Dad," obediently, he said as his eyes fixated on his bowl of rice, afraid of looking up. No sooner he said that his stepmother jumped in.

"Why bother! Why forcing him if he is not hungry." Her mocking voice now triggered his dad's madness.

"Shut your filthy mouth up," his dad told her. "You lost all of my money at your gambling while you were at the market. I want you to give me all the money right now."

"I won't give it to you. I don't have it." With her defying, challenging voice, she leaned forward and continued, "I don't really care. If you think you can hit me, go! Hit me."

Bang! Not the gunshot, but a whole bowl of soup flew to her face from his dad's hand, broken into pieces. The green mung bean soup smeared with blood, running down from the left side of her forehead, which terrified the soul out of him. Like wounded animal, she stood up, wiped the messy, bloody soup with her hands, and uttered her loudest voice from the top of her lungs, screamed for help.

"Help me, anyone out there. The bastard is killing me."

Scared, shaken, he cried out loud for help, he woke up, sweating. Thank God, it was just a bad dream! Still trembled from the horrible dream, he tried to calm himself down and prayed that it would never happen in reality. Even though he had witnessed their fighting more than once, in and outside of the house, but he never saw this bloody extent. He truly understands the meaning of what once said: "When two elephants tussle, it's the grass that suffers."

He could not go back to sleep; the nightmare still got a hold of him. He did not know what time it was in the morning, but the cocks crowed from the houses above the riverbanks, letting him know that it was almost day light. He decided to stay up and join the churchgoers for the morning mass when the bell at the church rang.

Two weeks later, little did he know that the nightmare, the terrifying dream he had had, was a foreshadowing of what became one of the most unforgettable moments in his life. The fight broke out between his parents at the dinner table. The bowl of mung bean soup did get broken. Her forehead did get smeared with blood. The reason to start out with was minor things in the household and then escalating to the sticky issue of money, which his dad blamed on her gambling thrills. It was a war in his house, a battlefield in his home.

He just wanted to get out of the house, to be away from this chocking air of hostility, which he felt so heavy in his heart. He knew very well from the core of his being that he had become not a bridge but a block, a wedge between his parents.

She hated him. He knows that. She wanted to get rid of him, dead or alive. He is aware of that. If so, why did she make a big deal about his going away to school? Perhaps, just going away but not schooling? Why did she want him around to become like any boy, anyone else, a farmer, a fisherman in the village? He is utterly confused.

True to his words, the following day, after that bloody confrontation, his dad took off to the city early on the morning bus to work on a place for Lin stay. By the time he got home, it was late in the evening. He looked tired but content with what he had found in the city for his son.

"You will stay with my friend Mr. Sau," his dad told him while both of them sat on the bench in front of the house.

"You will call him Uncle Sau. He knows more about the city, the school, than I do. I want you to listen to him. He will take care of you; he will show you what needs to be done before the school starts," his dad continued.

"Yes, Dad, and thank you. I will not disappoint you. I will listen to Bac [Uncle] Sau," Lin said softly. His heart danced with joy, indescribable, unspeakable joy. His yearning and dreaming of going to high school in the city have come to materializing.

It got dark quickly. Mother hens were making lots of noises, calling their chicks to their home, their cage, next to the kitchen. The kerosene oil lamp was sitting on the table, flickering, sending out faint light through the front door. The evening breezes helped cool off the muggy summer evening in this valley village.

While Lin was wondering when he and his dad would be leaving for the city, his dad told him,

"We will leave in the morning on a bus. Get up early; cook some rice to bring along on the road. You do not have any good clothes. Bac Sau will buy some for you when we get there. Go to bed early, son."

His eyes moistened with gratefulness for his dad's courageous love despite all the hardship and hurdles. Like a hero he had seen on that flight coming to south years before, his dad now stood up for him and secured the road to his future against his stepmother's giant shadow that cast darkness over it. How can he express this? How can he tell his dad that he loves him? When does he get the permission to do that? he wondered. Someday, he hoped.

He crawled on the big bed tonight feeling empty inside the large rectangular-shaped, rustic-colored mosquito net hung from the four poles attached to the four corners of the bed. His stepmother and his little brother had gone to her parents' house and stayed there for a day or two. This had happened in the past, and unfortunately, it became a routine when things did not go smoothly in the house, when verbal and physical contention had taken place. There is an emptiness in him that he could not explain, the vagueness in his felling he could not pinpoint, could not put his finger to. The stillness, the quietness of house was obvious when half of his family was missing. He lay there in bed but could not get himself to fall asleep. He was thinking about not seeing his stepmother, his little brother in the morning. He would be sad for it would be a long while before he could come home to see them, especially his brother whom he loved dearly. He hoped that his time, being away in the city, would help bringing about the healing at home, mending the ruptures in his family as well. Her grudges against him would be less, or, by the grace of God, be gone!

Nervous apprehension about life in the city, about school, about the unknown crept into his little mind and made his sleep almost impossible. He had told a few friends in the village that he would be allowed to continue his schooling in the city. Every one of them whose faces came to his mind at the moment, their innocent well-wishing smiles touched his heart. He will sure miss them, miss the games he played with them, whether at school yard or at the sandy beaches, chasing, wrestling along the river. He will miss the time in which a few of them on the boat, anchored out in the middle of the river, under the moonlight, fishing. He will miss the fish soup he cooked right on the boat with his friends the moment they pulled up a fish on the fishing line. He was telling himself that whenever he came home, he would definitely do it again and again with his friends. What a childhood experience! So beautiful, so innocent, and he finally fell asleep into such pleasant memories.

He woke up to the sounds from the kitchen. It was his dad doing the cooking instead of him. He remembered his dad had asked him before he went to bed last night that he would do the cooking. He felt the love from his dad that he let him sleep a bit longer. Maybe Dad knows that he had a hard time falling asleep last night. *Dad never says much but does more*, he thought. Maybe his dad wanted to make up for all the rough things he had done on him, from cooking to fishing, from listening to his wife's lies to almost killing him. Maybe altogether, all melted in one, a condensed love.

He sprung up, off the bed to the ground, and to the well outside. He felt the morning chill, the cold air from the mountains nearby. It is always cold here in the morning even it is now in the summertime, and much colder in other seasons. He washed his face and quickly went into the kitchen to help his dad.

"Good morning, Dad," he said as softly as morning breeze to his dad, who was raking the ashes out from underneath of the metal tripod and moving the rice pot, which was at the end of its boiling time, to sit on so that the rice could come to being perfectly cooked.

"Let me take over," he continued as he saw his dad's face shone with the reflection of the flame, flickering from the burning wood. His dark, weathered skin glazed unsteadily with the flame. He wished he had not grown this fast so that he could jump on the back of his dad, who's now sitting on the wooden log, used as a stool, and hold him as he used to. Was it because of a series eventful experiences lately that made him think and feel ahead of his age, almost thirteen? he thought. Was it because of his feeling that he was not sure if he could do it again? He was not sure, afraid? Maybe. Inappropriate? Maybe. Not accepted? Not sure.

"Almost done, son." His dad's voice deepened with emotion touched him; the word "son" from his dad made him feel redeemed. The smoke got in his eyes? He did not think so. He saw that the tea kettle was a few feet away from the tripod. He knew what he could do for his dad, fresh green tea! His dad is known, as far as he can remember, for the love of smoking tobacco, and the addiction of drinking fresh-boiled green tea. Years later in life, when his dad traveled to see him, faraway, he brought with him a bundle of green tea, fresh from his backyard, wrapped nicely in paper, newspaper, insulated with his clothes inside his suitcase for freshness. His dad is a very particular man, an eccentric character, one might say.

He dashed out into the backyard, in the gray-dark morning hours, grabbed, and picked a handful of the dew-wet green tea leaves from the aged, dwarf tea trees, grown by the hillside behind the house. He quickly washed them at the well, and into the kettle, he boiled after adding the fresh water from the well. Throughout the years, not only he had learned to cook rice, fish, veggies, the way his dad wanted, but also brewed the tea to his taste as well. Not too long, not too short, in boiling water, it has to be perfectly right for him.

Schooling In The City

He and his dad were at the bus station across the river before daybreak. His dad wanted to make sure that, by all means, they would not miss the bus even if they had to skip breakfast. Fortunately, they did get their hot freshly cooked rice. To him and to his dad, nothing tastes like fresh-hot rice. They both enjoyed their simple meal, rice and scrambled eggs, and it would carry them all the way to dinner in the city at Bac Sau's place.

He will miss this place a lot, he thought, standing, leaning against the wooden fence. The sweetness of morning air, especially by the river, would never be the same anywhere else. The fragrance of the leaves from the hillside, from the herbs and flowers in the field tickles his senses to make them come alive. This is the place of his childhood that bore him many memories, from school to home, from fishing to games on the sandy beaches. By this broken picket wooden fence, the crickets have already begun singing their sweetest melody, performing their concert in the underground hall, behind the grass curtain at this morning hour as if celebrating his new venture, his new beginning of his life and telling him, "Go forth and learn; go forth and celebrate life."

In his little mind, he was thinking of these little creatures, which have brought so much fun and thrills in his life when he had them fight. The winner poises on the platform with his triumphant singing, which is the very same concerting melody these creatures are offering, celebrating right now. Like a Zen student, awakened in seeing the monkey that happily splashing the water at a running creek in a story that his teacher had once told him, he, too, discovered, like these triumphant crickets, the meaning of, despite the circumstances, celebrating life. The bell at the church rang, echoing in between the hills. He looked up the morning sky, caught glimpse of a flying star across the immensity of the dark space. Lin, for the very first time, and the beginning of his new life, found joy in this epiphany, in this unfolding of his life.

His dad, pacing the field as if he were working on a walking exercise, finally came over next to him, and like any good father would do, he said, "Since you are going to be on your own, I want you to be diligent in your task, study and learn hard. You future is depending on schooling, your education. Make the best out of it, son."

"Yes, Dad, I promise you that I will give my very best not to disappoint you." He almost added Mr. and Mrs. Thong at the very end, but somehow they got skipped. His mind rushed, flashed to fact that many kids of his age in the village do not have this luxury, this opportunity of going to school. He felt grateful to his dad who has gone out of his way, who has sacrificed so much for the sake of his future. He wanted to share this feeling with his dad, but could not find words or courage to do so. Maybe someday he is able to do that; someday he is able to empty himself to his dad.

The lights were coming down by the hillside road, weaving like the eyes of a dragon in the dark, and then the sounds of the engine became audible. The bus was coming, but there were no passengers beside the two of them at this hour. *Will it stay and wait for more people to come?* He would not know.

Finally, as the bus came to a halt, the air brake made a sound like that of a giant blowing his nose, stirring the dust, floating through the streams and beams of light from the headlights into the air. The wave of dust came behind the bus now flooded him and his dad. Well, he thought, by the time he got to the city, both of them would turn into dust-covered walking robots, inescapable!

The driver stuck his head out of the window without moving from his seat, in his very friendly voice.

"Folks, if you want to go to the city, get on quickly. We will make a few more stops before we get there. Please, hurry," he said.

Immediately, his helper, a tall young boy, around fifteen or sixteen years of age, jumped off from the side of the vehicle, quickly got around to help him carry his small, worn, dark-brown duffel bag on the bus.

After a few bumpy stops, loading and unloading passengers and peddlers, their goods, and merchandise ranging from baskets of bananas, jackfruits, sweet potatoes to cages of noisy ducks and chickens, to name a few, along the way, they finally arrived at the heart of the city, where people and cars and motorcycles and bicycles flooded the streets, going in different directions in a dizzying speed. He was amazed at the city life and wondered if he would ever fit into this lifestyle. But he quickly asserted himself that he would learn and adapt to it, after all.

The driver made a few turns and circled his bus to an asphalt parking spot, guided by a navy-blue uniformed employee. Just as soon as the bus came to a complete stop, it was surrounded by an army of merchant ladies, waving, talking to their counterparts, still sitting on their seats that they wanted to purchase their goods. Immediately, he thought about his fish and how they got to the markets in the city. The fish, the goods have to travel many kilometers, must go through a channel of middle persons before they get to the ultimate consumers. It would be very expensive for him to buy fish and meat and fruits in the city. He had just made his first observation of how the goods and foods from a farm, from a river like his got to the market in the city.

Quite a journey, he thought.

He followed his dad, getting off the bus after his dad had paid their bus fees for both of them. His left hand held tight onto the bag, which was strung down from his dad's shoulder, keeping his pace with his dad's, making sure that he would not be left behind and lost in this throng of people. He had never seen that many people in one place in his life.

He finally got through this mass of humans. He breathed with a relief, for he was afraid of getting lost. What would he do if it did happen? His dad would be very mad at him. He would call him dumb, like he used to. He will do well in school so that he won't have to ever hear that word again from his dad.

After a very long walk on different dirt roads, weaving through many alleys, passing countless houses, his dad finally stopped at a small house sitting at the hillside. It was more of a shed than a house. At a first glance, it was obvious that it has a partially rusted metal tin roof, a wall boarded up with planks of wood of different shapes, sizes, and different lengths, leaving a huge gap at the top of the wall, which gave him an impression that it is not a warm house, or perhaps something that is missing. The back and both sides of the house were covered and shaded by a thick plantation of cassava trunks and their foliage. While he was observing and wondering if this was Bac Sau's place, a man about his dad's age, taller, short hair, in his faded military fatigue came out to greet them with a likable and gentle smile.

"So, you both are here. How are you?" he said to both of them.

Instead of answering to Bac Sau, Lin bowed his head as kids would do to their elders, while his dad said to Back Sau, "We are fine, brother Sau. Here is your boy." His dad put his hand on his shoulder as he was introduced.

As tradition, the Vietnamese man would consider and call his counterparts of the same age group brother, and for a female, sister.

"You two must be tired and hungry. Why don't you go to the back to wash yourselves up, and we will have a meal together."

"Yes, thank you, Bac Sau," he said to the man, at last, and followed his dad to the back where there is a very deep well next to the little kitchen. A large ceramic jar to hold the water from the well sits next to the entrance of the kitchen. A medium-size stainless-steel basin was placed on a wooden bench. He saw everything similar to his house and felt the connection and comfortable. He knew this place would be his home for a long time. The only thing he has to get used to is the red dust, the red dirt, especially when it is wet, when it becomes sticky-red mud, like a chunk of glues, to hold his feet down. He wished the areas around the well and the kitchen were a hard surface like that of cement. But that would cost lots of money, he thought. He was thinking that he could make a contribution to help Bac Sau by helping him harvest the tall cassava behind the kitchen. He could give him a hand to pull them up and sell them at the market too. He needed to help him out anyway he could to at least pay back his kindness of giving him a place to stay and food to eat. He does not know what arrangements being made between the adults, but he is determined to help Bac Sau so that he would not have to feel he became a burden.

He quickly got himself washed up and helped Bac Sau to get food on the table. A simple meal of rice, boiled mustard greens, and simmered-cooked catfish was super delicious. He was hungry! A long-distance walk from the bus station had burned up all he had early in the morning. He wanted to show Bac Sau that he could serve and he could cook and do the cleaning, which made Bac Sau very impressive of him.

The two men talked while enjoying their meal. Obviously, they came from the same village in North Vietnam, fled to South Vietnam about the same time in 1954, but different means. Bac Sau was on a ship, many days on the water, eating lots of canned sardines, canned tunas, and his dad fled by plane, a few hours' fly from north to south, feeding on crackers and cheese snacks, his dad told Bac Sau. They both met up a few years back through grapevine, word-of-mouth connections. His dad must have come to here to meet with him, for he had never seen him before; besides, kids do not know much about adults' affairs.

He also learned from the conversation that his wife had not made to the pier when the ship took off. He and his wife had made a plan to meet up at certain point of rendezvous, but the communist guards tightened their control and made their reunion an impossible mission. He had not heard from his wife despite letters to his village, letters to International Red Cross. He figured that the letters from him could get his wife in more troubles than helping her. Bac Sau prayed for her safety and hoped someday they could find each other—the two men, one lost his wife, the other, dead. He was not sure if his father was happier than Bac Sau with his stepmother in this marriage.

He cleaned up and washed the dishes while the men continued their talking. He did not forget to brew the green tea for his dad and Bac Sau, which immediately won him the praises from his new sponsor and host, who happens to be a tea lover himself.

The work was cut out for him from Bac Sau.

He would get up early in the morning to cook for Bac Sau so that he could bring his food to work at the lumber mill, outside of the city. He has a choice for his lunch, one he could come home during the break, siesta hours, or to take it to school. Dinners are set between 6:00 and 7:00 p.m. daily.

Homeworks are the highest priority and to be done before bedtime, no exceptions!

"This is your military boot camp," Bac Sau jokingly told him.

"Thank you, Bac Sau, I will do as you say." He felt blessed, for this is nothing compared to what he had to do at home.

Where is his school? What school is he going to? Was he not here to go to school? All of these questions were going through his mind, and then Bac Sau said he had an application for him to fill out for a poly-tech high school in the city. Bac Sau told him that it would be beneficial to him because it was a new pilot program in the country, and that he could become an engineer later on.

He was very excited with the program. The word "engineer" was too big for him to comprehend. It makes his head feel like spinning.

"Study hard and listen to Bac Sau, my son," Lin's dad told him as he was ready to go back to the village.

"Yes, Daddy, I will do my very best. I will study very hard for you," Lin happily assured his dad, who wanted to get home to go on a fishing trip the following day. He felt his guilt as he was thinking about his dad, lonely on the boat on a two or three-day trip on the river. His dad would not be lonely if he were with him, helping him on the boat. He promised himself to make his dad's sacrifice a worthwhile regardless of what came ahead. He silently prayed that his dad got home safely and that he would catch lots of fish on his trip.

He returned inside after his dad's short walking figure gradually became smaller and smaller at the end of the alley and then disappeared amid the houses in the neighborhood as he was on his way to the bus station. He missed his daddy already. This is the first time in his life the separation from Dad seemed real, and the void inside him kept expanding, moistened his eyes.

On the table where they had their lunch earlier, he saw the application form lying at the center waiting for him. This is something he had never done before. This is the beginning task of becoming a high school student. He felt a sense of importance of doing this, the filling out of the form. He could not help thinking of the earlier years in the village, when someone had asked him to write a letter for them since they were unable to read nor write. They were illiterate! He felt the pride and honored to be able to help these folks. The letters he created for them ranging from casual to sentimental, namely love letters, and they are fortunately, or unfortunately, not many.

The first ones are from those who have relatives from many parts of the land, and in a rare incident, from a remote village in North Vietnam. In many cases, he saw letters, which were faded, and the words sometimes became a guessing game in his mind. There are also ones with battered papers, separated at the folding lines, brought to him to write a response. He would read the letters out loud to them and write what they want to say and read it back to them. The last step of this letter-writing business is to write the address on a colorful envelope and give back to them to send it out. It is always a good feeling to do that, especially, to see their happy faces, to see them carry the letters with care and reverence as if their breath, their emotion, their love, all encapsulated in the envelope.

The second group of letters was not much he could brag about, except an incident that will stay with him as long as he is alive. It was not about the writing but the delivering of a love letter from a young beautiful girl, seventeen or eighteen years of age, a daughter of a merchant, an owner of a grocery store at his side of the river. Her name is Que, who fell in love with one of the young good-looking soldiers at the military post, which was located on the other side of the river to provide protection to the bridge against the communist guerillas. Knowing that he could, as little as nine years old, row his boat from one side to the other, effortlessly, Que bribed him candies from her mother's store to deliver her letter to her lover. Like a professional mail man, without a glitch, he hand-delivered the letter to the young soldier. The man was ecstatic! He showed deep appreciation for Lin's help, and she too.

A week later, Que asked him to do it again, which he was gladly to. However, little did he know that Que's mother had been watching her daughter day and night with her hawkish eyes.

Every move Que makes, every out of ordinary behavior, could not escape her mother's scrutiny.

It was early in the afternoon, siesta time, a lazy-quiet time. The sun was high in a blue cloudless sky, a very beautiful day. There was not anyone on the beach except a couple of birds in the air, chirping, calling each other. The water on the river was flat, mirroring the sky. Just as soon as he got to the boat, which was half-aground, carefully setting the pink-colored envelope on a flat surface of a plank, ready to push the boat into the water, a woman, in her early fifties, short and medium built, Que's mother, appeared from nowhere, quietly standing behind him, right at the edge of the water.

"Hey, blue bird," she called him in her low, choppy, threatening voice that jolted him. He was terrified as he turned around to see her angry face, which was reddened in the hot sun. "Blue bird" is something he had never heard before, but now, given the circumstance, he knows what she meant: "connecting the two lovers," he guessed.

He looked at her while her eyes were fixating on the colored envelope, lying on the boat in the plain daylight. He was frozen; he was petrified. He was searching for words, but they all escaped him utterly.

"Hand it to me," she commanded him as she pointed her index finger to the pink evidence.

He walked over to the side of the boat, stooped down to pick up the mail, and handed to her with both of his hands, respectfully.

"I am truly sorry, *mamma*," he said without looking at her. He could not find courage to lift his eyes to meet hers, for he was caught red-handed, a "blue bird." He was expecting a couple of slaps on his baby face.

Instead, she said, "I will tell your parents."

Oh no! That is even worse, he thought out loud. What kind of troubles he was going get himself into? His dad is going to whip him; his stepmother is definitely going to ridicule, to laugh, or even to have a better reason to torture him to death.

"Oh, please, mamma, I am sorry. They are going to kill me. I promise you I will not do it again," he pleaded to her, tears rolling on his cheeks, sobbing.

"You promise? Never do it again?" she asked, bending her head down, looking at him. Her eyes, squinting, met his. Her face almost touched his baby face, as if she were going to bite him. There's a pause between each short sentence, emphatically.

He felt a little hope, a tiny, teeny chance that he was going to get off the hook, judging from the questions she asked.

"If I ever catch you again, you will be very sorry. Now go home!" she said at last.

"Thank you, mamma," he told her, feeling like a bird, not blue bird, lifting his wings off from the trouble ground, up high in the air.

Whatever the consequences Que had after that unpleasant incident, she did not ever ask him to deliver her mails again. Maybe she never wrote him any more. Maybe she found a way connecting her love without a "blue bird," flying her mails across the river. Nonetheless, he did get off the hook that day. Thank God. Imagine if his parents knew about this, he would have experienced the hell on earth.

The filling of the application form was not hard as he had thought it would be. He needed to fill his name, date of birth, his parents' name, and place of residence. He was not sure if he had to put his mom's name or his stepmother's. But he quickly figured it out that he should put his mother's, and it was what written in the form, and not before long, he had completed the application.

He wanted to let Bac Sau know that he had it done and was ready to go to check out the school with him. As soon as he turned to the corner of the house to ask Bac Sau, he saw him lying on his side facing the wall, snoring loudly. He must have had a long day, very tired by getting things ready for him and his dad to come, making sure that the guests would feel welcome and at home.

Now in this quiet moment of the day, he has time to look at the house, a new place he would call home for the time being. It is not much of a house as he first observed. A red dirt floor packed down from in-house traffic, in addition to an application of salt, grained into the dirt to keep it moist and to prevent dirt turned into dust inside the house. It is a very creative way to make a floor look nice and solid next to cement at a fraction of the cost and is quite popular in the countryside. In the opposite corner, next to the dining table, is the bed, his bed, he presumed; otherwise, he would be sleeping with Bac Sau, which would be a big surprise. Nonetheless, it's a simple structure composed of three planks of wood about two inches in thickness, sitting on three horses, about forty inches in height, one on each end, and one in the middle. There are two small poles at each end of the bed for hanging mosquito net. *What a simply life*, he thought. In this case it is equivalent to being poor. Bac Sau does not have anything other than a roof above and a red dirt floor to support it and to walk on.

He wandered to the back to take a good look at the cassava plantation, no, make it a lot, a square one, about a third of an acre. It's so dense that it gives away such an inflated feeling. Down the hill, as far as his eyes could see, house after house in different sizes and shapes, and so are their roofs in different colors, some green, some white, some even in red. Talking about the mood in the city life, he felt dizzy!

Suddenly, he missed home, wondering what his little brother was doing at this time. Does he know that he is away for schooling? Is he mad at him for not saying good-bye to him before he left?

"Lin, are you out there?" Bac Sau called him from inside. Obviously he was up from his nap.

"Yes, Bac Sau," he answered as he dashed back inside to see him. He knew he would have to go to turn the application in at the school and do some shopping before the day was over.

"Get ready. We go to school, son." Lin was amused by the word "we" Bac Sau used, and he almost told him, "No, you don't; you are too old and too wise for it," but held it off.

Leaving the administrative office at the school, Bac Sau's had on his hands two pieces of paper, one white and the other pink. The white one is the acceptance paper, and the other, the list of items needed to purchase for school.

Lin was, in one way, joyful at the fact that he was accepted and officially becoming a student in the city. But, in another, he felt uneasy at the items he had to have before the school started in the next few days. The items that would take a chunk of money out of his dad's budget (if there is any) are uniform and shoes. They all are available through the suppliers at the school.

"It is just about enough from what your dad gave to me to get you going," Bac Sau told him. That is only one piece of information Lin ever had regarding money. He tried to quickly add things up in his mind based on the price, handwritten on the sheet of paper, that Bac Sau had checked for the order.

The loudspeaker in his head screamed out loud, *Holy smoke! That is a whole week's worth of fishing, given that you are lucky.*

"Bac Sau, thank you for helping me. I hope my dad will send some money to pay for my food and everything." Lin tried to express his gratitude as clearly as he could. He became a bit concerned of the amount of money used on him.

The joyful emotion filled him as he walked straight home from the school. The excitement ran through his veins, lifted his legs higher, faster, and, if it weren't for Bac Sau, who quietly, patiently walked behind him, Lin could have galloped and got home in no time. The road home from the school was rather a long one, but he enjoyed the walk. Lin noticed that on his left, there's a park, a large one, which he had not paid much of attention when he passed it earlier to school. He must have let his mind completely focused, totally absorbed in what could happen at school when he arrived there. Possibilities of rejection due to student population was at its max, and there was no more room for him, or perhaps his financial responsibility could not be met for school requirements, or millions of other things tumbled, jumbled in his little head that made him a nervous wreck that he had missed seeing everything around him. At a closer look, he saw benches scattered throughout the park, some with curved-back support, others just a flat, rectangular seat, and they are glazed marble inlay with subdue-colored pebbles in mauve, turquoise-blue, light-brown, and sand colors.

"If you want, you can stay here at the park," Bac Sau's voice echoed behind him as he noticed that Lin had shown much interest while looking at the park.

"You know how to get home, don't you?" Bac Sau continued in his soft raspy tone of voice, much of caring. He must have sensed that a boy, like him, growing up with rushing water in a river, surrounded with hills and mountains, enwrapped in with green tress, lush grasses, a full spectrum of colors of flowers, would appreciate this environment. And indeed, he was drawn into it as if there were a magnetic pull that drew him toward it.

"Bac Sau if you allow me," Lin said with full excitement hidden in his voice. "I will be home soon to cook dinner for you, Bac Sau." He continued with much appreciation conveyed to the old man's eyes.

"It is okay; take your time, son."

He bowed to Bac Sau, saying a good-bye, and in no time, he was immersed inside the park, flooded with late-evening sun.

What a treat! He wanted to scream out loud but did not want to startle the birds in the bushes or the young couple sitting at the benches nearby the tall blooming bougainvillea bushes.

The evening sun flooded its golden rays of light onto the entire area of the park, which covers the whole corner of the main streets, leading to heart of the city. It is so big that the serenity, the integrity of the park is not affected by the traffic of the road from its northwest side. Here and there, people, some in singles, some in couples began coming in for their treats of the day, leisurely walking, talking, laughing as they were slowly casting their eyes around to take in, to enjoy the nature's beauty of the park. Lin had never seen a park in his life, much less a farm of such a collection of flowers in one area. He was just amazed at a public place that has so many varieties of plants, of trees, and of flowers. Red and pink roses in full bloom along the sidewalk seemed smiling and inviting. He bent over to let his nose faintly touch the velvety petals of the pink and red roses. He never knew one could be inebriated by the fragrance of the roses. He was exhilaratingly intoxicated. His fingers touched the buds, the half-open roses, run down the delicate stem, ready to pinch it off. But he stopped, looked up, cast his eyes around, thinking of the trouble he could get in. He was thinking about the wild flowers in the field at home, back in the village, where he could pick them at his leisure. *Not here, farm boy!* he told himself and moved on. Pink and lavender dahlias together with giant white peonies seemed to be competing for man's attention at their circular, maroon-brick-colored blocks at the end of the sidewalk. Lin sauntered slowly from one sidewalk to another, giving his eyes the feast of the beauty of the nature, allowing his lungs a full breath of the fresh-scented air from the garden of flowers. He felt like being in heaven with blue sky above with stretches of white cloud, like shredded white cotton, drifting lazily high in the air. Birds wheezed above his head, dashing from one tree to another, chirping in the air, singing in the trees. They found their safe haven here for there is a sign on the ground, forbidding any kind of bird shooting. What a heavenly, beautiful evening! He knows in his heart this is a place where he is going to come to spend time to do his homework, to do his reading during the day, and home in the evening. It should work out perfectly because there is no one home during the day anyway. Lin decided to walk around the park to let him soak it in before he went home just for the sake of seeing everything and enjoy the quiet evening in the nature. He felt the joy seeping into his heart the first day in the city, the beginning of his new life, far away from home. He is too young to worry what is coming tomorrow or the next day.

"Did you enjoy the park? I am glad the Montagnards [the mountain dwellers] did not snatch you away," Bac Sau jokingly told him with a gentle smile and squinted eyes as Lin entered the front door.

"Yes, Bac Sau, I had a delicious time at the park. I had never seen so many beautiful flowers in one place like that in my life. I have learned a few names of these flowers too," Lin told him with all excitement in his voice and could not stop talking.

"And you know what? I am too skinny for the Montagnards; I am afraid that they might think they would have to feed me too much of their foods before I could become any good value for them." Lin continued with the same cheery mood in the conversation. Immediately he realized that it was late for dinner as he saw Bac Sau putting two bowls and chopsticks on the table; he told Bac Sau, "Oh, I am sorry, Bac Sau. Please let me do it. Let me bring the food out for you."

He dashed to the kitchen only to be engulfed in the aroma of a delicious beef stew in the air that certainly heightened his hunger and made his mouth salivate. It took him a few seconds to rest his eyes on a round ceramic dish covered with stir-fried beef, laced with fresh, green, water-crest, and sliced tomatoes, sitting on the stool ready to be served.

How deliciously it looks, a thought ran through his head. Bac Sau is surely a darned good cook, and he definitely wanted to learn from this man.

"Eat a lot, as much as your tummy can hold, son," Bac Sau told him as he sat at the table, facing him, beginning the evening meal, just the two of them.

"Yes, Bac Sau, I will and am hungry," he told Bac Sau. He let every taste bud dance in his mouth when the sweet, tender stir-fried beef melted on top of his tongue.

"There is no one here to watch you eat. I heard a lot about your stepmother," Bac Sau continued, encouraging him to just enjoy the food.

"Yes, Bac Sau." Lin's voice deepened with gratitude. He did not know if he should join the conversation about his stepmother. Obviously, Bac Sau had learned a lot about her through the grapevines, or through his dad, perhaps.

"It is a shame. It is a shame, my son." Bac Sau's voice packed with emotion and went on. "That is why people say what they say, *'May doi*...unless one finds." Bac Sau filled Lin's bowl with more food from his bamboo chopsticks as he was talking. It is the care that he experienced with his own father. He was simply touched.

"Bac Sau, you live all by yourself? Don't you have any kids?" Lin asked Bac Sau after he set the chopsticks across his bowl on the table, signaling he had finished his meal. He wanted to ask Bac Sau earlier as he had noticed the emptiness and loneliness in his house but did not have a chance, and he thought it was not appropriate.

"Yes, I had two boys. One was left behind with his mother when we tried to escape from north to south at the time in which the country was divided in halves back in 1954. The younger one came with me. It was very painful, Lin." Bac Sau had stopped eating and now told him his saga of the ordeal of the past.

"My younger son, I believe, is now somewhere in town; he left the house almost a year ago after a heated argument with me." Bac Sau paused in what seems like a long hour, perhaps, calculating whether or not to finish the story. His eyes now shifted back to rest on Lin's, in sort of hypnotizing.

"He is fifteen going on sixteen years of age, a few years older than you, Lin." In his maudlin tone of voice, he carried on with the story.

"He was never happy with me, no matter what I did for him, giving him. He wanted new nice clothes, new shoes even a brand-new bicycle. I bought every one of them for him; all I asked from him was to focus on study, do his home work. He refused to do that, and the next thing happened was a note from the school saying that he had not done his homework assignments besides multiple tardiness and absences. I asked him about what the school said. He flatly told me that he did not want to go to school any more. Oh my God, I tell you. That answer of his not only made me very angry, but also hurt me terribly. It tore my heart apart. I gave him what a good father would for his son: love and support to make sure he has everything he needed to grow, to become a good student, good citizen. But unfortunately, he wanted to hang around with a wrong crowd, wrong circle of people whom he calls friends, and, sadly, turned against me. Not only did he not listen, but he also argued back, talked back, and even screamed at me, and I was wondering if he were under some sorts of toxic influences. I could not take it any more. I would not tolerate this disrespectful behavior from him in this household. I told him he had two choices: one to be a good student, a good son, or he has to leave. It was not easy for me to give him the ultimatum. It was painful for a father to tell his son that. And guess what? Out of this house he went and never once came back. What has gotten of him, I wish I could know. I prayed and hoped that one day he would come home, he would walk in the door like a prodigal son, and I would throw my arms, wide open, to hold him and welcome him back." Bac Sau's eyes were moistened and welled up while his voice was quivering. His arms were up, stretching in the air, gesturing what he was saying.

Please, my Lord, do not let him break down, Lin silently prayed, afraid to see the man collapse. Lin wished that he could comfort the old man in this evening hour when he poured out his heart of his sorrow, of his misfortune of a lost son. Maybe some days down the road, just maybe, Lin was thinking that he could find his son and asked him to come back to his father. He made a point to pray for both of them so that the healing of their relationship could happen, soon.

Lin wanted to sit still in silence; at least in his thinking, that would help to give Bac Sau some comfort by just quietly being present here with him.

It was getting dark quickly. Mosquitoes were out, hunting, landing on his bare skin and his face. He wanted to slap them, chase them away. But he did not want to disturb the precious time between the two of them. He really wanted to say something to Bac Sau such as,

"Bac Sau, I do want to fill that hole in your heart by being a good boy, good student for you. And if you don't mind, I will stay here with you and take care of you as your son as long as you want." Not soon enough, Bac Sau had already stood up to light the oil lamp at the corner of the table with his match. Lin held that thought from becoming words.

"Tomorrow will be a busy day for you, son," Bac Sau told him under the yellowish light from the oil lamp. "You will pick up your uniform and your class schedule. You will also make sure your size is correct when the uniform is delivered at school. There should not be a problem because your name is sewn on your shirt."

"Yes, Bac Sau, I think I can handle that. That should be very easy compared to what I used to do in the village," Lin told Bac Sau with much assurance in his voice so that Bac Sau would not have to worry about him.

"I will go to work very early in the morning. You will take care of yourself. Make sure to cook some food for you to bring to school, and I will see you home in the evening." With that said, Bac Sau, a minute or two later, dusted off his bare feet by rubbing them together, climbed on his bed, hung his gray-white mosquito net on the poles at corners of his bed. The room quickly became quiet after Lin said yes to Bac Sau's advice.

Within moments of stillness of the evening and to his surprise, Bac Sau had fallen asleep, and his snoring, like a choked-up muffler, was audibly in the air. He felt he had accomplished a lot and learned a lot, especially about the life of Bac Sau whose life has not been easy or pretty. He was too young, too little to know anything to help him except that he wanted to pray for him tonight before he went to bed. He also promised himself to do anything he could to ease the old man's pains.

Lin was at the office of the school early the following morning even before the secretary arrived. He was anxious to try on his uniform and to get his school supplies. While he was standing outside of the office waiting, he noticed a bare flag pole, painted in white, tall, standing straight up to sky from the open ground in front of the office, which was flanked by two three-story buildings. He wondered if these were all classrooms or if they were dorms for students. He would soon find out when the school started in the next few days, two days to be exact. Behind these tall buildings were lines of aged-tall flame trees whose pink-red flowers start their blooming, like a faithful clock, year after year, to begin the summer break for school. And now the wilted, broken petals were covering and coloring the ground, signaling the break was about to be over and a new school year is to begin.

On his left hand side, far from the entrance, a giant soccer field, bared in red dirt, lonely poles at the ends of the field, awaiting patiently in the open air for the students to come back, waiting for those dark-skin, muscular, energetic legs running, pounding, chasing the leather ball, stirring the dust into the air, and the roar of screaming, yelling would be heard when the ball, like lightning, flew inside the net between the two poles. He felt the excitement of being out there, to watch, or to be a part of the team, dribbling the ball when the school started.

"Oh, I can't wait," he was mumbling.

A few students started coming in through the gate, at the entrance, bearing the name of a senator, a member of Rahde tribe, Senator Y-UT, who was assassinated years earlier by the communists. Some were walking, some on bicycles, leisurely approaching the administrative building. The door to the office was quietly pulled open inward, and there, inside, stood an elderly secretary, well dressed in beige-white traditional *ao dai* (long dress). The thick glasses on her kind face and her welcome smile made him feel at ease.

"Good morning, mamma, I am here to pick up my uniform and school supplies," he said as he bowed his head in a very respectful manner. "I am a new student, mamma."

"Oh, good morning to you too," she said to him as she walked over to her desk, which a glass vase holding a half dozen of red roses, accented with white baby's breath, cheerfully sitting on at the far right corner. She lifted her glasses up with her index finger as she looked for his name on stack of white sheets of paper after he had told her his name.

"Your last name is Le, right?" She was confirming his identity while her finger was moving down ward on the list, and to the end of the first sheet, and the second sheet, and the third.

"Hmm." Without opening her mouth, she then made a vocal sound; she glanced up at him as if saying, "Bear with me, son." She went back to the list the second time, slowly and carefully, line by line, name by name, making sure she would not miss his name.

Lin was nervous as he was helplessly watching her. A thought came to his mind that made him dreadful. Maybe his name was skipped out by a mistake. Maybe the school has decided not to have him because after all; the school is designed and built, particularly, for the minority tribal students. The government had recently promoted the education for the Montagnard youths, the white Thai, the Hmong, the Rahde, the Koho, to name a few, in an effort to gain supports from all tribes, dwelling in the central highland, and, ultimately, to produce educated young officers in the armed forces, young government officials in the local government. His situation is worse than a minority, he thought, and the government does not know how minor of the minority he has been. That could very well be the reason they denied him even thought they gave him the acceptance note, just yesterday. Mistake? His mind was ready to explode with all possibilities, one of which is he has to go back home to go fishing, farming like his dad, and the other is... He had not finished his thought when the secretary, without looking up, said, "Come on inside, I have found you." With one hand she pointed him to a wooden door behind her office while the fingers of the other were still on the page of the list as if she were making sure that the lucky name of his would not jump off the sheet. He chuckled at his own thought as she gave him a kind look and a beautiful motherly smile.

"Thank you, mamma," he uttered his appreciation as he entered through the door.

It was a small room with shelving up to about eight feet tall against the wall and a free standing one in the middle on a cement floor, lit by a single high-wattage lightbulb, dangled from the ceiling. The fresh smell of new clothes along with new books and new accessories brought him a new level of awareness of his very new beginning, which had just now begun. This was a pleasant feeling, which he had never felt before. The boxes with full names on white labels, stacked up neatly on the shelves, alphabetically. Row by bow, up and down, he let his eyes wander, searching for his name among the many boxes.

Not before long, he had his box on a bench next to the door, then other students began to come in to get theirs.

As posted on the wall on a handwritten piece of white sheet of paper, students may try their clothes here, or at the comfort of their home, as they wish. The decision had already been made when his eyes landed on the poster note. There is no way he would show his skinny, bare chest to all the starring eyes around him in the room.

Without opening the box, twenty-four inches and square, light-blue colored with a white label, which shows the name and address of the local supplier, he checked off his name on the list at the office and said thank you to the secretary, and off he was out of the office and ran straight home.

The clothes were ordered by ages, not tailored fit, but it came out almost perfect for him. Perfect because he had never had this nice set of clothes in his life. The navy-blue khaki pants and shirt rolled off his hands, piece by piece. He gently shook them loose from the folding. He pressed the shirt against his chest and put it on. *Perfect*, he said to himself. It fits him perfectly even the sleeves stop at his wrists without measuring. Incredible! Someone must have come to measure him while he was in bed. A funny thought, he told himself. He then tried the pants on. He felt, all of a sudden, shorter; the pants grew three inches longer, but fit him well. No problem, he said to himself, "I can fix this." In fact, he was used to mend his own clothes when living at home. He never thought the survival skills he had to have in the early years now became handy.

The next two items still sitting in the box, waiting, staring at him, were something he had never had, never worn in his life. A pair of shoes and a pair of socks, all were the same color, dark-green fatigue, like the ones he had seen worn by the soldiers. He took them out from the box, sat them on the bench where he was sitting, and he was not sure if he would be comfortable to put it on, or even to try on. He looked at them then he looked at his feet, covered with red dust. Hesitating for a moment, he knew what he needed to do first. He went out back to the kitchen, washed, and rinsed his feet.

The soft, silky nylon socks did not want to cooperate with him. He had such a had time putting them on simply: One, the socks were much smaller than his feet, even they were nylon. Two, his toenails were long, and the skin on his feet, from heels to sides, were cracked and rough, which all made the trying almost a joke. It sounded like the sawing heard from underground. At last, he had his feet and shoes in place and felt comfortable with the shoes. He tightened the shoelaces. He started to walk inside the house with his shirt on, without the pants. He bent down to look at the shoes on his feet and made a few more rounds to and from the kitchen, then decided it was great. The beginning life of a city boy, he chuckled with the thought.

Not too long after the school started, he came to learn that one set of clothes, the uniform, was not enough, but he could not afford a second pair. He did not want to send a letter home to ask his dad for help. Even if he did, he would not think his stepmother would be inclined to open her purse for a donation. He decided to make the best of his situation. He washed them in the evening every other day after school, hung them on the clothesline under the roof by the wall in the back of the house and let the breezes do the drying over the night. Most of the times, nine out ten, when the weather changed, rained, dampened, he either charcoal-ironed them in the morning, or he would fold it underneath the straw mat on his bed and sleep on it. The heat from his body would have it warm-dried by the time he got to school.

During the first half of the school year, he enjoyed the learning in the classroom as much as the friendship he had with classmates and others in the school. An incident that made his face known throughout the school, and it became his lifetime indelible memory. It all began when it was time to celebrate the Vietnamese New Year, the lunar year, also known as Chinese New Year, the first week of February of the western calendar. The entertainment and cultural department decided to do a show before the school break, before the students go home with their families for this important festivity time of the year. The show would include singing, tribal dancing, and a play.

Since it is a pilot school of polytechnical institution for the minority students funded by the government, it is primarily a male-student-only school. One can say that it is more like a nonreligious monastery than a school, sitting on top of the hill.

Therefore, no girls are available to partake a female role of the play. How to solve the dilemma? It did not take the thinking of a math teacher at the school to figure it out. They came to him for help. They wanted to have him play the role of a mother, a wife whose husband was sent to war, to the battlefield.

One day, during a lunch break, he was summoned to the music department.

"Lin, would you like to help us in a play for school?" asked Dan, the leader of the entertainment program.

"What can I do to help? What do I have to do?" Lin hadn't had a clue of what he was going to be up against to.

"We need your help to do a role in our play."

Oh, no, no, I don't think I can do a play or any part of a play, for I have never done such a thing, he almost said. *All I know is fishing. If it were fishing, I would do it for you.* But he held it off.

"Hey, brother, you are the best candidate for the role," Dan— the Hmong guy, dark-skinned, and tall, built like a Greek statue— continued with his persuasion.

"The teachers and everyone in the entertainment department agreed that you are the one."

THE ACTING He was elated with the recommendation, but something did not feel right, he thought.

"Tell me, why did you pick me? Do I look like a girl, act like a girl?" he challenged Dan in an amicable tone of voice. He knows in his heart that his name, a girl's name, gives way to it too. Sometimes he wondered if his parents were sober when they named him. Were they ever sure about his sex? Oh yes, he was teased hundreds if not a thousand times by the kids in the village.

"Hey, there are no girls here in this school. We all need to chip in to make it happen. Besides, you will do well. Trust me." Dan gave his persuasive ultimatum. "We all need to chip in." His friend's words, how can he turn him down; how can he avoid such a noble request?

"All right, I will do my best. Just tell me what to do." Lin gave in at last. After all, he felt he is a part of the community of the school, and so is his contribution needed to make it a better place for everyone to enjoy and to study.

"Great, I will give you a script to read. Training will begin tomorrow after school," Dan told him before he took off.

Back in the classroom for the afternoon session, his mind was wandering to a play, to the training, and the role in the play. Not just a role, but a female role. Oh boy, he was nervous. He will never hear the end of it. He would be known as Ms. Lin all over the school.

It was going to be a very grand celebration in which camping would be set up inside the school perimeter. Each class would have its own tent. The cooking, the cleanliness, and the decor would be graded as part of the competition among classes. There will be prizes awarded to the winners. Judges are selected among teachers and administrative officials.

The school has also invited the city officials. Word was that the mayor had accepted the invitation to join the school for the entertainment program. Everyone from the school officials to the students felt the pressure. "Every department, every part of the school has to run well. The school has to be well represented." The president of the school wrote in the school bulletin.

Lin received from Dan a five-page long, double-sided, handwritten script just before he went home in the evening. He, at the first glance, almost screamed at the pages.

"How in the heaven I can remember this? It is like a novel." But he calmed himself with one thought: *I will do my best. That is all I can.*

First thing first, that is, to read the whole script, ten pages long, to get an idea of what his role is all about, he told himself. And that was exactly he was doing while walking home. The good thing was there was no homework in any class. Everything was geared toward the celebration of the holiday. He appreciated the break and wanted to devote his time and energy for the acting the play. He wanted to do his very best on this assignment for the school, his school.

The story began with a young family of three, a husband, a wife, and a month-old baby boy. It happened during the wartime in the old days, which is very typical in the Vietnam history; simply she had been constantly at war. First, for over thousand years with China, her next-door neighbor, a hundred, no, make it a thousand times bigger than she is. Second, with France, thousands of miles far away, against its colonization for over one hundred years.

When the sound of the drums, the sound of the gongs were vibrating, shaking the air throughout the village, her husband, a young man, along with many in the region, followed the king's order to fulfill their duty, defending their country. It is an honorable duty to serve the king and the nation.

At the moment of their separation, in tears, the young warrior told his young wife that he will soon return and that she needed to take care of herself and their son. Resting her head against his shoulder, she was sobbing.

"Yes, my hero. I will wait for your coming home, soon." Her words, soaked with tears, hardly came out of her mouth.

"My darling, I will come back for you despite the circumstances," the young soldier told his wife with solid assurance in his tone of voice.

"I will stand at the door waiting for you, despite the time, regardless how long, months or years; I will wait for your return." The young wife, her arms were locking his solid-firm body, buried her face to his chest, reassured her departing husband to the war zone.

Outside, the drums, the gongs, continued their unrelenting fast-pounding sounds into the air, as if telling the warriors to get on the double, to get on their horses and on to the battlefield.

The sounds of horse galloping and other commotions faded into silence at the end of the evening in the village.

Then the longing, the waiting began. Days turned into week. Weeks turned into months. And year after year, he had not come home. Every night, after many hours laboring in the field, lying next to her son, now older, as the years had passed, she let her tears flow, blurring her man's image, his handsome face. The memories of their love, like a videotape, played back on her mental screen. She tried, in vain, to contain her sobbing, which became audible in the night between the walls. In the loneliness of a quiet night, she was wondering what had happened to him. His whereabouts? Does anyone know? She prayed and prayed to the heavens, to her God, regardless where he is, in the front line or in the rear to please keep him safe, please let him come home to her.

Every day in the evening, she would stand by the back door, watching the twilight sun, like an orange-colored dish, coming down, setting behind the leafless willow tree, and she would let her imagination take her, get a hold of her. Her warrior would be coming home on his horse. He is as strong and handsome as he was before going to war. He would jump off the horse, snatch her up, and away she and her man would be vanishing to their dream land. But the reality is so cruel. She shook her head and let her teardrops roll down on her cheeks.

Time rarely or never waits. Time never kept its promise, as one would say. Time is whispering to her, "My fair lady, why wait? Your beauty is like a flower, which is withering and fading. Don't you know?"

"I am forever faithful to my warrior. My fidelity to him is the utmost despite time and space," she whispered back.

The waiting continued on and on until one night, a stormy night, the winds were howling, blowing, beating, against the walls, outside of the house, and the thunders were rumbling, exploding far and near in the air; the lightning was continually ripping the dark sky. The young woman carrying her son, whose head rests on her shoulder, stood still in waiting despite the angry weather, despite the downpour of rain, defying everything that seems working against her. The magic moment had come; the mother and her child have turned into the stones, "the waiting stones," one leaning on top of the other. The faithfulness, the fidelity, the devotedness, all solidified, condensed, hardened to rocks, to stones. How beautiful the allegoric stones!

Lin engrossed in the story, and before he knew it, he had arrived at the park where he found a seat on a bench and reread the story and wondered if he could perform the role of a young wife, a mother carrying a child. Carrying a child? No problem! He is used to that in his younger years. But he would hope not a real crying, kicking, pooping baby. A fake one, he would prefer. Just like him, a disguised girl, disguised mother. He would have to wait to see what the trainer wanted him to do.

The following morning, while everyone busy digging holes, putting up tents for camping, he was inside the art department, grilled on his role playing by the trainer, none other than Dan, who got him into the acting business. By the end of the day, he felt comfortable with his role-playing. He remembered his lines and moved comfortably about the stage, pacified a crying child (doll) with his hands, stood still like a rock until magically turning into stones. One of the most difficult things seemed to be the lines of poetry that he has to remember by heart and recites in musical rhythms, which he thought sounds very spirit uplifting for the soldiers going to battlefield: "*Trong truong thanh lung lay bong nguyet*...the sound of the drum-beats seems vibrating the moonlight."

The D-day had arrived. The many hours of training, rehearsing now came to the real showing and performing.

The air of festivity, the atmosphere of celebrating were all over the school, from campground with erected military moss-green tents whose gates, built with tree branches, were trimmed with multicolored papers, to the stage, the center of all activities, which was decorated with two pots of green banana trees, one taller than the other, one standing on each side of the stage. A white ten-by-four banner stretched across the top of the stage, carrying bold-cut letters in black, welcoming the guests. Behind the closed dark-burgundy-colored curtain was a band of variety of musical instruments, under the direction of a teacher, the head of music department. The teacher gave a last-minute rehearsal, sending loud drumbeats, ear-piercing sounds into the air across the school buildings. On the floor, rows of chairs neatly sat in front of the stage, quietly waiting.

He was nervous wreck, despite the sounds of the uplifting music, despite the many times he told himself that he could do it. He was dreadful of the thought that he might not remember the lines, and he might forget to give appropriate gestures as he delivers the lines. His heart pumped faster than the ticking of the clock on the wall.

The show began with a short presentation from the principal of the school, who welcomed the guests and delivered the message to his students for the year to come. What really helped Lin, he thought, was a vibrant tribal dance followed by a Montagnard song, all of which were uniquely performed that eased his worrisome into his own play.

In the traditional Vietnamese outfit, a black kerchief, like bandana, formed triangularly on his head, a grayish two-piece long dress loosely worn on his body along with the makeup on his face, especially his red-colored lips, he surely looked like a girl, and his job is to act like one.

The audience roared with hand claps as soon as the curtain slowly pulled to the sides, showing his camouflage-shaped girl, carrying a baby doll, wrapping in the white cloth. He then emotionally sang his lines. He moved his pace about the floor, gestured his hands to bid a farewell to the man off to the battlefield. His performance went well along with others in the play, making it a huge success. The audience rose on its feet at the end of the play as the curtain pulled to envelop the cast. The trainer came over to personally congratulate him on his performing and on being a girl so realistically that which contributed to the success of the play. He felt quite a relief that it was over; it was done! However, he, at the same time, felt elated that he was appreciated for what he did and what he could do.

The last day at the campground before the school went into holiday break brought so much joy into his life. The students, the teachers friendly greeted him, and most of the time, heartily teased him by calling him "co Lin" or "Ms. Lin." which, at first, he felt a bit uneasy, perhaps a shade of insult. He took it too personal, defending that he was not a girl and not even a transsexual, but then, realizing that it was a compliment and because of what he had done, he became known to the staff, the teachers, and everyone in the school.

The people who had really shown interest in knowing him were the school principal and his wife, Mr. and Mrs. Dong, and the other couple was the school supervisor and his wife, Mr. and Mrs. Nam, and his whole family who all live inside the school compound.

At the campground, the food prepared and cooked from his tent did not make to the top of the judges' list, which he had hoped to see it would have happened. Nonetheless, it was so much fun, so much joy, so much laughter in the food and decorating competition, which he had never had or dreamed of having one in his life. The judge panel visited each tent, went through from one end to the other, glanced at the belongings, stacked along the walls of the tent, and, lastly, tasted the foods at the cooking area.

It was late in the afternoon, and after saying good-bye to his friends and teachers, wishing them a happy New Year, the year of dog, to come, he went straight home.

The weather has turned cold, especially in the high altitude of the central highland. It is generally colder here at this time of the year. Winds seemed to bring the icy-cold air from the depth of the jungle, from the forest to the city. Every now and then, a gust of wind pushed against his clothes through the pores of his skin make him chilled. A sudden loneliness engulfed him as his legs stretched on the dirt road.

The park on his right was barren without a soul around. The timing of the year and the weather have kept people stay warm inside their homes. This is also a sacred time of the year in which all should and must come home to be with their family for the New Year celebration. It is the time to be traditionally connected with the spirits of ancestors. It is the time to honor parents and grandparents for their roles in molding one's life. It is the time for new clothes and also the time for best foods to be cooked and served. It is the time for fireworks sparking up the dark sky and for the firecrackers, whose sound like machine gun, exploded from a string of firecrackers, hung on a pole or from the branch of a tree in front of the house, sending red-colored, tattered papers up in the air and quietly scattered on the ground. The white smoke from the explosive powder can be seen and smelled from far, far, away. He was thinking about all of these things that would happen in a day or two in his village. His mind was in the scene, celebrating, and yet his heart sunken. He knew he missed his home. He missed his dad and his brother. But he was not sure if his stepmother would like to see him home, let alone welcoming him. Although his heart had been healed from the past experiences and incidents, the scar of hurt and pains would not want to go away. As time passes and he grows older, and sometimes in the quiet of night, he pondered, wondered why some persons are so generous like Ba Thong, Bac Sau, whose kindness, like magnet, pull him, draw him closer to them, while others, the opposite.

Before he could make up his mind, Bac Sau was at the front door, standing there waiting for him with a big smile.

"Did you have good time at the camping?" Bac Sau asked him, and as if he knew the answer, he continued. "You need to get ready to catch the bus home for the New Year before it is too late, son."

It was all decided, the path has been chosen for him, the thought rushed through his head.

"Yes, Bac Sau," looking at the old man, Lin said obediently. But he was thinking that maybe, just maybe, he should stay with Bac Sau for the holidays to keep him company for he has been all by himself, very lonely, especially during this time of the year. He ventured to Bac Sau and told him, "Bac Sau, would it be possible if I stayed with you for the New Year?"

"No, no, that is absolutely not possible." The old man cut him short before he could finish.

"For your son is not with you."

He then added, "Your dad wanted you to come home for the New Year; besides, I am going to travel to visit friends in Saigon area for a week. I will see you when I get home. Be sure to tell your dad I say hi."

"Yes, I will definitely do that, and I hope you have good time with your friends, Bac Sau."

Caring For Dad On Newyear's

The year-end evening at the bus station was completely different from what he had seen six months ago. It was quiet with only one bus parking in the middle of a giant red-dirt empty parking lot, patiently waiting to pick up the last customers, for it did not want to leave anyone to miss the ride home before the New Year came.

The winter winds gushing seemed to give him a push as he picked up his speed, running to catching the bus. Papers, leaves, plastic bags, and trashes were blown, skidding along with empty cans, bounced and jingly sounded while rolling on the ground as if they were rushing to get the ride with him. It was not a lively pretty scene.

At last he climbed on the side of the bus, which was literally packed with passengers and merchants. There was hardly a space to stand in the middle aisle, much less the seating on the sides of the bus. His hands grabbed on a shining metal bar that runs along the side of the bus with his little duffel bag, rested securely between his legs. The high-pitched voices, especially from the merchants, seemed competing for airtime with the music blasted from the built-in speakers. The ducks and chickens in the cages hung from the back of the bus wanted their voices to be heard too. It was just a lonely, noisy fully loaded bus in the evening of the Vietnamese New Year's Eve. His mind now wandered to the village and wondered what everyone in his family was doing. He knew that his dad would expect him home and would prepare some traditional delicacies to celebrate the New Year. Dad is known for his specialty in making glutinous rice cake, shaped like a log. The white, overnight-soaked sweet rice, spread on banana leaves, were heat treated for flexibility and durability. In the middle of the patch of rice is a stretch of thick-seasoned pork meat, normally a belly part of meat, covered with well-soaked mung beans. The whole ingredients are now skillfully, tightly rolled and secured with bamboo strings. Each roll is about a foot long with a diameter of about three to four inches. The logs of cake are to be boiled in a big pot for hours before they are fully cooked, and when they are done, they are just simply delicious. He could not wait to give his dad a hand to wrap the cake and to cook as well. After all, he wanted to help and pay back for his time being away at school. His mind was busy with imaginary cooking without knowing that the bus had made a few stops and now approaching the uphill slope before entering his village. When the bus slowed down almost to the top of the hill, it stopped. It was like an old animal, exhausted his energy, used up his life force in climbing the hill, coughed, and coughed a few times, then decided to quit, stopped moving completely. Was it out of gas? Mechanical troubles? A dozen passengers looked at one another, wondering what the cause was. The young helper quickly jumped off the bus with a sizable wooden block; he wedged it behind the rear tire to stop the bus from rolling back down the hill. The driver impatiently tried repeatedly to turn on the engine but failed to get it started. Passengers voluntarily got off the bus just to make sure they were safer than sitting on the vehicle. He, too, was out and walked up to the top of the hill to gauge the distance just in case he decided to walk home, which he would not mind. The only thing he might be concerned with was wild beasts, not the robbers. There is nothing on his body for the robbers to get their hands on, but the wild animals, the tigers, the bears would have their New Year's Eve feast. The thought of facing a tiger would have his legs paralyzed, frozen in fear of being masticated under those fearsome teeth. The driver and helper were now working under the hood with a flashlight on, moving the light back and forth, left and right, checking on possible wire disconnections and other possibilities of malfunctioning. The evening light quickly disappeared behind the thick jungle of trees along the road. People began voicing their concerns, their complains.

"What an old junk we have on the road," said a short-tempered curmudgeon.

"I want my money back," disappointingly voiced another, a lone woman, a merchant.

"Let's give it a push to the top of the hill and then let it roll down to the valley," said a smarty young man of practicality without seeing the danger of being smashed by the back rolling of a heavy-duty vehicle. Anyhow, no one seemed to move at his suggestion.

Some whispered, wondering if they could ever get home at all. Nonetheless, the majority of passengers held their patience, their anxiety, and showed their respect to the driver and his helper who were trying their best to fix the problems. Like the rest of the crowd, they would never want to be stuck here on the road, out of nowhere. They have a family waiting for and to be with too.

As the temperature dropped in, at the peak of the hill, the chill from the forest seeped through his clothes onto his body. While everyone sat on the ground and grumbled about the circumstances and the cold air, he decided to move about, up and down the hill, not only to keep his body warm, but also to be not the victim to the mosquitoes that came in by hundreds if not thousands. They seemed always showing their forces in the beginning of the night, blood hunting. All was quiet; all came to still except occasional wheezing of the birds, flapping their wings over the air from the trees, from one side of the road to the other. The sky faded into darkness. He has been told many a time that the night of the New Year's Eve of the lunar calendar, tonight, is the darkest night of the year. It is said that one would not be able to see one's hand in this night, even in front of one's face. A cartoon he saw in a magazine awhile back depicted how dark this night is. In the middle of a whole sheet of paper, painted in black, a three-inch-long bar in solid white, with a half of an inch in thickness, stretched horizontally. It says in the bottom, "Can you guess to see what it is? Guess, guess, and guess." Then the answer is, "It is a smile of an African in the night of the New Year's Eve." It was a very cute cartoon, and it has stayed with him until this day.

Time seemed stand still. People stopped talking. Maybe they were tired. Maybe they were meditating, praying, which he was. He was praying for all to be able to get home with their families, soon, before the New Year started. Otherwise, he thought, it would be a bad luck, an unfortunate thing, which would have unlucky influence on the whole New Year, as any Vietnamese would say and believe. The only sound heard was coming from under the hood, where the two diligently tried to solve the problem. It seemed like eternity, and no one would know if they could change the situation, could fix the mechanical problems.

The roar of the engine came to life, at last, that vibrated the air, tore off the silence of the cold night and brought cheers to all distressed passengers, young and old. He believed his prayers were answered, and he silently said, "Thank you, Lord."

All rushed climbing onto the bus to avoid the icy-cold air, which seemed colder into the night, and to congratulate the driver and his helper for their success. Sitting behind the steering wheel, rubbing, cleaning his greasy hand with a half-clean rag, under the ceiling lights, the middle-aged driver turned back to his passengers, with his proud and kind smile, apologized for the troubles that put everyone in a bind, and thanked all for showing their patience. He then asked to make sure everyone was on board, for he did not want to leave anyone behind before he rolled his bus off up the hill.

The bus picked up its speed as it rolled down the hill, the atmosphere inside the bus came alive as people started their conversations.

"What if we had stay inside the bus all night?" a man would ask.

"I would just fall asleep, why such a question? Anything else would you or could you do?" matter-of-factly answered the other. They all talked almost at the same time to one another, unlike the mood just minutes ago on top of the hill.

From the bus station, after uttered his sincere appreciation to the driver, Lin began his walk home, almost running to surprise his parents for he knew his dad has been waiting for him since the dawn of the day. His dad has probably been sad because he had not come home. Ahead of him and around him were lights twinkled from houses in the village as if they were waiting for the magical time of the year, and he was almost certain that one among them, ahead of him, on the left side of the bridge, on top of the hill, was his, twinkling for him. He found his way onto the bridge without a glitch even in the darkest night like of tonight. He knows this area like the palm of his hand and could walk home even blindfold. The air was so fresh with fragrance of the earth, of the herbs, of the trees, of the leaves from the valley—all of which now came alive to him, for he had been away for so long. The water rushing audibly underneath the bridge reminded him how much he had missed his childhood life in this place. Just as soon as his legs got him almost over the end of the bridge, his soul, his spirit was flooded and lifted with choir of crickets as if welcoming him home, even at this late hour in the night of the year. Oh, he thought to himself, there was so much he missed from this beautiful simplicity of life. He saw some lights on the boats by the river and wondered if Ba Thong's was one of them. It was hard to tell in this thick blanket of darkness. He comforted himself with a thought that he would come to visit with her and her husband the first thing in the morning on the New Year's Day, which would be against the culture, the tradition to pay a visit to someone other than the immediate family members, such as parents and siblings. Ba Thong and her husband, as far as he is concerned, are more like parents to him; therefore, it is an honor and duty to do so.

While he was walking, thinking, expecting a house full of activities, lots of cooking, instead, he found a very quiet house. An oil lamp was shedding a weak, faint light through the crack at the front door that made him wonder if it was his house and if his parents were home, or they were in bed sleeping already. It dawned on him that it was very late in the night, and his dad might have thought that he was not coming home and then went to bed. Now it became his dilemma that he did not know what to do. His stepmother would certainly not be happy to be disturbed at this hour of the night on the New Year's Eve, and he would not, on his life, want to get her upset. On the other hand, he could not just stand outside of the house and turned into iceman in the morning. He paced back and forth in front of the house; he then pulled up his courage, and through the opening of the door, softly, he called up his father.

"*Thay oi* [Daddy], I am home." Pressing his ear against the door at the opening, he was hoping for his dad to respond, perhaps excitingly, to jump up at hearing his voice. But it was quiet, not a sound heard from inside.

All of his concern, his fear of waking up his stepmother went numbed in the cold; he turned the volume up on his voice, calling his dad repeatedly.

"Daddy, Daddy, I am home. Open the door for me!" He even ventured to knock on cold surface of the wooden door.

As he pinned his face against the door, peeking through the short, narrow, vertical crack, he saw the mosquito net moving, and out from it was his father who stepped on the floor, wobbly to the door. His heart sunk as he saw his dad in such a poor health condition. He must have been ill, he though, and he must have been home alone.

As the door was pulled open, he stepped inside to greet his dad.

"How come so late? I was waiting for you all day," his dad inquired in his weak and raspy-sleepy voice and began coughing.

Instead of telling his dad what had happened on the road, Lin was very concerned about his dad's health, and it appeared that he was home alone.

"*Thay*, are you not well? What is wrong? Where are my brother and mother? Can I get you something?" he asked a series of questions as if he would not have a second chance.

"They are at your grandparents' because I have been sick. It is a bad flu. I should be okay in a day or two. Besides, we do not do anything for the New Year. I have not been well." His dad went back to bed as he was talking. He felt sorry for his dad and worried about his health. Why is his dad home all by himself when he is ill? What happened to his stepmother? Why did she have to go to her parents' while his dad was not well? He wanted to ask his father for an answer, but hearing the coughing, he held it off. He felt the guilt for not being around to take care of his dad. He felt something was not right in his family. Perhaps he is the very cause to the rift in between his parents. The whole room became quiet as his father fell asleep. He felt sorry for his dad but did not know what to do. He does not know if his dad had eaten anything before he went to bed. Was he able to eat anything? Was he taking any medication? He will not find answers to those questions now. What he could now, even this late, is to cook some rice soup for his dad and make him eat when he got up during the night.

Lin went to the kitchen, carrying the oil lamp with him. He tried to get himself familiarized with his old kitchen. Nothing was changed, but he could not find any leftover food at all. He wondered if his parents ever cooked. In no time he got the fire started. The pot filled with water and a small cup of rice. Sitting by the fireplace, watching the flames caressing the side of the rice pot, he felt the warmth from the burning firewood, which was cracking, snapping under the tripod. He was grateful that he got home at last. He would never have thought to see his dad sick on this day. But this is the reality! All the things he had imagined on the way home were still his imagination. No glutinous rice cakes, no firecrackers, no greetings, no welcoming home, no laughter. But those things are not important, he thought. He was glad he got home to see his dad, especially when he was ill. He went up the house to check on his dad to see if he could get him to eat the soup he just made, but his dad was sound asleep. He went back to the kitchen, helped himself a small bowl of soup. He had not eaten much all day, but somehow he did not feel hungry. He was tired from seeing his family falling apart. His heart saddened.

After making sure the fire is completely out, the food is put away, not much anyway; he was debating whether or not to sleep on the bed with his dad. But he did not want to disturb his dad; he crawled onto the straw mat on the floor, next to the bed, to be sure he stayed close to his dad and fell asleep.

He woke up to the sounds of firecrackers and of occasional explosions from the supersized ones, which sounded like that of a hand grenade, in the neighborhood. He remembered he had not had a blanket on when he was lying on the floor, for he did not see one around, but he now was under a moss-green blanket, feeling warm, and he did not want to get up. He turned his head to look up and saw the opening of the mosquito net wide open, and his dad was not up there. He looked at the blanket on him, and there was no blanket on the bed; he knew his dad had put it on him somewhere in the middle of the night to make sure he would not get sick, or catching a pneumonia. His dad gave him the very blanket he had while he was sick, in bed. He wanted to cry.

He sprung up, ran to the kitchen to see his dad sitting by the fire, making his tea.

"Thay." He squatted next to his dad and continued. "Are you feeling better? What did you have? When did you have it?" He has the tendency to ask series of questions.

"Cam thoi," his dad told him mater-of-factly. (Just a cold.) "It has been the third day and…" His dad looked at him inquisitively, cutting short of what he wanted to say.

"Are you just back from the jungle?"

Jungle? The same old tricky, sarcastic way of questioning from his dad has had for him. Why didn't he just plainly, simply, ask or say, "Hey, son, your hair is too long. Go get your haircut!" He thought it was cute, for he had not heard it for a very long time. It bothers you, but after a long time, you are kind of missing it. He cannot help thinking of an analogy to that effect, a story of a buffalo and its owner, a farmer working out in the field, a rice paddy.

Every day the buffalo gets the yelling, the hollering, and getting whipped on his sides, on his back whenever a yoke is placed on his neck so that he could do the work, the plowing, and the raking of the soil. One day the farmer was ill. He stayed home. The buffalo, however, out in the field, felt that he had been missing the rod, the whipping from the hands of its owner, the farmer.

"*Thay*, I have been very busy at school. Besides, I like it the way it is." He actually wanted to say he was short on money, but held it off in time. He did not want to have his dad worry about money for him. He will figure out how to make money and pay for his school, he thought it out loud, even though he hadn't a clue how.

The tea kettle was boiling; the steam escaped through the spout up into the air like that of a steam ship, making the black, round cap of the kettle puffed up and down noisily, as the pressure of the boiling water increased. Lin was wondering if his dad had his green tea leaves in the pot, for he did not smell the fresh green tea in the air. He is always proud to have a sensitive nose from which he could tell if the corn is done when being boiled. He got up and said, "I go get some green tea leaves for you, *Thay*." He dashed to the backyard without waiting for his dad to say yes or no. He just knew what to do. In less than a minute, quickly filled his lungs with morning fresh air with a touch of fragrance from white flowers of the tea tress, he had a handful of green leaves, washed, and then inside the boiling kettle. The fact that his dad was boiling water without tea tells him that his dad was not well. However, his dad still got to the kitchen to get himself warmed up in order to share the blanket to him. He wanted to hold his dad, climbing on his back as he used to when he was little, and to tell him how much he loved him.

Lin now sitting next to his dad in the kitchen, enjoying the warmth from the firewood. He noticed there was a dramatic change in his dad's well-being, in his appearance. He looks a lot older since he last saw his dad in the city, at Bac Sau's house. Dad's cold has probably added more to it. He also noticed that his dad had not coughed this morning. That is a good indication that the cold has come to the tail end of it. He got up to fetch a ceramic bowl from the rack for the tea. He knew instinctively it was done and ready for his dad. Judging from his past experiences, the scented green tea in the air, and the time it was boiling, he knew it was perfectly brewed, and that would please his dad and help his cold.

He handed the hot bowl of tea to his dad and told him, "It is hot, be careful, *Thay*." His dad gave him a look of both appreciating and amusing as if saying, "Ah, you sounded like a big boy now to take care of me." He received the tea with both of his hands, which were a bit quivering around the bowl. It tells him that the illness did take a toll on his dad.

The slurping of the hot tea from his dad made his heart gladdened. It is the sign that he is truly enjoying what he is drinking.

This hot tea will make Dad feel better, he thought. *It will make him sweat and the cold will be flushed out of his body with the sweat beads.* He remembers this sweat-driven remedy is used whenever someone has a cold. Let that person eat a bowl of hot plain rice porridge, a white rice soup, heavily sprinkled with black pepper, garnished with chopped green onion, then the cold will be driven out, gone. He felt his heart packed of joy.

"I will warm up the rice soup I made last night for you. Since you were sound asleep, I did not want to wake you up. You will eat it while it is hot to bring the sweat out of you. Besides, you have to have some food in your tummy so that you could get your strength back. Do you remember you used to make me do it whenever I got sick?" It seemed as if it was the longest piece of conversations he ever had with his dad all of his life.

Surprisingly, his dad finished his soup, obediently. Maybe he wanted to please his son who has been far away from home. Maybe he realized that he needed to get well quickly to enjoy his son's company, or maybe because it is the New Year, and the Vietnamese people are quite superstitious. Things that happen on the New Year's Day will influence the rest of the year. It is said that one should not sweep one's floor during the first three days of the year. It is also believed that whatever on the floor is wealth. Do not sweep it away. Frankly, he did not have any intention do it anyway.

He saw beads of sweat on his dad's weathered forehead as he began to walk back to his bed. *He is getting better and looking better, but needs some rest*, he thought as he was walking behind his dad.

After he helped cover his dad with the blanket, he whispered, "Mung Nam Moi, Thay." (Happy New Year, Dad). Then he went back to the kitchen, thinking what to do next. It dawned on him that there was nothing at his house to bring about the flavors, the colors, and the atmosphere of the New Year. No pinky cherry blossoms, no yellow flowers (*hoa mai*), an exotic type of flowers, in the pot or the vase as he used to have in the previous years. The hoa mai yellow flowers, also known as flowers of the spring, whose shapes and sizes very much looked like those of apple blossoms, are popular and in high demand at this time of the year. Some people make good money on this by devoting their time to harvest and to cultivate the trees, mostly bonsai, and the branches to make sure they would produce flowers. The Vietnamese do believe, or they are superstitious, that if the buds on the trees or branches are open on the New Year's Day, it is the very sign that the whole year is favorable. It means wealth, health, and longevity. He was told that some of the adults stayed past midnight, waiting to see the blooming of the hoa mai yellow flowers in the early hours of the New Year. Someday down the road, when he gets older, he would like to experience the waiting for the buds to open. It must be a lesson of being patient, a virtue after all. He could get on the boat, dashed to the other side of the river, by the rocky gorge, where he used to cut the hoa mai, and sell them weeks before the New Year came. They grow and bloom wildly in this part of the riverbanks. However, given the circumstance, he might not be able to get to it today.

He mentally made a list of people he needed to visit and to do the happy-new-year wishes. Somehow he became aware of the two distinctive parts of the visiting. One, traditionally, on the New Year's Day, everyone turns one year older on this day. It does not matter what day one was born during western or lunar calendar; today is his or her birth day. So if you go out in the street, seeing any person, young or old, male or female, it is customary to utter the greeting "happy birthday" to that person, and that person will reciprocate the happy-birthday greeting as well. The other part of the visiting is the wishing for the New Year in which he finds very uncomfortable to say the endless items on the mental wish list. He feels the wishes uttered are empty, perfunctory, and not well meant at all. It is a scripted, memorized speech and used on every one encountered.

He decided to go to his uncle's family first, then Mr. and Mrs. Thong's, and wherever else he could get to later. Perhaps, he could go to the grandparents' where his stepmother and his little brother were supposed to have been. However, he did want to be back home with his dad, instead.

The morning air was wintery fresh, but chilly even the sun was high. The breeze must have brought "the cold home from the heart of the jungle," as his dad used to say on the day like this. The breeze here always brings fragrances of the soil, of the hay and the herbs combined, like no others. It makes him feel at home after a long absence. The sound of firecrackers was sporadically echoed back from the middle of village, enticing him to explore the New Year's events and activities, not to mention their smoke and smell, which would please his nostrils. The dirt road to his uncle's was not far, and within a few minutes, he was at the front door of a small-sized thatched-roof house, waiting to see if anyone home. The door was wide open, but no one was in sight. He wondered where they would be at this hour on the New Year. There were no dogs barking to let them know that there is a guest at the house. He decided to holler to make himself noticed.

"Uncle and Aunt, this is Lin. Are you home?" It was quiet. He ventured inside, feeling that he was a part of the family, and it was perfectly okay to do so. Besides, he felt that they would love to see him anyway for he had been away to school for so long and now came back as a student. Appeared and merging from the kitchen was his aunt, short and small built, who stared at him for a long time, until finally, like a magnet, she flew over and held him, sobbing with joys.

"Oh, this is my dear nephew. How are you? Look at you! Grown up and a student." There was a quick flashback in his head on the day his dad was really rough on him, and if it were not for her, who yelled and screamed at his dad to stop the beating, he would have probably been dead or crippled. This is the aunt who saved his life. He would never forget her motherly protection. She did not say much, did not interfere with his family's affairs even though she knew how mean and how wicked his stepmother was to him. There must be wisdom to it, he thought. She and his uncle are just a very quiet, kind, loving couple, very unique pair of human beings. They are like two philosophers under one roof. They are known throughout the village as couple of loving kindness.

"Oh, Auntie, you haven't changed a bit. I am just fine. Happy New Year to you, Auntie. Where is my uncle?" he asked her with a quavering voice, holding the moisture in his eyes. He realized that love, the tie within the family, bound together by an invisible string, thinner than any fishing line, is stronger than any cable conceivable. His pent-up river of tears was ready to flood the desert of his hunger and thirst for mother's love.

"Your uncle should be here any minute. He had to go fetch the fish he had caught and saved for this day to celebrate the New Year. You will have to stay for lunch with us and take some food home for your dad. I heard he has been under the weather. Is it a cold, a flu that your dad has?"

"Yes, Auntie, I think he's got a cold, but he is getting better now. I made some rice soup last night when I got home. It was late, and he was not well to eat. But he finished what I gave him this morning. I hope he is well soon so that he could enjoy the Tet [New Year celebration]."

"Poor thing! He is all by himself and sick. Your stepmother went to her parents with your brother. It is a shame to see her do that on him at this time of the year. The addiction has gotten a hold of her. God only knows." His aunt stopped short saying what she had in her mind. But he has intuitively known that his stepmother had involved in the gambling addiction even long before he left for school. That is another reason for his parents' rift and unhappiness.

"Pray for her and for your dad, son, so that she could change and your dad, the endurance to bear the cross," she said as any good mother would, "and believe in the power of prayers." And that was the only thing he could and must do.

"Yes, Auntie." As he was saying, he noticed her eyes were gazing toward the front yard that made him turn, and there he was, his uncle with a big perch on a bamboo string, jumping, shaking, trying to get off his hand.

"Uncle, good morning! Happy New Year and happy birth day to you," he bowed his head and said his wish joyfully. "What a nice-size fish you have," he added.

"Wow, it is nice to see you home, boy," his uncle said with a big smile on his face. "And look at you! In your school uniform, looking good." His uncle continued with his loving compliment and obviously showed some pride in his nephew. Uncle But (pronounced: boot), his name, which literally means "pen," was his dad's younger brother, who is his nicest uncle on earth.

He wondered if his name had anything to do with his personality, which, at any given time, is found loving, kind, and happy.

He thought of the names his grandparents had given to his father's siblings and could not help chuckling. He had never asked his dad about other uncles and aunts who got left behind in North Vietnam when the country was divided.

His father's name is Nghien, which literally means "ink pot," and his youngest sister's name is Viet, which is a verb and literally means "write." He had a feeling that at some point of his past generations, his grandparents had had an intention of changing the future of their offspring from traditional fishing to a better one, namely, schooling, education, to be able to read and write. That is why they named them in that order.

"Let's get this fish cleaned up and cook lunch," Uncle But said as he gave the fish to his wife, and turned to him. "Stay for lunch and tell us about your schooling in the city."

"Yes, Uncle. I will be happy to do that."

"But, Uncle, please let me help Auntie to clean the fish; that is the least I can do. Besides, I haven't done that for a long time."

"I don't mind, but I don't think your aunt will let you do that." Like a happy child, he quickly disappeared to the kitchen where his auntie was ready with the fish. He took a knife and saw a cutting board on the bench, and the fish was lying flat next to it. Without a word, he went right to it and started doing what he was trained to do a long time ago. This caught his aunt by a surprise, for she was at the other side of the kitchen, by the patch of herbs, to gather some chocolate basil and green onions, which were not doing well this time of the year, as told by his aunt.

"Son, let me do it; students should not do this kind of work," she told him, but he had already started and was almost done. He felt the love and honor in what she said. Like his own parents, both of them were taking pride in him, their nephew, who was going to school and loving every minute of it. They are, like his father, who would like to invest in him, to give him love, and to support so someday in the future he will break the cycle of being a fisherman.

"Auntie, I should be done with it in seconds. I would like to do it, to help out. Besides, students need to work too, in addition to studying." He was going to tell her that he would be looking for work when he got back to the city to support himself and, ultimately, to reduce the tension between his parents. But he felt he should not have her and his uncle worry about him.

During lunch, which was the best in months with fresh fish from home cooking, the crunchy fried fish with fresh veggies was outstandingly superb. He told them the things he had been doing at school, from subject to subject with different teacher for each of them. This alone made them feel in awe, for in their mind, all they have seen is a teacher in his village who is on every subject. He also told them about the school play, acting as a girl, carrying a baby, and at the end, magically turning into allegoric stones, which made them laugh unceasingly. They asked him about his life at Bac Sau's, which he told them how good a man Bac Sau was to him. He also told them about Bac Sau's spit family and that he had gone to see his friends for the holidays.

It was an excellent meal, which he enjoyed immensely. The food, the company, the conversation—everything was perfectly right. It was definitely a good sign for the New Year, at least in his superstitious mind, for him. Just before he said good-bye, they gave him an envelope, a red one; it was traditional lucky money, regardless of the amount, from the elders in the family hierarchy, from the parents to their children, and tapered down to the end at the bottom of the rung. Along with the envelope was a care package for his dad from auntie. She wanted to make sure his dad had some food, good food for the holidays. He was deeply touched at their care and love.

"Uncle and Auntie, thank you for your yummy, tasty lunch. I do appreciate very much your lucky money and the food for my dad as well." He also told them he would see them before he return to school.

On the way home from his uncle's, he recalled the comment from his uncle about the uniform he was wearing, which he had completely forgotten about. He was just so comfortable having it on because of its coarseness and thickness of material for this wintery weather. He just might have to do what he had been doing, that is, to wash it at night and put it on in the morning. Besides, he was proud to have it on to see the relatives despite the fact that it has been badly faded.

His dad was sitting up in the kitchen to keep himself warm as he walked in the door. Lin went right in to join him by the fireplace where the three big logs of wood joined at their ends to give the fire for the cooking and the warmth to the kitchen.

"How are you feeling, Thay?" he asked as he noticed his dad's alertness, and he looked a lot better.

"Much better, son," His dad told him. "Where did you go?" He looked at the container on Lin's hand.

"I went to visit Uncle and had lunch with them. They were concerned about your health. I told them you were getting better. They also sent some food home for you to enjoy." Lin grabbed a small bowl from the rack as he was talking. He wanted to make sure his dad had food and got his strength back.

Lin sat next to his dad while he was enjoying his meal.

The flame was quietly flickering at the end of the logs underneath of the tripod where the tea kettle was humming. Streaks of the smoke were lazily floating up in the air. It was good timing for his dad to have a bowl of hot green tea after his meal. He knew it would be a treat to his dad better than anything else he could think of, including sweets and deserts. Quiet as usual, men of few words as normal between him and his dad. The only comment his dad had was, "The fish tastes great." And he continued enjoying the meal. He was wondering if his dad had any plans to go anywhere, to see anyone today, granted that he was now better. He wanted to ask if he could go visit Ba Thong and grandparents, but he did not want his dad to venture out in the cold and ended up catching pneumonia.

"Thay," he broke the silence when his dad started pouring the tea into the bowl after finishing his meal. "You will get some rest here by the fire. It is warmer here. I would like to go visit Mr. and Mrs. Thong. Do you know if they are still staying on their boat?" he continued, hoping that his dad would not join him.

"Yes, son, they should be. It is New Year," his dad said mater-of-factly. "They should not be on the fishing trip yet; besides, I just talked to them a few days ago. Tell them I am sorry that I could not make it down there to see them with you."

"Yes, Thay, I will definitely tell them. Get rested and I will see you soon."

His legs were faster than his mouth, for he was out in the daylight before he finished talking to his dad.

The sun was high in the blue sky, with hardly any clouds drifting above his head, casting his shadow, which was moving along his right side as he paced down to the river. It must have been about two o'clock in the afternoon. The sun surely helped break the chill earlier in the day. There were people in their colorful, festive clothes everywhere in the street. They were laughing, talking loudly as if they were the only human beings on the road, or as if it were their happiest day in their lives. Indeed, it should be because, for the Vietnamese, there is a saying that goes "As happy as the New Year's Day." It was a young couple, with their children running, chasing around happily. It was a lively scene. He felt the joy permeated from those happy faces. He bowed his head as he was passing by those whom he knew in the village, uttering the customary greetings of "happy New Year," and then he heard the same echoed back to him. He just made a quick exit to a shortcut, a tiny trail descending to the river.

The sand beach stretched far out in the river, bathing under the sun. The water is always low at this time of the year because the rainy season was over, making the beach lager, extended almost to the middle of the river.

A group of white cranes and egrets, like a big family, scattering, wading along the edge of the water, catching their dinner.

Here and there on the air, brown pelicans, like air fighters against the blue sky, swooped down, splashed the water, and then for a second or two shot up in the air, with the fish on their bill, flying to perch on a branch, rewarding themselves and enjoying their meals. What an air show for the New Year! A divine coordination, he thought.

At the usual spot was the boat he came for. Streaks of white-grayish smoke floating up in the air from the "kitchen" in the back of the boat made him wonder if it were late lunch or early dinner cooking time, or perhaps it was for driving the cold weather off. Whatever it was, he's determined to join them on their boat. Shoes off, barefooted, he sunk his feet into the sand, ran to the boat with all eagerness to meet up with his second mother, Ba Thong, whom he had not seen in months.

Even yards away, he lifted up his voice, calling her, "Ba Thong, Ba Thong, I am home to see you. Are you there?" His voice was filled with tenderness and anxiousness.

"Yes, I have been waiting for you, son," she said happily as she was emerging from the "cabin" of the boat and continued as she stood up next to the kitchen.

"I was wondering if you came to see me or you just stood there on the sand to enjoy the scenery. I saw you came down, but, then, you seemed to have gotten lost into the nature to somewhere." He did not have a chance to say a thing as if she wanted to empty all the pent-up love for him.

"Good grief! Look at you; you look exactly a student I had imagined to be. I am very proud of you, son. "Happy New Year! Come on, get in the boat. I would be very disappointed if you did not come today. You know why?" She looked at him, paused for a moment, and punctuated with her voice, "Because we wanted to celebrate the New Year with you."

"Thank you, mamma, I missed you too." He felt loved and touched as he was climbing on the boat.

"You look great, mamma, haven't changed a bit," he said to her and wanted to ask her if her husband was home but immediately saw him sitting with a book in his hand, reading.

"Happy New Year to you, Mr. Thong," Lin respectfully uttered the greeting to Mr. Thong, bowing his head.

Taking his spectacles down from his reading, Mr. Thong wanted to see the boy at close-up as if he were taking his time before he said anything.

"To you too, a very Happy New Year, and guess what, you have grown since I last saw you off to school." His speech had not gotten any better because all of his front teeth were still missing, gone since last time he saw Mr. Thong.

Sitting next to Mr. Thong was his famous musical instrument that he made it himself, unlike any from the modern world. It is made out of a clove bamboo trunk, about three feet in length. At the one end erected a small twelve inches wooden rod, from which a silk string is strung all the way to the other end of the trunk, tapering down from two-thirds of the rod. The sound of music is made by vibrating the string. Mr. Thong is a master of this primitive instrument. Lin had some fond memories listening to Mr. Thong's passionate playing of the instrument with one hand holding the rod, and the other plucking the string with a long plectrum, and Lin had hoped some day he could learn how to play it as well.

"Oh, thank you, Mr. Thong, it has been a while. You both look great, and I missed you all." Lin gave the old man a big smile as he continued his conversation. He took a glance at the book Mr. Thong was reading. To his great surprise, it was written in a language that he had never seen before. It has characters instead of alphabets as he has been learning. Wanting to learn about the book, about the language, he wanted to ask Mr. Thong, but Mrs. Thong was ahead of him, grabbing his attention by telling him to have a seat on the mat.

Once he sat down across from Mr. Thong, Ba Thong started to tell him that she would like to treat him the best New Year meal, which she had started the night before. She had rolled the glutinous rice cake herself and boiled for hours till this morning. Along with the cakes, she made simmered-cooked caramelized pork with dry bamboo shoot, one of the New Year favorites on the menu in most Vietnamese households. She also saved a nice catfish, which she knew is his favorite, especially the way she prepares and cooks.

"All these dishes are to celebrate your coming home for the holidays," she told him from the kitchen, getting ready to serve. "We figured that you would come to visit with us in the afternoon so we waited to celebrate the New Year on the boat. We are happy

135

to see you, son. I know your dad has been ill. That is too bad; he could have joined us here."

He felt love and honor, all packed and condensed in her voice and the dishes she prepared for him on this special day.

"Yes, my dad is still fighting his cold. He has asked me to say hi to you both."

He gave her a short report on his dad condition, which eased her concern.

Lin was glad that he made down to see them. It would be heartbreaking if he did not show up for any reason because she and her husband would continue to wait for him. She must have trusted her intuition that her "son" would be coming for her. His heart was filled with gladness and gratefulness.

During the meal she inquired about his school, about his place of stay, about his food. He told her about Bac Sau whom he has been staying with and felt very at home.

Like a mother, she was concerned of his well-being, his food, and his living conditions, which he assured her that he was glad and happy with everything, including his school works. He could not help telling them about the play where he had become a "waiting stone," which delighted his audience immensely. In fact, Ba Thong was so ecstatically thrilled that she laughed to tears.

"You , you...you," she stammered, "you could act...in a play? That is...incredible! With all things I thought you could do, the thought of your acting had never come across my mind." Lin smiled sheepishly. She also mentioned that not only was she familiar with the story but also loved it tremendously for the moral, the teaching that the story offers. Lin inquired about their life, their business of fishing, which she told him it has its own moments—one day up, next day down. Nonetheless, they both enjoyed the togetherness, especially in their twilight age.

"Son," she looked at him with seriousness and asked, "I wanted to save this question to the end of our dinner, and that is, I have noticed that your uniform is so badly faded, frayed, and worn. It looks to me as if it is the only pair that you have. Correct?"

"Yes," Lind softy answered and nodded his head, thinking about his situation. He never ever allowed himself to compare his situation with others at school. They all have nice clothes, some have motorcycles, and some even have their parents drop them off from their shinny, polished cars. They all are lucky kids, and he is too. He felt he has been blessed to be able to go to school, and that is all he needed to focus on, for there are many kids in this village who do not have what he has to change or to improve their lives. Everything else can come later, he thought.

Ba Thong reached into the pocket of her dark-burgundy shirt; pulled out an envelope, a red one, the color of the holiday; gave it to him, and with her usual motherly caring voice, she said,

"Son, this is not just the lucky money, but of course, you could think of it that way because it's here on the New Year's Day. But I want you, as soon as you get back to school, use this money to buy some clothes for yourself. However, you must get a new set of uniform. I know you need it, badly."

He did not want to keep the envelope, even it was in his hand. He did not have a clue how much she has put inside the envelope, but it was her savings, her hard-earned money, and she might have a need to use it later when she gets older. He nonchalantly rubbed the red envelope, which has a sketch of a black dragon, between his thumb and his index finger while his eyes were looking at her as a child would to express his love and gratitude to his mother. He knew he should not keep the money, but he also knew very well that her authority should not be challenged.

"Mamma, I should not take any more of your money, for it is your savings. I shall keep a portion of yours as 'lucky money,' but not all," he said as his hands were holding the envelope up.

But she quickly scolded him for not listening. Her voice became grave. "Son, listen! Be obedient! I want you to put the money to a good use. You will not make it on your own. Every little bit will help you on your way to a better tomorrow. You need to understand that, and besides, my savings is for you. It is a small investment in you, my child."

He became speechless, letting his emotion rise and well up his eyes. He really wanted to cry. He deeply felt the motherly love from this woman even though she is not his own mother. He knows how the entire family of his dad, his uncle and aunt, and Ba Thong and her husband invested on him. It was not just in the finance, but also in their trust and love, and he has the responsibility to bring them hefty returns, that is, becoming a good student.

"Yes, mamma," he said softly to her, revering the connectedness between them. "I will not let you be disappointed."

A kind, happy, and loving smile returned to her face, after all.

The evening sun sneaked through the back of the boat and shone on the water, which was ruffled under the breeze. He told Mr. and Mrs. Thong that he needed to go home to check on his dad and hoped that he would be well enough to go around, enjoying the air of the new year.

"Take this home for your dad, a little flavor of the New Year from us. Tell your dad we will come to visit with him soon." Ba Thong said as she handed him a covered pot, full of food to take home.

Lin thanked both of them for the food as he was getting off the boat and told them he would be by before he left for school.

As he was walking home, he thought about paying a visit to his grandparents, a duty of a grandchild on the New Year's Day. He never felt the deep connection, but rather an obligation as a child to the elders.

More so, he wanted to see if his stepmother was there with his brother or if she was still at gambling tables somewhere. Of course, he would never be able to find out simply it would be disrespectful to ask his grandparents' about her whereabouts on this day, and he would never want to put himself in such a position to do so.

His dad was up and sitting in the kitchen as if waiting for him. Perhaps, he was thinking about his days like these without his wife, without his kids, and wondering what happened to them. Where are they? What has gotten into her? How much has she lost? Has she borrowed any money?

Lin was glad to be home for his dad, for he had been worried and lonely.

"Thay, how are you feeling? Ba Thong asked me to bring you food. You should eat because it is late, and you should be hungry by now," he asked his dad as he walked into behind him.

"Much better today. Did you have good time with them? They love you, son. They talked about you every time and all times." Lin was happy that his dad had sounded better. His voice was almost back to normal.

"Sometimes, I wondered if she were your own mother," his dad continued with deep voice of content. "I wouldn't be surprised someday if she would ask to adopt you as her son." Lin did not find any teasing nor did he find any humor in what his dad just said. There was no such an indication to that effect. Perhaps, his dad now realized that his wife would never love him. Ba Thong is the only person who could give him the motherly love as she had been doing.

"Thay, Ba Thong really cares for me. She loves me very much. She wanted me to be a good student, a good person just as you do." He said nothing further. He did not want to have his dad think, in any way, that he has not fulfilled his duty as a father to love his son, nor did he want his dad feel that he has failed to protect him from the vice of his wife.

He went outside, after setting dinner for his dad, to gather some tea leaves to make a new batch for his dad, knowing that he would be wholeheartedly enjoying it after his meal. The air was so clean; he took a deep breath, filling his lungs with the fresh air that has a faint fragrance of something he could not figure out, perhaps a mixture of wild leaves and winter flowers or just the air of a new year. Whatever it was, he simply and truly enjoyed it.

"Thay," Lin asked while his dad was slurping his hot tea after his dinner. "Do you want to go anywhere to see anyone before the day is over, or even tomorrow?"

"Not at all, son," his dad told him. His voice was absent of any sense of enthusiasm. "I might head out on a fishing trip in a couple of days."

He felt the loneliness in his dad's heart and his own helplessness at the same time. He wishes he could stay to give him a hand on the boat, keeping him company. But he also knows that he has to make a sacrifice for a brighter and better tomorrow as he has promised everyone who has helped him.

"I am going to visit with some of the relatives tomorrow. You should stay home and get rest, get over the cold so that you could go on fishing. I should be going back to school too. Besides, Bac Sau has gone to visit his friends; I need to watch the house while he is away, vacationing."

He told his dad the money Ba Thong gave him for his clothes and his uncle's lucky money. He had not checked to see how much the gift he had received. They are still in the envelopes and well kept in his pocket. His dad told him to be frugal on the money and should spend only when really needed, which he has been doing all along. He did not know why his dad said that; maybe things were tough on the river, and he was not sure if he could continue to support his son's schooling, or maybe the things between his parents were not much of harmony, especially with her gambling habits. Nonetheless, it was a very good advice for his own sake from his dad.

After saying good-bye to everyone he needed to and helping his dad with his supplies and nets to his boat for the trip, he was on the bus back to the city to get ready for school.

It was odd, he thought, as far as he could remember, that never in years of the past had his dad gone fishing on the third day into the New Year. In fact, rarely anyone had done that. It is the time for everyone to relax and to enjoy family and food, which should go together, or complement each other. In some parts of the country, especially among the farming communities in the north, it is said that they dedicate the whole month of January to celebrate the New Year, doing nothing but playing, gambling, and enjoying holiday foods. In this case, however, his dad might have found what was missing on the ground by getting on the boat, emerging into the nature, the blue sky, and the running water of the river. The casting of his nets would help heighten his spirit and ease his pains.

He could have stayed an extra day or two to keep his dad company or perhaps go on fishing with his dad, but since Bac Sau's house has been unattended and anything could happen during the holidays, he needed to hurry home. In fact, this is the prime time for illegal, unlawful activities ranging from theft to robbery. One cannot be sure who and where would be the next target of the gangs, the hoodlums.

As the cool breeze was brushing his hair, caressing his face, something just sparked his thinking, his interest—that is, those people, men and women, boys and girls were on bicycles everywhere along the road. What if he could get a bicycle, a used one? He could go home to visit without having to pay bus fares—a savings every time. He put that thought on his mental list to save enough money to purchase a secondhand two-wheeler. It does not matter how old, how not so pretty it looks, as long as it is strong enough to get him home and get him back to the city without falling apart, he would be happy. He knew he had to find a job to support himself first, but he was clueless on what to do. And who would hire him at this tender age? He will pray and hope for something to happen to keep his dream alive.

From the bus station, he took a shortcut home. After getting used to the life in the city, Lin got to explore the city's landscape, the stadium, the soccer field to know the roads, the streets—the ins and outs of them. There is a public dirt-walled swimming pool, more of a large-size pond than any conventional public swimming pool, which draws the water from a stream up from the mountains miles away. It is a landmark halfway home from the bus station. The water in this pool is almost always reddish and constantly moving, in and out, not circulating nor filtering. At the spot where the water flows out from the pool, it gathers people, mostly women, who do their laundry. They scrubbed and beat their clothes on the flat surface of the boulders and then rinse them off. And as if they were the true water conservationists, they often bathe themselves right there.

He passed the pool area down the hill and zigzagged through some uphill alleys before he got to his house.

Lo and behold! He could not believe his eyes. What lay in front of him was an empty lot, full of ashes, black charcoals, and a few spots of smoldering smoke. What happened to his house, Bac Sau's house? Who burned it down? Where is Bac Sau? Lin stood there in shock; he did know what to do what to say, except let tears of anguish and fears well up his eyes. He looked at the houses in the neighborhood, which were a distance from his house, and found them safe, and he was glad for that. What happened to it while he and Bac Sau were gone? Did Bac Sau ever come back while he was gone? He did not think so. But if he did, where is he now? Is he safe? Is he all right? Question after question were asked in his little mind, and he could not find an answer. He was wondering what happened and who burned it down as he walked over the neighbor to see if they could help to shed some lights to his darkest moments of distress and misfortune.

Becoming Homeless

Upon seeing him, the couple, Mr. and Mrs. Tanh, whom Bac Sau had mentioned about his neighbors, in their late thirties came out from their house to greet him for they know of him. Mr. Tanh told him: "It happened the night before last night at about two in the morning. We were very concerned at the fact that the flames might travel to ours. But luckily, there was no wind that night, and it stayed where it was."

They went on to tell him that no one knew the cause at the time. But the officials who came the following morning stated that it appeared to be a gang-related activity and that they would try to find the arsonist who was involved in the burning. He asked the couple if they had seen Bac Sau before the incident or even anyone around the house at all. They said they had not seen a soul. He thanked the couple and walked back to the pile of ashes, thinking what part of the ashes were of his belongings, which wasn't much to begin with. His books and his school supplies and materials are now just dust and ashes. He was trying to hold his tears off to where they belonged. Where does he go from here? Where is he going to stay for the time being? All of a sudden, he now became homeless! It is a terrifying thought but a reality.

When Bac Sau gets home, of course, not only is he going to be in shock, but also devastated to see the ashes instead of the house he used to own and live in. Where will he stay? Is he able to build the house up again? How can he and Bac Sau connect with each other when he gets back in town? The only way possible is if Bac Sau would come to school to find him, which he prayed would happen.

It now dawned on him that this is the beginning of the year, a lunar New Year, and to have a house burned down to ashes is not a good thing, not a very good start for the moon calendar. It does not matter how nonsuperstitious a person is, but this is not a lucky year for the entire year.

The sun was straight up high above his head. He had been dejectedly standing by the scene of ruins for quite some time. People walked by, looked at him, wondering if he was part of the ashes for he must have looked terrible, a homeless boy with no belongings, no suitcase of clothes. He is now a student with no books, no pens, and no bicycle. What he has on his body is what he has got: a pair of shoes, a pair of pants, and a shirt. Where will he go from here? Going home for the time being? No, no, not a good idea. He flatly rejected that thought, for it's going to be more painful than what it was going on right now in his life. His stepmother would be all over him while his father was away fishing. He thought of going to some of his friends to stay for a few days until he could find a place, but then decided against the idea. Finally, he left the place of ashes and smoldering smoke, dejectedly descended down the side of the hill, and emerged onto the main road, walking toward his school, knowing very well that it was still a holiday in the New Year, and chances are everyone from the school—principal to the teachers, the curator, and the janitor—have gone home to their families. But he was hoping with a little hope that his luck had not been demolished and mingled with hot grayish ashes at Bac Sau 's house. He silently prayed that, out of a miracle, the curator's family was still at school, and because of his rapport with the curator and his wife, they could open their hearts to let him stay in one of the dorm rooms, at least, until the school resumed after the New Year's break.

The winter winds pressed the cold air against his frail body as he walked past the gate of the school, which now stood quietly in the sun. Every now and then, a whirlwind of red dust raced across the empty, open dirt field, as if someone had just turned on a giant fan, then disappeared into the lines of bare trees behind the school buildings. He quickly lifted himself onto the cement sidewalk of the admin building and peeked through the glass windows, which now was covered with dust from the wind. He sauntered past every room to the end of the building, and then something caught the sight of his eyes at the side of the next building—the handle, the metal bar, of a bicycle, which was lying on the ground, glaring in the sun as if beckoning him to come over? It was the first indication to let him know that someone is around in the school building, and that was a sign to keep his hope alive. With ounces of energy and excitement left in his body, he picked up his pace, jumped off to the ground, and walked fast to the next building, where he now remembered as the place where the curator was staying with his family. He was nervous as he was now standing at the steps to the front door and did not know whether he should let someone inside know that he was outside, needing help. He glanced at the bicycle and looked at the closed door, wondering if he should wait until someone came out. The size of the bicycle gave an indication that it is not an adult's, and if it is a kid's, then kids would come out to play. But he did not want to stay outside, making him look suspicious of doing something dishonestly. Perhaps, someone might think that he had an eye on the bicycle. Nonetheless, the wind and cold had gotten to his skin. He shivered.

Finding New Family And Home

He knocked on the door once, twice, and three times, and pressed his right ear against the door, listening, and slowly, nervously, he stepped back after hearing footsteps approaching the door. It was a young boy, one of the curator's children, who immediately recognized him, and in his happy, cheery voice, he said, "Brother Lin, Happy New Year." And without waiting for Lin to say a word, he dashed inside to get his parents. The boy must have thought that Lin had come on his special visit to wish a happy New Year to his family on the New Year's days. Indeed, it was a very special visit; he amused himself at the thought, if only the boy knew what Lin had gone through and what he came at the door for.

"Oh heavens, my child, come inside, it's cold out here." The curator, Mr. Nam, kindly opened his door, his heart to let him in. Mr. Nam looked at him curiously after closing the door behind them. Instead of asking Lin the circumstance that brought him to his place, he asked him to come into the dining room where they were having a family dinner and said, "Lin, join us; we have just started. Happy New Year, my child."

Mr. Nam was quick, and his fatherly voice full of care carried the authority. Perhaps he was seeing Lin's circumstance through his appearance, which was miserably shabby, not to mention cold and hungry inside. He bowed his head in greeting his wife, Mrs. Nam, his daughter, and son and sheepishly said, "Yes." And as if he remembered the lines to the greeting in the New Year, he continued with a nervous smile, "Happy New Year to you all."

He noticed an extra bowl and chopsticks were added, sitting on the round table along with a wooden chair for him. Lin was an unexpected guest to the family. He, however, received a warm welcome, warm to his heart, warm to his soul and to his body, as everyone at the table gave him a genuine smile, especially Mrs. Nam. She asked him as many questions as many times she filled his bowl with food. Not only did he truly enjoy the food but also the family love and kindness they had given him.

The conversation at the dinner table began with his life and his family in the village, which he told them. They showed much interest in knowing his boyhood life by the river, growing potentially a fisherman. Their daughter, younger than he was, judging from her look, was fascinated with his life on his boat on fishing trips. She laughed her heart out as much as she frowned at the twists of his life story.

Since everyone at the table was familiar with his role in the play, now was the time for comments and critique of his performance.

"What a great job you did in that play. Everyone commented on how good your acting was," praised Mr. and Mrs. Nam as they both looked at him kindly.

"I wished you could change your voice to a girl's; you would be a great wife. And by the way, you looked very womanly pretty with the makeup on." The girl giggled and teased him. She seemed comfortable talking to him and teasing him. He now remembered having seen her once in the past when she was on her bicycle, coming home from the market, and the second time when he walked by this building.

"Be (pronounced: bae), you are a naughty girl, how dare you tease your brother?" lovingly scolded by her mother, who also gave him a smile and an affectionate look as if saying, "Don't pay attention to this little baby sister of yours. She is mischievous!" Nonetheless, He now knew her name. It could be her nickname or her real name. It works both ways. He was thinking, *Be* means "little, petite, and small." It is definitely cute as a nickname, or it could also be what is written in black and white on her birth certificate as well. He felt touched and loved to hear her mother say in such a way that makes him feel as a part of her family. This little Be is like a doll with black eyes, long black hair, curly at the end, cascading beautifully over her shoulders. He would not mind having her as his sister, he thought. After all, that is what her mom, Mrs. Nam, had suggested.

He wanted to tease her in return that she should have her parents change her name to something else because her name "Be" does not complement her physique. In fact, it could be an argument! But he did not want to get himself in trouble at the beginning of the New Year and decided against it.

The dinner and laughter kept him occupied that he had not even noticed a giant yellow blossom, the hoa mai tree, planted inside a very beautifully hand-painted gold-colored china vase, standing against the white wall at the corner of the room. Seeing the flowers fully open, the sign of prosperity for the New Year, he wanted to comment on this very symbol of good fortune.

"Master, the flowers are in full bloom. It is a great sign of good luck. May your New Year be filled with prosperity, happiness, and longevity." He addressed Mr. Nam as "master" for a good reason, that is, all school faculties are to be addressed teachers or masters. There is a saying behind this beautiful philosophy that goes like this: "One word he teaches, he is your teacher. Half a word he teaches, your master too." Besides, Mr. Nam sometimes substituted for hygiene teacher as well.

"That is very nice of you to say that," Mr. Nam told him. "We wish you luck and that you will do well in school this year and many to come too." He looked at Lin and continued.

Yes, I need lots of luck, Lin thought as he was thinking of his dire situation. He will have to tell Mr. Nam his circumstance but did not know how to start. He certainly did not want the whole family to worry about him, especially after such a great family dinner.

"What is it in your little mind? You look worried of something?" Mr. Nam beat him to it, beat him at his own game, and asked him while he did not know how to open up the conversation on his homelessness.

"Yes, master, I just became homeless. The house I was staying got burned down to ashes. I just found out this late morning when I returned from visiting my family. I just wondered if I could stay at the school dorm for a few days until I could find a new place to stay."

The entire room fell into a complete silence. The evening sun had crept through the window; gusts of wind were heard bellowing outside the wall. Eight eyes were on him, concerned, worried, and caring.

"There is no problem to put you in the dorm." Mr. Nam broke the dead silence and said, "We must find a long-term solution— not one or two or three nights."

"You can stay with us," said the boy, looking and smiling at Lin. Cu (pronounced: coo), his name, who had been on his quiet side all the dinner, now made his voice heard.

Mrs. Nam turned her eyes to her daughter and then to her husband as if saying, "That is a good idea for Lin to stay with us."

It seems a man is made the head of his household, and he is destined to make important decisions. In this case, Mr. Nam is also a curator of the school; any decision he makes that involves school property or relates to school policy, he needs to consult with the school principal.

"Let's put our boy to one of the dorms in the first floor for the time being, and I will talk to Mr. Quang, the principal, when he gets back from the New Year's break to see if we can keep him in the dorms."

Mr. Nam not only addressed him directly but also to everyone in his family after a long moment of weighing the options.

Deeply touched with what he just heard from the curator, Lin got off from his chair, went down on his knees to the cold cement floor, facing the elders, and said, "Master, I will never be able to thank you enough for your love and your kindness. Thank you, and thank you." Lin bowed his head to Mr. and Mrs. Nam. Lin wanted to show his heartfelt appreciation to all of them, who have just rescued him from the sinking boat of distress.

Mr. Nam got up from his chair, bent down to pull the boy up from his kneeling posture, and said,

"Oh come on, boy, don't do that. You are like my child." He held Lin to his chest and kept him there for long moment. He now dearly looked at Lin, whose tears welled up his eyes, and said,

"I will see what I can do for you. Just enjoy the evening here with us, and I will take you to the dorm."

The curator paused for a few seconds, and as if he did not want to forget something important, he continued. "By the way, would you have any problem staying all by yourself in the dorm in the big building?"

Lin did not have a clue as to what Mr. Nam had had in his mind, but what immediately came to Lin's mind was the city hospital is just across the street. And the dark-red, brick-walled morgue—which was densely covered with ivy vines, dead and brown and green leaves and other kinds of climbing denizens from the walls to the roof—is built right next to it. In fact, it is directly opposite the dorm on the other side of the street. What separates them is a line of giant flame trees behind the dormitory. The rumor among students is that in the quiet of a half-moon night, the whining, the moaning could be audibly heard from the morgue. Not only that, they say often that floating in the air was an image of a girl in a long *ao dzai* (long dress), black hair flowing in the ether. It is the image of an unsettled soul, a girl's soul, wandering, levitating. However, he told himself that at this very moment, he was not anywhere near a position for bargaining, nor was he to show weakness of a girl, even though he did act as a girl in the play only weeks ago. So, be brave!

"Master, there shouldn't be any problems at all. I am used to be on the boat all by myself on fishing trips on the river that runs deep in the jungle." Lin told the curator and cast his eye across his audience. He noticed the girl's wide eyes gazing at him in awe of what she just heard of him.

"Great! I am very proud of you, son. Now would you please tell us about your family, your parents, and siblings?"

Mr. Nam wanted to learn more about him and his family. Lin was not sure if he should tell them everything, but in a split second, he began the story of his life, his unhappy childhood from the loss of his mother to an infection after giving birth to his sister when he was seven years of age, to the days of hell, having a stepmother into his life. If it were not for his father, who wanted a better life for him, he would not be able to go to school. It is the very big sacrifice that his father has made for his sake. It's here where the path of his journey and his audience now cross in his life. He did tell them about Mr. and Mrs. Thong, one of the many angels in his life, who supported him from the very beginning and who also considered him their own child. He tried to condense his life story but failed miserably to the extent that the many details of his childhood sufferings have deeply stirred up the emotions and welled up some eyes in the audience, especially those of the girl. She tried to dry them with her little, white hanky a few times.

The room became still and quiet as he ended his storytelling. He also punctuated the day's event of meeting them, of their kindness they all extended to him. He also looked at each member of the family and told them that he would treasure every bit of these wonderful, loving experiences in his heart.

The evening was winding down with the whispering between the mother and daughter, and it resulted with an armful of clothes for him to take to the dorm. They all realized that he was a bare-boned homeless boy, and they wanted to make sure he was warm in his room and in their loving care.

"These are some clothes you could use tonight. We will go shop for your new ones tomorrow, my child," said the mother as the girl handed the clothes to him.

"They will be too large on you, brother. But, at least, they keep you warm tonight. I want to wash your clothes tomorrow. You have them on you all day today, and they definitely need a wash," the girl said.

His heart sank and melted at her words, her loving compassion, and her care. He hoped someday he could return the favor to her.

"Thank you, my sister, Be. I think I can handle the washing myself. Besides, I am used to doing it," Lin told her, and he could see a slight change on her face, a frown perhaps, and feel a sense of disapproval in her. He tried to make up for what he said that caused this emotional friction but do not know how. He felt short of clumsy, not knowing what to say or do, for he had never a sister to deal with, much more a grown-up one like Be. He could not go back and say, "Okay, okay, babe Be, you can do my laundry." But that would be too obvious that he gave in. He could say to her that he would do half of the job, that is, she would do the rinsing, and he, the soaping and scrubbing.

However, before he could offer any of the options, the mother, as if seeing an air of tension between the kids, or perhaps wanting to rescue him, said, "Son, let your sister do it for you."

Phew! He breathed with a relief, and looking at the mother with the eyes filled with gratitude, he then said, "Yes, I hope she doesn't mind."

Lin saw a wisp of a smile on her lips and a playful look in her eyes as if saying, "Brother, I won, did I not? You should have just listened to me." He acknowledged her smile with his, and as if in a whisper, he said thank you to her.

It was getting dark, so Mr. and Mrs. Nam and their boy and girl walked Lin to the dormitory. The wind was dying down, and the air was cold as the whole family approached the front door of the building. With a long-handled flashlight in one hand and a ring of keys dangling in the other, Mr. Nam flashed the light both sides of the door as if to make sure no one or ghost would be standing by waiting. He fumbled a few keys before he could get the right one to unlock the door. He shut the door behind after everyone had come inside and the light was on. In front of him were a huge kitchen and a large dining hall for the students who stayed in the dorms. He had no idea how big this place was until tonight, and it seems a lot bigger when no one is around, and that is exactly what the kids were commenting about. They got to the room on the second floor after passing through the kitchen, a half of the dining hall, and climbed two flights of stairs. It was a very large room with two sets of bunk beds. He can choose of any bed he wants.

Lucky me, he thought as he was observing. There was no key to the door but a latch from the inside, which he could not figure out the wisdom to it, but he felt safe for the night. Like good parents, Mr. and Mrs. Nam got him set up with a blanket, a pillow, and a mosquito net, which Be and Cu quickly helped him mount on the poles in no time. Be teased him, saying that the mosquitoes will be singing outside of the net so that he could fall asleep faster, and he should not have to think, to worry about anything at all. Well, he would hope so because he had thought about the rumor of the floating white images.

Mr. Nam then showed him the washroom, the shower room, and how to exit in case of fire and emergency. He told Lin that he would come over in the morning to see if he needed any help, but during the night, if he needed help, he could come over to his place any time.

"Good night, son," the parents said to him as they were leaving the room.

"Good night, brother," Be and Cu said to him. They both reached for his hands, squeezed, and added, "See you in the morning." He felt loved and wished he could go home with them. Nonetheless, he counted his blessings.

As the sound of the footsteps on the wooden floor faded away, the light downstairs was turned off, and the sound of the front door slammed shut, he retreated inside the room, latched the door by lifting up the wooden bar to rest into its bracket. A feeling of loneliness engulfed him after his hand reached for the switch to turn the light off. He had debated whether or not he should leave the light on while he was in bed sleeping. The light would definitely help him less scared, but he did not want to show it; besides, it would cost the school money.

Once in bed, in this immensity of void of the building, his mind rushed back to the village where his father was all by himself on the fishing boat at this hour, anchored at some point along the winding river, perhaps wondering about his scattered family—him, his son in the city, learning to be a good student, and his wife who decided having nothing to do with his son whom he loved. Lin could feel his dad's loneliness too. He felt the world of the adults is too complicated beyond his young thinking mind, and many a time, he wished that his father had not remarried.

He still could not figure out why his stepmother treated him the way she did. Is she expected to do what she has done? Is it something the society has culturally influenced her to do, to behave the way she did to fulfill the prophecy—"Unless one finds the bone"? He thought about Bac Sau and his house that now became ashes. Where is the man at this hour? he wondered. Lin said his prayers for his safety, and he thanked God for guiding him to where he was. Tears of gratitude rolled off the corner of his eyes as he turned on his side to fall asleep. It had been a long day emotionally and physically for him.

Lin woke up to the honking of horns from the cars in the street behind the building. It was already daylight, no clue of time, he thought. All he knew was he had slept like a log on the bunk bed in this strange room and place. It took him a few minutes to bring himself to reality. He remembered now that Mrs. Nam had mentioned to take him out for shopping. The dilemma is, as he was thinking, there is no way he would go shopping on this baggy, blue-and-white pajama, which is more likely owned by Mr. Nam, who was more than kind enough to let him wear for the night. He would rather die! He would have to go shopping with what he had. He sprung up from the bed and rushed out to get himself washed up before anyone came over.

"We did not want to wake you up because you had a rough day yesterday," Mr. Nam told him as Lin walked in the door at his place. "And did you have good sleep?" he continued.

"Yes, sir. Indeed, I slept like a...rock," he told the elder amusingly. Everyone laughed at his rocky analogy.

"We were a bit concerned about you being there alone last night. But you handled well. Proud of you," said Mr. Nam.

"Were you scared at all, brother?" admirably asked the girl, with her black, big eyes wide open and a smile on her face. He wanted to tease her by telling her that he had seen a long-haired, white-dressed girl ghost floating in the building. But he decided not to because she would be scared to walk in the dark at night around the school; in addition to that, he would, for sure, get a stern look from her mom for frightening her daughter with fairy ghost stories.

"Not at all, sister, I am quite used to being alone. Besides, I did not have time to worry. I just turned myself into a log and fell asleep," with both palms of his hands held together against to his face, tilted, gesturing of sleeping, he assuredly told her, letting her know that it is okay to be alone sometimes. She gave him an admiring look and a kind smile that made his day.

Lin pulled out the money from his pocket and walked over to Mrs. Nam and said, "Would you please help me? Here is all the money I have to buy a few things I need today—"

Just before he could finish what he was going to say, Mrs. Nam held up her hand, and with her smile, she said, "Put it away, son. It is going to be our New Year treat for you, just like Be and Cu, who all have got their own treats. Besides, you will need a new set of uniforms when the school starts."

Lin was speechless at the love and compassion this family has given him. His heart was ready to melt again in this room in less than twenty-four hours. It was very hard for him to keep the tears where they belong. A boy like him with an unhappy, abused childhood, without a place to stay, without any relatives to lean his head on, without any belongings has received warm and pleasant surprises, one after another, along his journey. Ba thong, Bac Sau, and the members of this family were all angels in disguise, who showed up to give him a cup of cool water to quench his thirst in the desert of his life. He was hungry for care and thirsty for love and these simple, kindhearted beings went out of their way to fill his hunger and slake his thirst. He knew in his heart that there were no accidents in life. He hoped that someday he would understand the wisdom and mystery behind the things that have happened in his life. He felt that the kindness from these beautiful beings and other folks has come to fill him up so that someday it flows out from him into others to keep the kindness going, forever giving.

"Thank you, Mrs. Nam." His heart cried out to address her "mother," to call her "mama." But, not now; he just would have to wait till someday when her cup of love for him was overflowed and his heart burst from joy, he would be able to utter the word "mother" to her. He deeply felt the divine is in the works to bring these mothers in to his life to ease his pains.

"Here is the plan for today of what we're going to do. I will go do some shopping to get things for all of us. I know what you are in need of, and in the next few days as the school resumes, I will get you the uniform. You can stay home and rest," the mother said to him.

He planned and wanted to come along for the shopping. But he sensed in her tone of voice that she preferred him stay home; perhaps she did not want him to know how much she spent on him, or maybe she did not want to deal with him, arguing about his paying for the goods. After all, he told her that he'd like to stay home, hanging out with Cu to either do the reading or to play some soccer out in the field. The mother was pleased with his decision, and off to the market she went with her daughter.

Another beautiful sunny day into the New Year, it was much warmer, for the wind had decided to stay elsewhere behind the mountains and hills and forests. Up in the air, a few swallows were stretching their wings against the clear blue sky, inviting the boys to chase the ball in the soccer field, or to wander in the park. After getting the permission from the father, they decided to walk straight to the park. What Lin did not expect was a familiar figure approaching the gate looking for him. It was Bac Sau! Lin ran to him as he recognized him from far away.

"Oh, Bac Sau, you are back. I have been worried about you and prayed for you. Where are you staying now?" Lin asked, assuming Bac Sau had found out that his house had been reduced to ashes.

"Well, son, I was worried about you too, not knowing if you had returned from your visit. And if you did, where would you stay after seeing our house was no longer a house. I just happened to check with the neighbor about the fire, the burning, and the cause to it. They told me that they knew nothing about the fire, but they mentioned that you had come by to check with them as well. I figured you might be hanging around at your friends, whom I do not have a clue on their whereabouts, or your school, or you could have probably gone back to the village. But I am so glad to see you here."

Lin then told him what happened yesterday after leaving the scene of his house, and that he did not have a slightest idea where he should go. But, as if guided by a divine, he headed for the school and is now being cared for by the curator and his family. In fact, he introduced Cu to Bac Sau, telling him that Cu is the curator's son.

"Where are you staying now, Bac Sau?" he asked the man, his voice full of concern.

"I will have to stay at the place where I work. They had offered me a living quarter next to the plant since I did not have a family of my own. I did not take it because I wanted to take care of you, as I had promised your dad. However, since you are now staying at the school with your teachers, I feel a lot better and happy for your. I am even happier because you have a family to stay with now. The whole idea is for you to go to school, and now, you not only you go to school but stay in school as well. I will stop by to see you whenever I have a chance to come to town."

"Yes, Bac Sau, please come to see me often. I missed you, Bac Sau," Lin said as Bac Sau made a quick turn to walk away, hiding his emotion. He had lost his place to stay and now separated from the boy whom he considered his own son.

If it weren't for Cu being next to him, Lin would have probably run into Bac Sau's arms and cried his heart out, for he came looking for him. He knew Bac Sau loved him very much, for he remembered one time, at a middle of the night, Bac Sau came over to his bed, pulled the blanket over him, and made sure that he was warm in his bed while sleeping. Either Bac Sau was thinking of his own son when he did it, or he did it because of his love for him. Either way, a great father he was to him. He let his tears loose in the dark of the night. He had never known behind this stoic appearance and demeanor of Bac Sau lay the spring of love and kindness, ready to flow.

Lin and Cu continued their walk to the park as Lin filled Cu about his stay with Bac Sau.

"You are very fortunate to have a place to live and a loving family of mother and father and a sister to be around and to look after," Lin told the young Cu in such a way that it did not sound like an envy, but rather a young philosopher to his disciple. "Be thankful and appreciate what you have, and so, too, treasure it."

Young Cu took what Lin said to him at face value, smiled, and nodded his head as his legs stretched along Lin's side to the park.

"Thank you, brother, for taking me to the park. Because without you, my dad would not allow me to go by myself. Thank you, thank you," Cu said to Lin, expressing his joy for the chance to be in the nature with a friend.

Lin gave him a smile, along with a wink, and continued to the park where there were people in nice, colorful, festive clothes moving about already.

Behind the trunk and under the shade of a giant, aged tree gathered and stood a group of youths. There were about ten of them, boys and girls, wearing light-orange-colored uniform with fuchsia-colored scarfs neatly worn on their necks. They were playing guitars; they were singing cheerfully the songs with themes from welcoming the New Year to the one packed with New Year wishes. They were smiling, hand gesturing while singing, entertaining the crowd. Lin then found out that these youths came from the Buddhist temple, all the way from the other side of the town too. Besides what they were doing, they promote the annual event to be held at the temple. The features of the event would include the dragon dance, which every kid would love to watch. He loves the puff of smoke coming out of the dragon's mouth, as if the dragon were breathing. His head would swing from one side to another while the drumbeats were pounding in the air, vibrantly. There would be a feast of all vegetarian dishes, which look and taste like the real meats of pork, chicken, or beef. It is truly an artistic work to make these kinds of foods to please even the king's taste buds. The wisdom behind this make-believe meats is something he would never be able to understand. In addition to that, the desert of all kinds of delicacies of sweets, such as mung bean cakes or purple kidney bean in sugary soup, to name a few, is to be served at the event. His imagination now suddenly got a hold of him. Lin excitedly tried to comb through the handwritten five-by-ten, lined yellow flier, which was handed to him by one of the youths to find the time and date of the event at the temple.

His jaws dropped wide open as he discovered that it was this very night; tonight at 5:30 p.m., the program would begin, and it would go all the way to midnight. But how could he go when he was with Cu's family unless they decided to go too.

"Hey, Cu, since the event at the temple is at five thirty this evening, would you like to come? Perhaps you and I can ask for your parents' permission, or perhaps, we all can go as family too." He was counting on Cu to make the move, asking his parents because he did not want to make them feel that he had become a pet only a day or two being in the family.

"Oh yes." His voice full of excitement. "Are you kidding me? You do not have to ask. I do want to go with you." His black eyes were wide open, and so was his big smile. He then continued, "I am very sure my parents and my sister would love to come. Maybe they all knew about this and ready to go tonight."

"Well, let's head home right now to see if your mom and your sister are home so we can tell them about this all at the same time."

Lin pulled Cu's arm and made a quick exit out of the park, leaving the singing band behind with the crowd, and rushed home before Cu could say anything. Lin was praying that Mr. and Mrs. had known about the program and decided to go so that he could join them on this special event as a family. This is the time of the year when special foods are offered in conjunction with entertainment at temples and churches in the region, if not around the country. It is not only to celebrate the goodness of nature in bringing the spring, the beginning of life after dormant cold and shivering months of winter, the season of colorful blossoms and fruits and foods, but also to show man's generosity and appreciation for what was received from the Creator of nature. There were so many activities, which he enjoyed in his village during this time of the year in the past, and, obviously, he had missed them this year. This is the chance for him to rediscover the fun, the joys of the celebration of the New Year here in the city, which he knows is a lot bigger, perhaps more sophisticated than what he used to know. It was hard to contain this burst of excitement inside him as he wished he could fly. Lin and Cu seemed to have a race rushing home, and, indeed, they arrived home in a very short time. Trying to catch their breath from the running, their mouths were wide open when they saw the mother and the sister had already been home along with what they brought home.

Cu ran to his mom and held her as he screamed from the top of his lungs, "Mom, Mom, what did you get for me?"

His mom gave him a look as if she was going to scold him. "Slow down, my boy. Why do you have to yell so loud?"

In the meantime, Lin was hoping that Cu would tell his mom or his dad about the event, which would begin at the temple in just a few hours. But he knew Cu is going to do it for sure in his heart. Be patient, he reminded himself.

"You have everything already, son. The things I bought today were for your brother. He does not a thing on him. I hope you understand," the mother told him softly as if reminding him that he should be content with what he already had so that someone else could have some too. It is the art of sharing.

Cu gave his mom a smile, nodding his head in a complete agreement with what his mom had said.

"Yes, Mom," he proudly said as he understood the meaning of what his mom told him. And then he ran over to Lin, holding his hands, and with a big smile, he said, "Brother, you are the one who needs the things, not me, right?" Lin did not know how or what to say to Cu. From the outside, he found himself speechless at the kindness of this boy who is younger than him, while inside him, his heart was utterly melted at the loving kindness that was being practiced at all levels of this family, amazingly including the youngest Cu. How can he express himself to show Cu and everyone in the family his heartfelt appreciation? Words had totally failed him. He cast his eyes up to meet everyone's in the room and rested at Cu's and said "Thank you, my little brother."

From the corner of his eye, Lin saw Be, who was sitting by the wall, grabbed the shopping bag from her side, walked over to him, and said, "Mom and I bought these for you. Would you please try them on? I am very sure they'll fit you." She added, "By the way, if you want, you can go to the room in the back to put them on. You can let mom judge how good I am on picking the sizes for you when you have them on out here." Her big, black-brown eyes rested on his as if saying, "I care for you, brother, and you deserve some nice clothes for a change—now get going."

A prisoner of love and kindness, he felt as he held the bag in his hand, obediently walking toward the back room, a mix of emotions engulfed him. He remembered the words his mom had told him when he and his dad, at the last moments, found her after days of waiting for her to show up at the airport in north Vietnam to join them on their last flight from north to south, running away from the communists years ago. He was so happy to see her that he cried his heart out because everyone was ready to board the plane, and she was nowhere to be seen. His dad had told him that they might have to go without her. Her words were as crystal clear then as they are now: "Boys are not to be soft with tears." But he could not help it, for his eyes are now moistened. What has he done to deserve this caring and blessing? he wondered. He had not done a thing for them.

As he sat the large, light-brown paper bag down on the cold, grayish cement floor, he was shocked to see a stack of brand-new clothes in nice, cheerful spring colors, looking at him from the bottom of the bag. He carefully lifted each of the folded pieces out of the bag, one by one, as if they all were in a dream world that he was afraid they might quickly vanish like those of a fairy tale. Two pullover shirts, one in light cyan and the other in beige white, and a pair of dark-navy-blue pants were something he could never ever dream of. The fresh smell of the new fabric of the clothes added the sense of awe into his drunk-like feelings. It took him a long while to get over this feeling before he could put the new clothes on, one at a time. He decided to leave the beige color one on him for the showing. A feeling of uneasiness of new clothes bore down on him. He felt awkward as he paced back and forth between the walls of the room. He was not sure if he wanted to show everyone out there the new clothes on him.

While Lin was mustering his courage to walk out into the living room, he heard something like thunderstorms outside in the air. He did not think it was from the storm; instead, it was more of a heavy-duty–size firecrackers, which enhanced the mood of the holidays. He then thought about the event at the temple tonight, which he did not know if anyone knew besides him and Cu. In any case, he did not want to go with the new clothes on. He just felt not normal. In fact, he felt like walking on the air.

In the living room, Lin was in front of his admirers and judges who all commented on how good and how cute he looked in the new clothes, which made him very shy. He felt like he had come down with a fever that made his cheeks hot and blush.

"You look so good, my son," said the mother. "You look good on anything and everything. Remember the role you play?"

"Thank you, mama," he said softly to her. "Yes, I remember that too." He looked at the mother and gave her an appreciative smile.

Now he wanted to say a big thank you to Be, for she had picked out the perfect colors and sizes of clothes for him. He pulled up every ounce of courage and decided to come over to her, let his eyes meet hers, reached out to hold her hands with his, and said, "Sister, I want to say a big thank you to you and mom for the wonderful gift of clothes you have picked and chosen for me. I am indebted to you, Be."

She gave him the biggest smile, squeezed his hands, and said, "You need to change often so that I can wash them for you." She looked at him as if she wanted to say something else. Perhaps a comment such as on how could he have his clothes on him for days without being changed and washed, or perhaps, his clothes have now acquired a strange smell. Nonetheless, he felt he had read her thinking and said, "Yes, I will try to do better, sister."

With an approving look, she gave a smile, understanding his circumstance, which she would not like to be in at any time.

"Could I borrow your clothes some time too?" asked Cu, smiling and looking at Lin in a teasing voice and demeanor. He had been observing the comments, the raving about how cute his brother Lin looks with his new clothes on him, and he agreed. But he could not help derailing from what everyone was thinking and saying. That is his nature! He is mostly quiet, but he gets attention when he says things out of ordinary or teases people in a humorous way.

"Anytime, Cu. After all, I would love to share them with you even though they are a bit too big on you. Do you want to try them on, brother?" Lin teased Cu back, and they all laughed at the exchange of the teasing between the boys.

Lin noticed something was missing in the atmosphere. That is Mr. Nam's presence, and he was wondering where he was and what had happened to him. Why did he not come to join his family on this occasion? Did he not approve the spending on his new clothes? Is he here a burden to his family? Lin did not think those are the reasons, for he could intuitively feel the love, the care Mr. Nam gave him. As his young mind was wondering and his narrow brain searching, the old man walked in the door with his left hand on the knob, pushing it open. The look on his face was not anything that indicates good news. Before any of his members could utter a word of greeting him, Mr. Nam told them that something disturbing had just happened minutes ago, and as a result, the curfew inside the city limit had immediately become affected. He said that there were several explosions and scattered skirmishes at the border of the city adjunct to the highway between the government troops and the National Liberation Front guerillas fighters. He commented that for so long, the fighting had always been somewhere far away in the remote areas, many kilometers from the city. But now, it happened right next to the heart of the city, where he thought it has always been safe. He said he had been in his office working to get the school ready when it resumed, but the explosions led him to turn on the news on his radio in the office. It dawned on him that he had heard of the sounds explosions and thought they were some sorts of thunderstorms or even the supersized firecrackers.

The Air Of War

"The province chief has ordered all the festival activities inside the city to be canceled, including the well-publicized event at the temple." He looked at everyone in the room as he announced the news. He said that he was planning to take the whole family out to the temple as a surprise to get the taste of the New Year flavors and to see the many activities of the holiday, especially for Lin while he was in the city.

"I am sorry," casting his eyes, full of concerns to each member of his family, the curator said in his solemn voice. "This is the very first time it happened, and I am afraid that it would be getting worse. We all need stay inside because of the curfew and also for our own safety," he instructed his family.

What he did not want to tell his family was, as it later hit the newsstands, the main highway, which runs through the city, was closed off. As a result, everything, including food supplies from the south and the capital, could not come to the city.

The mood in the room was suddenly changed from being upbeat, full of laughter and energy, to that of a deflated balloon. They all looked very worried. Within a minute or two, conversations began between the elders and the youngsters all around the possibilities of the city being attacked, and then the gunfire in the streets, and to the worst-case scenario of the bombs being dropped from the sky to save the city, in which case, they, as civilians, are the poor victims—"the suffered, the smashed grasses between the two elephants that tussle." The mother and the daughters were more sensitive about the livelihood of the whole family. They worried about the food to put in the mouth of everyone in their family of which he is also of their very concern. They talked how to get the basic food for tomorrow from a bundle of green mustard to a mud trout or dried fish. They have enjoyed the luxury of all fresh veggies and meats offered at the open market every day, twice a day, and year-round, and now, all of a sudden, this might not be a possibility. Or if there was anything at the open-sky grocery market the following day, would there be any food that they could afford at all? She, by her motherly instinct, knows that the price always goes up according to the law of demand and supply. This is one of the perfect situations where the sellers will get what they want for their products.

"My lady and my children, don't you think it is such a waste of time and energy to talk about something that is not happening and might not happen at all?" Mr. Nam cleared his throat as he voiced his wisdom of life. "Change the subject, please," he continued as if he were the professor of philosophy on the platform, chastising his students for their unacceptable thinking and behaviors.

As if awakened from a nightmare, all had realized they did not use their time wisely and perhaps not put their wisdom to test.

"Thank you, Dad, for pointing it out," said the girl, looking at her dad with a complete sense of admiration. "This is the only time we presently have for one another. We are certainly using it for tomorrow in worrying, which may not happen."

Lin could not help thinking, *Huh, like father like...daughter. Does it sound right?*

Lin and Cu were the ones who had put all the hope and expectations coming to the event, and they now really felt bummed out. Oh well, there was nothing anyone could do. The old saying that his father used to recite on the river while fishing now came back to him: "Man proposes; God disposes." It does fit into this situation perfectly.

Mr. Nam projected that the traffic would resume by tomorrow because, according to his valuation and estimation, the government cannot afford to let the blockage of this strategic city happen, much less the guerillas occupying it. It is like choking one of the main arteries of one's body. It needs to have it cleared up, or it will die. Therefore, at any cost, for politics' sake, the highway has to be freed so streams of transportation will flow through. He also suggested that it is a test of strength from the members of NLF (National Liberation Front) to the local government military might to see how much resistance they encounter. It is a very good thing so that their troops would always be alert and stay ready for any attempts to run over the city. Lin and the rest of the audience were in awe at the old man's political analysis, and his knowledge had made all feel comfortable at the time and situation of unrest like this. Everyone—the mother sitting on the chair and the kids on the floor—looked at him, waiting for more words of confidence from the man, the head of the family, because his voice, his tone, is like that of a pilot, calming his passengers while gliding his plane through the stormy weather. That is exactly why everyone's eyes were on him for—to find comfort and strength. His courage, his knowledge, and his kindness have earned Lin's admiration tremendously. During the past school months, Lin had seen the old man, here and there, all over the school buildings, and he is also responsible for disciplining the students with behavioral problems; his name is known to all in school. Lin would never want to be summoned to come to his office by all means. Never in his dream had he thought about being here in his household, becoming a part of his family and being cared for by him and his family members. It is truly a wild dream that came true. Mr. Nam is in his fifties, the age of his own father;

the thick spectacles on his nose seems to be always the victim of gravity, which keeps his forefinger a bit too busy to give it a lift, or else, you would see his eyes roll up as his glasses would slip down to the end of his nose when he talks to you. His white hair all over his head earns him a title of Curator the White Hair. No one knows what school he came from or what college he went to, but he is very strict in disciplining and keeping the troublesome students in line. Otherwise, a caring, loving gentleman he is.

As if forgetting something important, he turned to look at Lin and said, "My son, I have been carried away with things happening outside of the house and had completely overlooked the very things in our family. I am sorry, but look at you, my boy. You look very nice, perhaps, what's the word? *Handsome*, yeah, it is the word I should use. The clothes fit you just perfectly well, and by the way, I love the color of your shirt too. It looks and feels springy."

"Thank you, Mr. Nam," he said as he looked up at the man and cast his eyes to Mrs. Nam and, at last, rested his eyes at Be's, as if saying, "Thank you for your loving, caring, and choosing the colors and the sizes of my clothes. Do I deserve all this, especially, in the situation we are in, for the war is entering into the city? There will be lots of uncertainty." As the things were unfolding, he does not feel comfortable with the gift, which he knows cost a lot of money, from their budget as a school official whose income is fixed, monthly. He was wondering if it were a possibility to return the merchandise at this point in time? The question is if he had the guts to ask those who extended their love through their gifts. He looked at Be for a long while with a hope that he could convey the feeling in his heart, the thoughts he had in his mind. She gave him a smile, and that was the end of his debating. He would never find courage to say what he wanted to say.

"Oh, you are very welcome, son," said the old man to Lin. He then turned to his wife. "Let's have our dinner early tonight, my dear." He did not say why, but Lin could sense and read his mind that things could happen in the evening when it is dark. The fighting could break out between the government soldiers and the communist rebels, and when it happens, at least everyone has had their meal. The old man did not want to alarm his family members or remind them about the eminent threat of war that they had talked about earlier. But men often forget that women do have what is known as the sixth sense or, who knows, maybe more.

Mrs. Nam and her daughter quickly went to the kitchen after saying yes to the old man. They wanted to have their loved ones' tummies filled first regardless what the circumstance or situation. It is the motherly care that was designed from and by God, from birds in the sky to beasts, and to humans on the ground.

While the ladies were back in the kitchen, Mr. Nam softly asked Lin and Cu to come to sit with him on the chair across from the dining table and said, "I did not want to frighten your mom and your sister. But things could get worse, meaning there would be gunshots and explosions. Stay where you are and never run around outside the house, unless it is on fire. The reason is— listen carefully, sons—you don't want to get caught in the gunfire from either side. Remember, stray bullets are blind and have no mercy. In addition, there is something of importance I want to talk to both of you. Since you are boys, and Lin is the oldest, I will have to depend on you if anything happens to me; you would be the head of the family."

This startled Lin and troubled him deeply but did not know what to say. Mr. Nam then continued, "Since I am a government official, I am an enemy to the communist rebels. They could come to get me even though I am not armed to fight against them. I just want to make sure that you both are aware of the possibility that it could happen. Promise me that you would do what I just asked you." The old man looked at Lin and then Cu for answer.

"Yes, Dad," said Cu.

"Yes, Mr. Nam," said Lin, and he felt a heavy load of responsibility bearing down on his shoulders, and at the same time, he felt honored to be bestowed with such a task. Mr. Nam did not think of him as an outsider, but a son to him and family. Perhaps he was considered as a student to a teacher, and knowingly, there is a sacred relationship between the two that brought forth his decision. He, all of a sudden, felt older and proud to accept the responsibility even though he hadn't had a clue on what he should be doing if he became the head of the family. He almost laughed out loud with a childish thought that it would be almost impossible to make Be his subordinate and to ask her follow his orders.

He thought it would be too complicated. Now he prayed that nothing would happen to Mr. Nam.

Lord, God, please keep him safe.

The old man continued to tell him that the principal of the school and his wife were scheduled to fly in from Saigon the following day to get the school ready when the students returned from the holiday break, but it might not happen because of the curfew and the fighting. If it were the case, he would be in charge of the facility and respond to the situation accordingly. He knows very well that he has to take care of every student who made it to the school, especially the ones from the tribes, and put them in the dorms and feed them. The school was built in their behalf, and the training, instructions, and curriculum were structured to make them leaders and officials in their communities. In a nutshell, they are the government's interests; therefore, Mr. Curator has a big job and an awesome responsibility ahead of him.

True to his prediction and his institution, the sounds of sporadic gunshots were heard, and then a series of big explosions shook the ground, rattled the house, and scared the soul out of everyone in the family. It happened while the members of the family were enjoying their dinner. Shaken in shock, Be and her mom sat their unfinished bowls of food on the table as their hands trembled; their faces turned pale with a look of horror displayed on them. Cu started sobbing and covered his mouth with his hands in an attempt to contain his cry, as if he were afraid that if he made any noises, any sounds, he would endanger his family. Nonetheless, he was terrified.

The old man now, at best, tried to calm and comfort his family by saying, "It sounded like it is next door. But it is not, it is the sound of artillery round that came in from the suburb, or perhaps the sounds were from the counterattack from our military installations. Don't be too alarmed. It is still far away yet." Mr. Nam's voice was calm and clear in his evaluation of the situation. Lin felt that he needed to show his support to the old man by staying and showing calm. After all, Mr. Nam had wished him to become the man of the house. He looked at the father, cut his eyes to the mother and Be, and faintly nodded his head in agreement.

He threw his right arm around Cu's shoulders to reassure him that Daddy is right and whispered to him, "Everything will be all right, don't cry and stay calm."

To show as an example that things are okay as he had said, he asked all to continue with their meal. He then quickly picked up his bowl and encouraged them to do the same. Lin noticed that the ladies were quiet and seemed still letting the fear and anxiety hang over their head. Be's eyes were moist and welled up as his eyes slowly met hers.

Don't cry, sister, he quietly said in his mind. Immediately, he made a point to break this thick silence of fear and nervousness by saying, "Mama and sis, I don't know who is responsible for making this incredibly delicious beef-veggie stir-fry. It just makes my taste buds singing and dancing." He had a big smile and a playful rhythmical vocal sound of "uh uh uh" that drew laughter not only from the two chefs but also from the father and Cu. He knew he had won the emotional battle on the ladies.

"Would you like to teach me how to cook this very dish?" Lin looked up at the mother as he asked the question, which won him a smile on her face. The air of anxiety and fear has finally escaped the room."

"You? Cooking? I don't think so," the mother told Lin and in her teasing voice. "Besides,

it is a secret recipe. I will have your sister teach you with a price."

"Will you charge me, sis? I will have to give you an IOU until I get a job. I hope you don't mind." Lin teased her again, hoping to bring her into a conversation and get her mind off the fear of the gunfight.

"IOU? From you? No, no, COD, cash on delivery only or nothing!" In a playful tone of voice, she finished her frolicsome thoughts with, "That is why I am short because I don't have enough patience." Be smiled, almost laughing, and brightened up herself as she found her way to making fun of him.

Wow! Lind did not expect this playfulness of words coming out from her. What a surprise! He admired her for the witty comeback, and he also was glad that laughter has returned to fill the room. He prayed that it would last for a very long time. He could not remember at any time in his life he had been in such warmth of the loving family setting like the one of this family, despite the fragility, the uncertainty in time of war. He just wanted to soak himself up, to immerse his whole being down into the nectar of this very moment of life and to stretch it to the eternity. Oh, how much he wanted to treasure this precious moment of his life.

"Okay, okay, as poor as I have been and as homeless as I am, I will do the dishes for you to begin with in exchange—"

Raising her hand, palm facing him, a universal stop sign, Be would not want him to say any more of what he had in his mind. He immediately knew that he was in trouble, for her face had changed, become saddened. Taking her eyes off from him, she turned to her mom and said, "Mom, I just don't like the way my brother talked. I do not like it."

Immediately, Lin said to her and her mom, "Forgive me, mama and sis. I am heartily sorry for making you upset with my words. But what I said was an honest truth. I have planned to find a job, a part-time, to support myself and continue my education. Things are tough at home, and besides, I do not want any more friction between my parents because of me. My stepmother, who never wanted me in the family in the very beginning, would never be happy if I kept receiving my dad's support. It does not matter how hard I tried to do everything she asked me to do to win her mercy; even a meager meal, she would not let me. Therefore, I have decided to be on my own and learn to survive and to be a good and better person. I know in my heart, which of a young person, a determination to face the challenge of my life. I am so grateful for your loving compassion and for considering me a part of your loving, caring family. Please allow me to do anything a son would do and could do for his family. I will do it with grace and gratefulness."

As he finished his heartfelt speech, he noticed everyone's eyes were on him, but with different reactions. Mr. Nam did not expect him to give a lengthy speech but gave him an eye of approval by slightly nodding his head. A smile from the mother's lips gave him comfort and love. Cu kept his mouth half-open as he stared at him as if saying, "Good job of speaking, brother." Be was dramatically opposite from everyone else's. She was drying her tears with the sleeve of her shirt. She was probably feeling sorry for making him pour his heart out or perhaps empathizing with his eventful life.

Whatever was the cause, she said to him in a remorseful teary voice, "I just don't want you to do the dishes. It is my job, brother. I am sorry."

Is that it? My little sister? he was thinking in his head. He had a lot to learn, for he had never had a sister to deal with.

"Then smile!" he playfully said as if he ordered her. That did it!

The laughter had returned to the room, and the conversation had resumed. Lin now breathed with relief that Be was not upset with him anymore as she was gathering the dishes off the table to be washed at the faucet outside the kitchen by the wall. It was getting dark; Lin could hear the winds gusting outside the house. The cold air flooded the room as Be pushed the door open to haul the dishes outside on a big, circular aluminum tray. She had stacked up small bowls in a short column and the two big serving bowls, one on top of the other, next to it along with chopsticks and spoons, lying flat on the tray. He looked at the tray and then at her; the whole picture was not balanced. The slender figure of hers was dominated by the enormity of what was laden on her two hands, and the danger of her being swept or even knocked down by the gusts of the wind would not allow him the luxury of sitting there, watching. Inside his head, a voice, like a loudspeaker, was screaming, *Go help her!*

Like a big brother in the house, he sprung from his seat, followed by Cu; both dashed out of the door to make sure Be was not swept away by the wind, which was gusting stronger. He immediately grabbed the tray from her and safely took it to the wash basin by the wall. He asked her to go inside, for it was getting cold, mostly because of the wind that intensified it, making it a lot colder. He did not want her to get pneumonia over the washing of dishes. For him, cold? He is used to it. Do dishes and cooking? They never bother him. He could do it any time, dutifully and joyfully. As soon as he was sure that Be stayed inside, he and Cu started washing and rinsing under the amber light from the single bulb of incandescent light on the wall.

"You are doing a very good job, Cu. You must have helped you sister a few times doing this, right?" Lin asked in a very praising tone of voice, which drew a smile from Cu's face.

"The next time you do, I love to do it with you," Cu said enthusiastically. A thought came flashing to his mind that he and Cu had to fight with his sister for the dishwashing job; it is because of the bias from the mother who would never let the boys do the dishes while her daughter is around. That is rooted in the culture.

Just as Lin was about to give Cu the answer and to tell him that he should be going inside, the whole sky above him lit up and startled the boys. Immediately, he knew it was one of the flares that the military used for their surveillance, just like the ones the soldiers had used in his village. He told Cu not to be afraid; in fact, he pulled Cu away from the house so that he could look at the flare slowly drifting away in the air. He told Cu that he had seen this before in his village.

"Brother, what holds the light up in the air for so long?" Cu asked.

Lin did not know the answer but quickly told him what he had in mind, his guesses, that it must be attached to a small parachute. Maybe Mr. Nam can answer that once they go inside.

While they were admiring the air show of light, which was now fading away, they noticed the streaks of light crossing the dark sky in different directions, and then sounds of gunshots echoed in the air. Lin realized they were tracers, he pulled Cu back inside the house, and, in horror, Cu told his parents and Be what he had seen and heard outside. The look of worry once again returned to their faces as the night fell. What would be happening next in the night? No one wanted to know. Each had something to keep their mind occupied and to worry about. This time they all became silent, and they repressed their fear as they went to bed.

Mr. and Mrs. Nam have decided to have Lin sleep on the floor with Cu, for they both felt uncomfortable to have Lin all by himself in the dorms up on the second floor in the empty building.

"It is much safer to sleep on the ground because the bullets will fly and travel on the air," the elders told him. Lin did not mind the dorm but was glad to stay on the cement floor with the family. Cu was happy. He was, in fact, excited to be inside the mosquito net with Lin, leaving the worry to the adults. He whispered to Lin as he lay on his side on the straw mat, "Hey, brother Lin, you stay with me forever, all right?" The nightlight by the wall cast a faint light on Cu's face, revealing his innocent smile and his nice white teeth.

Cu's soft expression touched Lin deeply. He felt that he had found a brother for himself as well. He looked at Cu in the eye, smiled, and whispered a word deep from his heart, "Yes, since we are brothers." Lin playfully rubbed his brother's head with his hand. He smoothed his hair. "Sleep tight, brother."

Cu smiled, closed his eyes, and fell asleep. Outside the brick wall, the winds were still gusting, mixing with sounds of sporadic gunshots echoed in the air, perhaps from far, very far way. He said his prayers, thanking God for his newfound family, the brother and sister, Mr. and Mrs. Nam, who took him in their arms and loved him as a son. He prayed for their safety, for the war ceased right away. His eyes welled up again as he lay next to Cu, and he covered him with his blanket.

Lin woke up to the bright daylight and to the whispering of the adults, as if they did not want to disturb the boys' sleep. He kept his eyes closed and realized that nothing had happened, for he slept all the way through the night. He did not hear any gunfight or any explosions. Maybe the fighting was over, he now hoped.

Mr. Nam's voice was audible even though he had intended to keep it down.

"I bet you did not have a wink last night," the husband said to his wife, who was sitting next to him on the chair for comfort.

"Neither, did you. And by the way, how could we with all the sounds of gunfight all night long? Some were just like right in our neighborhood, others very far away. Did you hear them all last night, dear?" the wife asked. Her voice was tired from lack of sleep. The worry did take a toll on her.

"The closest ones were not too far from us, maybe a couple of kilometers from our school buildings. In fact, it is the provincial radio station that the communist rebels tried to take over. The radio station is so very important to either side. It is the breath, the livelihood, and the voice of the government, central and local alike. For the rebels, if they ever got to it, you could not imagine the damage they would do to our government. They can broadcast all the propaganda they want in order to confuse the people throughout the area and, worst of all, to dampen and crush the fighting spirit of our government officials, our fighters, and our soldiers. It would be very devastating to all of us. I am glad that it was now over. The reinforcement of many battalions of troops, from rangers to the red berets, the parachute troops, or the sky angels, had come early yesterday afternoon. They coordinated and tightened the grip to choke of the enemy from the outside."

This was reported on the morning news on his radio. Mr. Nam gave her the news report of what had happened in the process of taking back the control of the area and the city, and ultimately to clear off the arterial roads and freeways. Impressively, he was almost correct with what he had predicted about what the central government would have to do to gain the control of the city and outskirt areas.

Lin felt the relief from what he just heard. He had slept so well that he did not hear even the smallest sound of the gunfire. He must have slept like a dead log. He decided to get up to help with the family chores or anything Mr. Nam might want him to do to get the school ready before it resumed.

"Good morning, Mr. and Mrs. Nam," he said as he rolled himself out of the mosquito net.

"Good morning, son. Did you sleep well? Did you hear anything last night?" asked Mr. Nam as he gave Lin a bright smile, which lifted him up with all the enthusiasm for the new day, especially the news report that he overheard while he was debriefing his wife.

"Yes, sir. I did, much like a rock, I must say. Had you rolled me out into the street, I would not have even known." The parents laughed at his answer, which had a touch of playful exaggerations. From the corner of his eyes, he caught a glimpse of Be out in the kitchen, where the smoke was rising up to chimney. She must be doing the cooking for the family. He thought he could give her some help.

"May I come out to give my sister a hand?" He asked to be excused from the parents. They were pleased with the idea. However, the mother asked him to get Cu up to give help too. Being the youngest boy in the family, he gets the perk to sleep in, and there was not much that he has to do around the house. The mother realizes that, and now since Lin is around, she wanted Lin to shape him up to be more helpful.

"Cu, get up. We have work to do." Lin wanted to tickle Cu to get him up; instead, he pulled the blanket off from him. That did it! Cu sat up, rubbed his eyes, and gave Lin a sleepy smile. They both cleared up the sleeping area, exited to the washing area, and went to the kitchen to help their sister.

"Good morning, sis, you are up early. Did you sleep well?" Lin asked and gave her his big smile. She returned him with hers and a nod while staying busy with the cooking chores.

"Sis, let us give you our manly help." He faked his voice like a grown-up, raspy male voice, which brought laughter from her. "Tell us what you want to do and leave it to us. Cu and I can do it for you," Lin continued.

The smoke got in her eyes while she was adjusting the flames from the burning firewood underneath the stove. This is exactly what he had been through when he does the cooking for his dad—teary eyes. Oh, how much he sympathizes with her in this moment of the task of love for everyone in the family. He needed to take over. But stubborn as she was, it would be almost impossible for him to take over her work, which she loves.

"I am done, please help set up table so that I can get the food in," she finally told him what to do. She would not let go with what she was doing. How could she anyway? One just can't take over someone's cooking—the style, the seasoning, the heat, the control of temperature, and a whole lot more. It brought back the painful experience on the boat with his dad on the river. Someday he would probably share that experience with Be.

"Boys, I have work for you to do," the curator announced right after meal, which wasn't a breakfast nor was it a lunch. However, it was just delicious, and he again thanked his sister, Be, for the very tasty meal. Mr. Nam wanted to get all the classrooms cleaned up. The chairs, the benches, the desks—all need to be rearranged and dusted, getting ready for the students when they returned. Besides, the boss is flying in twenty-four hours. He and his wife are returning from their vacation. Of course, he wants to see the school in good shape and that it survived the war, no damages.

Lin was happy to help and even happier when he got Cu excited to join him as well, which made Mr. Nam a very happy man on earth for he sees his young kids eager to help, to work, to make a contribution in life instead of being idle and roaming in the streets and getting bored. He had at one point complained about the work ethics among the young children, especially in the city, who do not have a smidgen of desires to work, to help, to earn a living, nor do they have any concept of contribution to the society where they belong. He had mentioned that he came from a very poor family in a farming community down south in the Mekong delta, the region of lush, green rice paddies that spread for miles. He had to pack his own lunch and walked ten kilometers to and from his school every day, rain or shine. That means he had to get up very early in the morning to get himself ready to leave his house at the first rays of dawn on the horizon, and he did not get home until it was dark. On weekends and the days that he did not have school, he would tend his parents' herd of ducks in the field, feeding them when the harvest season of rice was over, collecting the eggs they lay in the field. He was so proud that he had worked so hard to support his schooling and to help his parents. Many years later, at this age, he still talked about his boyhood with such pride in his voice, and no wonder he was happy to get the boys involved and to pave the way for them to become a contributor instead of a taker, a parasite to the world they live in.

"Should I bring brooms and dusters along, Mr. Nam?" Lin asked eagerly.

"We will stop at the stock room to get what we need. But, definitely, we will need them," said the curator pleasantly.

Just as the three of them were ready to march out of the house, Be, with all excitement in her voice, asked to join them. "I want to come to work too. Dad, may I?"

Delighted, the old man felt like the happiest man on the planet for his children, who all have the desire to help and to work.

When did all of this begin? he is asking himself. Where and when did his son and daughter find this enthusiasm and be this energetic? He obviously knows it is from Lin, whose good nature has nonchalantly influenced them.

"Yes, you may, my girl. Make sure you tell your mom that you are coming with us so that she does not worry when she finds out you were not around."

"Yes, I did already, Dad. Mom said it was great to go help, Dad." Be was so proud of herself to tell her dad about her newfound energy.

The sun had anchored straight above his head. It must have been noontime, for he and his shadow had become one. The sky was clear and blue, hardly any clouds in the giant vault. The winds had died down, and the air—yes, the air, which was not only fresh with a touch of wintery herbs but also greeted the new day after all anxiety and uncertainties—had been evaporated at the dawn of the day. Within minutes, they were on their way to each classroom in each building, doing exactly what they all had planned, cleaning and straightening tables and chairs and desks. Lin helped Mr. Nam lift or move the furniture while Cu and Be were doing the dusting with feather dusters, the ones made with real fluffy, smooth chicken and peacock feathers in different colors. They were tightly glued together layer after layer over a bamboo stick, which became the long handle of the duster. Every now and then, out of his boredom, his naughtiness, Cu used his duster to tickle his sister by poking the end of the duster, which has one or two long feathers, to his sister's ears. Would she put up with this kind behavior of his, or would she tolerate her younger brother out of her sisterly love? No, not really. She told him to stop it the first time as a warning even though she laughed at being tickled. But he stubbornly continued to annoy and distract her from doing her work; she disciplined him severely. Cu bore the punishment by standing, facing the wall with his arms stretching out on the wooden wall like a mannequin or a paper poster for ten minutes, until he was in tears, begging for mercy. Neither Mr. Nam nor Lin wanted to interfere with the discipline, which Lin finds interesting and meaningful. Since Cu's hands are the ones that caused him mischief, then his hands are also the ones to be penalized. She has earned his respect!

"Is it your classroom, brother?" Cu asked after being released from his punishment and coming to this classroom in the middle of the building, which is located adjunct to the administrative building. The classroom gets a half day of sunlight, from noon till sunset. It has a clear view of the front court, where the white-painted flagpole stands patiently and dedicatedly like a quiet school official throughout the year. There are times when Lin could see during class the whirls of wind, like invisible cylindrical vacuum machine, sucking up red dirt, brown leaves, and debris into the air, and then, like a deflated balloon, losing its helium, its momentum, dumping them at the end of the court, by the line of tall trees, as the wind tapered off.

"It is one of the few, depending on the class," Lin told Cu. "When you are in high school, you get to go from one class to another. You will know what I am talking about." Lin proudly continued his explanation as if he was giving his younger brother a heads-up on his endeavors in years to come. It dawned on Lin that in this very classroom, months ago, he met his Vietnamese literature teacher, Mr. Phat—young, learned, and handsome, wearing an eyeglasses with dark burgundy frame buried under his long black hair, which ignored the barbershop in town. His teacher has an average height and built for a man born in Vietnam and spent his time paraphrasing, dissecting, explaining one of Shakespeare's works, the famous "love story." Mr. Phat captivated his audience of young male students with his spellbinding storytelling skills that kept the students thirsty, hungry, and craving for more of the exquisite details and intriguing plots as he let them unfold one at the time. Lin was always looking forward to coming to this very space of this classroom, sitting in his chair, in his usual spot to hear his teacher's voice, one with inflection, flowing low and high with the story. He was simply enchanted! Not only was he fascinated with the story, but also hypnotized with the voice of his teacher when he sang the love story in Vietnamese, in French, and in English. What a talented young teacher he was!

By the time they got to the last classroom of the last building, it had been late, and Be was sent home to give her mom a hand in getting dinner ready. She came over to Lin as she was leaving and said, "Brother, I will see you at dinner, but in the meantime, keep an eye on Cu and make sure that he is not spoiled by making you do all the work." She gave him a smile and quickly left the room.

The three-man party now headed out to another building to which there's an equally large place to inspect, rearrange, and get it ready. First, they went to the huge kitchen and dining hall on the main floor and the dorm rooms on the second level, one of which he would be staying tonight if not at the curator's. Lin came to a sudden realization that it is not a small job; it is an awesome responsibility for Mr. Curator to run this aspect of the school. When the school resumes, Mr. Nam would have all the cooks, their helpers, and the janitors to give him a hand to get things done.

Lin had been in or around the kitchen more than once during the school year to ask from one of the cooks for a piece of light-brown burned rice, which tastes like a snack, and for him, it does fill him like a meal. The cooks are all very nice and generous with students. He felt grateful to them and their tools, the wooden-handle, flat-lip shovels; they used to pry up sheets of caked rice at the bottom of the supersized cast-iron woks. Lin also appreciated their ability to cook such a large amount of rice in a wok on the woodstoves like the ones in front of him, every time, every day, without a flaw. Overcooked, you get your rice burned, black like charcoal. Undercooked, a dull taste of porridge. They have definitely earned his admiration.

Lin turned to Cu and asked, "Have you tasted the burned rice from these woks, Cu? I sure missed it."

"How can I not, brother?" Cu showed his white teeth in his biggest smile as if having a light-brown piece in his hands. "The cooks often give it to me in a handful, nice and warm, and very tasty. But my mom does not allow me to come nearby the kitchen. They would sometimes save and bring it to me."

It is one of the rules at the school that no students were allowed nearby the kitchen during the cooking hours for safety and for the sake of order in the classrooms. It would be chaotic to have young students, hungry or not, herding at the cooking area for a handout of foods, or it may look like a charity house.

Mr. Nam was ahead of the boys in this building, for he had gone upstairs to inspect the dorms after a brief check at the dining hall. There was not much that the boys could do other than keep the curator company.

Lin could not help wishing that he could have the privilege of staying in this building, enjoying the meals prepared from this kitchen and walking right over the classrooms in the opposite buildings. He would not mind becoming a minority, a Montagnard, to get this opportunity to further education and training because he does not know if will he be able to stay around here in the next few days when the school starts. He is, in a way, a homeless person. However, he just remembered a saying from a guru who says, "The secret of living is to live one day at a time" and "Today, right at this moment, I am happy."

"Brother, we are done. Let's go home." Cu's voice lifted him out of the deep thinking. A friend in his class sang the song "Que Sera Sera" and told him the meaning of it. It fits his circumstance, and he just now liked it. As he was about to answer Cu, he noticed a little library at the far end from the dining hall. It is like a reading room, which he had never seen before. How could he? He has just been in this building less than twenty-four hours. It has a large number of books on the shelves. He asked Cu to come over to check them out and maybe he could ask Mr. Nam to let him read some of these books if they fit him. The clock on the wall by the kitchen struck five thirty, as the sunlight shone through the large panes of glass windows set the mood for the boys to explore. There were books on the history of Vietnam that goes back to thousands of years at the beginning of forming the nation. There are also books on automobiles and steam engines, but what interested him the most was books on Vietnamese literature. He made a point to ask Mr. Nam to let him check one of these books out to read. While the boys were busy flipping, turning, and enjoying the smell of the pages of the book, the father had come and stood behind them, watching his kids with the eye of approval. He understands very well that a child who shows interests in reading books will become a person with knowledge because wisdom comes from reading, from associating and learning from others. He felt a sense of gratefulness that Lin was there in front of him to influence Cu to desire learning and reading. No wonder he loves the boy, Mr. Nam thought.

"I am glad that you show the love for books," the father told the boys, at last, from behind their back. "You can go back here to read and study anytime you want."

Lin made a quick turn. His eyes were wide open and in shock of what he just heard. What held him back from coming over to give this slim, aged man a hug, he did not know, but in that instant, in that moment in time, he felt the surge of emotion that he had found the father's love. His eyes met the old man's, and he uttered in deep emotion, "Thank you, sir." He then turned to look at Cu, like a big brother guiding his younger one, and said, "You come with me at any time, but say thank you to Daddy."

How delightful he was to see and hear what he just heard from the boys. Indeed, Mr. Nam was a very happy man. It showed in his voice, in his eyes, and in his smile.

"Let's go home for our meal. I am hungry, kids," he jovially said to the boys.

Carefully setting the books down, jumping to their feet, they picked up the joyous, merry mood from Dad; their voices rang out like singing, "Me too and me too." And out to the door, they dashed out.

Leaving the old man behind, they were out in the red-dirt field yelling, chasing each other, stirring the dirt up in the air behind them. They finally arrived home after a full round of running, passing two buildings and the soccer field, burning up their youthful stored-up energy.

Panting, catching their breath as they walked in the door, everyone was at the dining table ready and waiting for them, not impatiently but in a good cheerful mood. In fact, the parents and the daughter were having a conversation where his name was mentioned. All the eyes were on him as he bowed his head and respectfully greeted them.

"Brother, I am so proud of you. Aren't you hungry?" Like a singing bird, Be was eager to talk to him after what was a praise from the father, who reported to her mom just as soon as he walked in the door about Lin's work and his becoming a "young model" for Cu. He told them his observation of the boys at the library in the building next door. He was just simply impressed with what he had seen of them.

"Oh yes, I am starving, sister," he told her as he rubbed his hand on his tummy in a circular motion and made a face as if he had been hungry for days. "Do you know why? Because I worked hard and chased our little brother all over the soccer field."

"Really?" Raising her voice, she smiled and rolled her eyes as if she was surprised at what he had said were true, but then she squinted her eye, looking at him and softly said, "I believe only half of it because you are acting very well." Was it a compliment, or she knew of his exaggeration, stretching a bit from the truth? he wondered.

"Well, let's eat, boys and girl. We old people are starving," the father broke in so the dinner could start and save Lin from being teased by the daughter.

The dinner, served with laughter and conversations, was filled with what went on in each classroom and all the buildings during the day. Cu made a confession that he had learned a valuable lesson from being punished for not putting his heart and mind into what he was doing and distracted others with his naughty behavior. He looked at his sister and softly said, "You were mean to me, but I did learn my lesson. Thank you, sis." Cu's confessed in a childlike way of saying it with a smile and an expression that touched everyone at the table, and his parents enjoyed the huge transformation in their baby boy, the youngest and a spoiled child, but now, a tamable person. They both laughed with gladness and joy throughout the meal, and they occasionally gave Lin a look that says more than words, and he felt it. He felt the love they had for him.

Lin, however, every now and then, caught a look from Be's eyes that was half-teasing, half-twinkling, with a touch of devious ray from the corner of her brown eyes. "You are a star in the family now, brother. But do not let your nose boom with your ego, okay? We all love you." He wanted to tell her how deeply he felt the love for her family and the gratefulness that filled his heart. But instead, he gazed into her eyes, and let it rest for a long moment to say it all to her.

"Sis, I almost caught a bird that was trapped inside one of the classrooms for you. The bird was small, black, and very cute. He has a bright-yellow strip at the edges of his bill. He could be a bird that one day would talk to you, but Brother Lin would not let me catch him. He freed the bird out of the room." Cu told his sister about the incident of the bird that somehow got into the room and could not find the way out; he was simply stuck between the walls, scared and hungry. Cu chased the bird from one side of the wall to the other and from one corner to the next with the handle of his broom. Lin could not just stand and let this poor bird get injured and suffered and die. He had seen enough of this game in his village where kids of his age and older used net to trap all kinds of birds and pluck them. He finally told Cu to get the door wide open, and with one swift, the black bird whizzed out of the room, up into the air to freedom.

"Your brother did the right thing, Cu. You should never do it again," Mrs. Nam told her son in a grave tone of voice. "Never hurt a being, a life, even an ant. Do good karma."

"Yes, Mother," Cu said remorsefully. He never knew he could get into trouble by mentioning the incident of catching the bird.

Be looked at Cu and felt sorry for him, but also glad that he knew what he did was not acceptable. She cast her eyes upon Lin's and gave him a look of approval.

Lin wanted to lift Cu out of the hole he was in by finally asking the parents if he could go take Cu and Be to the library to read after dishes were washed and put away. He immediately got the smiles from everyone, the approval from the parents, and the relief from the rest. He and Cu helped Be to get the washing and cleaning chores done, and the three of them rushed to the reading room.

It was late in the evening. The air was fresh and a little warmer, for it was not as windy as days before. The birds were flying, crossing low in the grayish evening sky, noisily chirping, calling one another as they disappeared in the canopy of leaves of the big tree by the end of the building

It turned out that Be was attending a public high school at the other side of town. She loves to read as well. But being in the all-male student school, even her father has the key to the library, it was not appropriate for her, nor was she comfortable venturing into the reading room with many eyes staring on her. Therefore, she did appreciate the opportunity to come along for the reading.

"Thank you, brother, for asking me to come along. I do love to read books," she told him with a soft voice of appreciation, which made him feel that he had discovered his own worthiness. He needed to tell her that he was very glad that she was happy too. He realized that the role of girls in the society in the culture is quite different from that of boys, where the girls are mostly to be kept inside the walls of the house and in the kitchen. She is to learn to master the art of cooking and serving her husband and his family. She is destined to be a housewife, a homemaker; therefore, time for reading is generally not recommended. On the contrary, it is completely different for boys. They are bound to be warriors, officers, and statesmen; therefore, it is a must that they read and write and learn and earn education.

"I am glad that you come and that you are happy," he said softly, almost as a whisper, as she came in, followed by her brother while he was holding the door, unlocked since his first sleep, to the building to open for them. He felt he had earned the role of being a big brother, guiding and protecting them. She looked up at him, and for a very short moment in time, she rested her gaze on him as if telling or expressing her deep appreciation for him.

Through the glass windows, a faint light of the evening still lingered inside the room. Lin reached to the switch on the left side wall of the entrance to turn on the main light, an incandescent light, hanging on a long black electrical wire, dangling from the lofty wooden ceiling. Cu quickly got to the corner of the library, and with a quick click from the switch, he had the amber-warm light from the two one hundred watts bulbs flooding the whole reading room.

The three of them were quietly absorbed into their books after a moment of astonishment of being surrounded with so many books in their lives. There was a sense of awe while letting their fingers move and do the feeling, touching the soft and hard covers of the books as if the wisdom and knowledge in the pages were awakened to the young seekers. There was a moment of lively debate as to what book would be their first choice to read. The three of them, brothers and sister, were sitting at a separate table knowing that as kids, they could get into talking naturally. Lin innately took the role of a big brother who exemplified the serious business of reading to Cu and Be, and they quietly followed his lead and manners. It was all quiet except the occasional faint sounds of the page turning. All of a sudden, there was a sound of the front door being open, and footsteps coming toward the reading room. Lin was first startled and then surprised at what he saw. He could not believe his eyes! Mr. and Mrs. Nam had come for a visit. Mr. Nam had his index finger at his mouth as a sign for him to stay silent. Be and Cu finally sensed something out of ordinary, looked up from their reading, and caught sight of their parents being in their midst. They almost screamed with joy and surprise, but the sign held them silent as well. They were both delighted at seeing their kids reading and enjoying the books. They have every reason to be happy about their kids. With a quick visit, they detoured to the left and climbed upstairs to the dorms. Lin was wondering what could be up there for them to come at this late in the evening. Everything was worked on and inspected today during the afternoon hours. What else was there that was needed to be done? There must be things kids should not be involved and are not supposed to know, and he shifted his mind back to his reading his book, *The Importance of Living* by Lin Yutan, which had been translated into many languages, and Vietnamese was one of them. It is a fascinating book in which he knew he could learn and benefit from tremendously. In just a few pages of the book, he found the soothing run through his veins and his heart. While his eyes were on the pages, his mind drifted back to the parents up on the second floor. Their footsteps could be audibly heard from where he was sitting. Judging from where the movement and the sounds above him, Lin could tell that they were at the room or, at least, in the area close by it. It must be it, the room where he had had his first sleep right after he lost his shelter at Bac Sau's a few days ago. He could not help let his emotion rise up to form a lump in his throat, as he now realized why and what brought them here. They were checking on his temporary sleeping spot for this night, or perhaps it could become a spot where he could consider his regular nightly shelter. He does not know if the curator could make that decision on his own without consulting with the principal of the school, but he could have his opinion and suggestion in his favor. However, he must realize that it would be an uphill battle because the school was built specifically for the students of minority, the highlanders, and he was nowhere near the status, even though he could tell the whole world that his situation, his circumstance, was worse than any student of the minority. He just had to pray that the principal would not kick him out when he arrives in a day or two. Nonetheless, he found himself at this very moment soaking in the blessing, swimming in the pool of loving care from Mr. Nam's family, without which he would have been miserably homeless, hungry, and perhaps already back to his village to face his reality of no school, no education, and, worst of all, the repugnance from his stepmother. He tried to shift his mind off from this mixed emotion to be present with the pages he was reading, but then he nonchalantly slipped himself in a tug-of-war between sounds echoed from the dorms upstairs, where he had the urge to go up to see if he could be of any help, and the pages that were staring at him. He managed to wait what it seems like forever for them to come down.

"We arranged the furniture in your room so that we could put a small nightstand with a table lamp for you. You can now stay up and read as much and late as you want," Mr. Nam told Lin as he and his wife came to the reading room. They both were delighted in seeing their children use their time wisely in reading and hopefully learning.

"Dad and Mom, can I stay with him too?" Cu jumped in as if the offer were for him.

His dad gave him a stern look and a long gaze, but in loving voice told him, "It is for your brother temporarily. Perhaps just a few days until the students return. But you can come with him."

"Really? Dad, thank you. I am not going to stay up there." Cu widened his eyes, smiled, and reassured his dad.

Mr. Nam nodded his head approvingly and cast his eyes on Lin, on Be, and around the room.

Thank you, Mr. and Mrs. Nam, for taking care of me. Lin wanted to tell them as they were about leaving the room. He was again speechless at what they gave to him by taking their time to come, making sure he is comfortable even temporarily. They had gone out of their way to do it for him in the name of love. He wanted to express his deepest appreciation but did not know how other than the gazing from his eyes and the bowing of his head.

After the parents left, Lin went right back to his reading as if the pages of *The Importance of Living* were calling him. He felt he could learn a lot from the book of which he could for sure apply to his situation and enjoy living a meaningful life for himself. He felt the need to finish it before the school starts.

He had been enjoying every moment of life with Be and Cu, who gave him the brotherly care and sisterly love until the students returned from the break. He had been told and expected of the reality that he had to move out from the cozy dorms. Mr. Nam had been his advocate to keep him where he was but could not persuade the principal and other members of the school board. The argument was very simple: "If Lin, a nonminority, could stay, then others could too. You cannot give to one and deny the other." Besides, the government policy does not allow that to happen. Mr. Quang, the principal of the school, more than anyone else, was well aware of that and did not want to get himself in trouble by violating the law regardless how big a heart he has.

While Lin was in the distressed mood of being homeless again and with the shock he was in, Be and Cu were both next to him and gave him support by even suggesting that he should just stay with them. It was fine with them, but it could become a problem, for their space was too small for a long-term stay, not just for him but also for everyone else in the family. The cold cement floor, which he does not mind, will and can be warm after a moment he lays body down on it, but the inconvenience he might cause to the family is something that he needs to think about, and he is sure the parents were well aware of it.

Lin was considering a possibility of going to a friend to ask for help to see if could stay with him temporarily till he could find a solution for his situation. The friend, Tan, is one of his classmates whose dwelling place is a big government building, all by itself, about halfway between the school and Bac Sau's. In fact, it is situated at the corner of the two streets across from the park. Tan's father is the director of the provincial treasury office, and, therefore, his family of four, his parents, and his older sister and a maid have enjoyed the luxury of staying in this big mansion, a brick-walled structure, beautifully painted in white and trimmed with dark-brick-red color matching that of the scalloped brick roof. Tan had mentioned in the past, knowing Lin's situation and circumstance, that he could come stay with him and his family. They could walk to school together or chauffeured on his dad's car on a rainy day. He had come to Tan's place a few times and had a couple of meals with his family but felt intimidated at the bourgeois air of the family. He had thought about having his dad working for Tan's family when Tan told him that his parents were looking for a good gardener, trimming the bushes, taking care of a very large-size garden full of dozens types of flowers and vegetables, but decided against it for various reasons. One, he is a full-time fisherman with family in the village miles away from the city. Two, he has never been a gardener and knows nothing about flowers and how to care for each type of the plants, and chances are, he might kill them or let them die. Lin did not want to put his dad or his friend in an awkward situation and, in turn, ruining their friendship.

While Cu and Be, not in their best mood, sitting quietly by the dining table, were all concerned about their brother's possibility of being moved out and if he could ever continue his education here in this school, Lin was there in their midst, but in his own world. He was thinking, pondering on finding a way out of his dilemma. What he did not know was the principal's wife, Mrs. Dong, and Mrs. Nam were in Mrs. Dong's office, discussing and looking for ways to help him stay in the school buildings. Mrs. Dong said that she and her husband were very worried whether or not they could get back in time before the school started because of the fighting, and mostly, they were also concerned about the safety and the well-being of Mrs. Nam's family. They all breathed with relief when the news came to them that the fighting had been over and the government troops had crushed the communist rebels' attempts to take over the city and its radio station.

"I would not mind to keep the boy with me, but as you can see, our place is so small to have an extra person. I just do not want him to sleep on the cold floor every night," Mrs. Nam said to Mrs. Dong and gave her the detail of how he got to her place in the first place and that Mr. Nam had put him up the students' dorms temporarily. She did not miss any detail about Lin, along with her kids, helping Mr. Nam to get the classrooms and the entire kitchen and dorms cleaned up to get them all as ready as they were. She went on to give her his circumstance with his family in village where his stepmother was his nightmare.

"I now remember him from his performance on the stage. Oh, how much I love the boy too." the principal's wife commented on his identity. The room all of a sudden became quiet. The two ladies, sitting across from each other with a clear glass vase full of red roses and white baby's breaths in between, each in her own mind, her own world, were searching for a solution for the one they loved and cared for. It was Mrs. Nam who, after hearing he husband's concerns over Lin's predicament, decided to come to Mrs. Dong to get help for him. They were the only two ladies living inside the school compound, giving motherly care for all, the wives of the two essential figures of the school; one has two children, and the other, none. One was a few years older than the other. Mrs. Dong was the younger one, who had been married for a number of years but never been able to bear a child. She loves being around the children, especially Mrs. Nam's kids, and here, she could feel Lin's pains and the urgency and the needs to get him out of his situation. Like a lightbulb that got turned on in her head, her eyes wide open, she slightly turned to look at Mrs. Nam and said, "Sister, I think I have found the solution for him." Confident in her voice, Mrs. Dong softly told Mrs. Nam, and that got all her attention. "I will ask my father to let the boy stay with him. He loves the boy too. He made that comment during Lin's performance on the stage." Mrs. Dong's father, Mr. Nguyen, the sole French teacher for all classes in the school, among a few privileged teachers, stays inside the school. Maybe because of his age the school allows him such a favor so that he does not have to travel a long distance to do his job. By having his own room, he could just walk to and from classrooms to do his teaching conveniently. Mr. Nguyen is in his late sixties, white-haired, skinny, and slightly hunchbacked, who wear silver-rimmed glasses. It all made him look like a scholar and philosopher.

"That would be great! A blessing for the boy and us as well. It would be heartbreaking if he had to go back to his village, enduring an oppressive life under his stepmother's vice," Mrs. Nam said with excitement in her voice. She breathed with such a relief, knowing that would be an excellent solution for the boy; not only does he have a place to stay but also a learning environment and a role model he can look up to. And as far as Mr. Nguyen is concerned, she thought he would accept the proposal, without any reservation, from his own daughter, who has not given him a grandchild. She was entertaining an idea: What if Mr. Nguyen would adopt Lin to be his grandson? Yes, what if? And she could not hide her chuckle.

"Sister, did you mention that Lin wants to find a part-time job for himself to support his living and school supplies?"

"Yes, it was his ideas just days ago when his lodging place got burned down. He wanted to be on his own, self-supported, and I cannot help admiring him for such a noble thought at his age. What do you have in mind?" Mrs. Nam asked inquisitively. She felt that Mrs. Dong has had something to share to offer.

"Well, I have a very close friend, Michelle, half-French, half-Vietnamese, who owns a large coffee plantation right outside the city limit. She also has a son, a young boy, perhaps, a year or two younger than Lin, and she is looking for someone who can come to her place to tutor her son twice a week, weekends preferably. She did mention she would be happy to pay five hundred piasters a month, a very generous compensation, I must say. I thought Lin would be the best candidate for the job since we know him well. He is our student and a good boy." She paused to gather some thoughts about the job Lin would be going to embark on.

"Lin would be at about the same age range with the boy, a perfect match to encourage the learning environment for my friend's son for, only a year or two differences, one is a tutor of other. That would inspire the latter to strive to do better. Math is the main subject of concerns, as Michelle had mentioned to me"

"Sister, since the plantation is quite away outside in the rural area, my question is how is he going to get himself to the plantation? It would be a very long walk, hours on his feet, don't you think? He definitely needs a bicycle to get around to and from the plantation. Do you have any thought on this?" Like a good planner, great mother, Mrs. Nam voiced her concern.

"Oh, that? I think I have a solution for it too," said Mrs. Dong. And with a benevolent smile, she continued, "I have a fairly new one that I have not used for quite a while. It is up in my room. It is a shame that it has been sitting there and collecting dust. I would like him to put it to use. It will make me feel very happy."

"You have big heart, sister. Very, indeed," said Mrs. Nam at last, praising her friend for her generosity and a kind heart.

They both decided not to let Lin know until Mr. Nguyen, the French professor, agreed to the arrangement, which they know in their hearts that he would not have any objection to the proposal.

They both walked out the office, feeling that they had accomplished something from the meeting, even though they knew there was much more work to be done before the mission was completed. They parted their ways from the office under a sunny, cloudless sky. It was a rather warm day, and the students were roaming about in the court, in the field, talking, laughing, and chasing one another. Some kept the soccer field warm after many days of being empty, bare, and cold. Mrs. Dong felt the energy now being returned to the school with activities, and that is what she and her husband wanted to happen. As a wife to the head of the school, she shares the responsibility with her man of five years of marriage to make sure he has her support for his success. She is the woman behind the scene, a very traditional woman of Vietnam.

She was not sure if she needed to run this by her husband first before she came to her dad on this issue. But she got the thinking that she had to let her husband know what she was doing because, after all, he is the head of the facility and her family. She was pleased at that decision and headed out to his office only to find out that he was out with Mr. Nam on a tour around the school buildings. She then decided to talk to both, her husband and her dad, at their dinner in the evening. She was very sure of winning their approval.

She just thought of something she must do right away, that is, to inform her friend Michelle, the coffee plantation owner, the mother of the boy, that she has found the tutor for her son. She will tell Michelle that the tutor is none other than her husband's student at the school. Lin is the tutor she has been looking for. She decided to mail her a note to that effect and would meet up with her in person. She is sure that after Lin started his tutoring business, she would have Mr. Quang take her to her friend's place for a weekend retreat to catch up with friends. She loves her friend's house, which was built right at the heart of acres of coffee trees. It is an ideal getaway place after stressful days of working in the city. She and husband and other friends of the owner had come here many a time to enjoy its tranquility and serenity and freshness of nature the place has to offer.

From the main road, there is an entrance, a paved driveway leading to a three-bedroom, thatched roof house built on a very large, flat cement floor, which was extended from all sides of the house not only for sidewalks but also for drying coffee beans after harvested from the trees. Built next to the house is a very large kitchen, which includes a room for two full-time keepers, a middle-aged couple, to stay and to tend the property. The keeper's wife is an excellent cook who offers the owner's guests with her specialty of both Vietnamese and French delicacies. A flock of dozens of hens and cocks keeps their young and baby chicks of different colors from black to spotty to dark maroon to white, roaming, chasing, crowing, making all kinds of the noises around the house all day long, and they are the food for Michelle's guests and her family all the times. Harvesttime of coffee beans can be a feast to the eyes for their colors. The hue of red and green of the beans along with the fragrances can be a treat to the visitors and friends who are used to city life. This is a perfect or at least a good place for Lin to tap his life into, a good environment, good people, and friends to be around and make a living with tutoring. She thought her friend was very generous in giving such a compensation, but she, of course, expects a good return.

Lin was moved to tears when he was told with the news that he would be moving in with Mr. Nguyen, the French professor. Mrs. Dong, after her dinner, came to the curator's place to deliver the news in person after she had secured the approval from her father and her husband. The news was like a stream of cool fresh water to everyone in the household, dying of thirst in the hot desert, especially for Lin. He had been thinking very hard and not sure if he could ever find a place to stay to continue to go to school. The mood in the family had been gloomy, and the air was thick with uncertainty and worry. Mr. Nam was not in any better shape either. He had felt defeated for not being able to get Lin a place to stay, which was the dorm he had hoped for. He knew that there was a fine line that he had to cross, and the chance was very slim, and as it turned out, he did not have ground for his support and argument in getting Lin the spot to stay. It came down to "if the school offered to one, it is obligated to others." And his heart sank, broken, not knowing what to do to help his boy. And as a result, the mood spread and affected all in the family. Be did not say much, but her eyes welled up when she looked at Lin and felt helpless. What happened to the cheers and laughter of yesterday and days before it? Cu was not even animated or joking either.

They all felt something of importance to have Mr. Dong to come visit at this hour in the evening. Only Mrs. Nam was aware of what was going on and what was about to happen. She gave Mrs. Dong a biggest smile, for she knew that it was going to be the greatest news for Lin and her family, which she had counted on. She knew in her heart that Mrs. Dong—a kind soul, the kind heart, whom she loves as her own sister—would be able to do it for Lin, given the fact that her father and her husband are all good-hearted men. The talking, the laughter, and the joy now returned to the dining room where a dismal dinner took place moments ago.

Mrs. Dong, as if she were an expert in handling the news, came in, apologized for interrupting the dinner, said, "I have great news for Lin and everyone too." The principal's wife gave Lin a loving gaze in his eyes and to everyone else. "I found a place for Lin to stay inside the school so he can stay with us." Lin took the news with great surprise as his eyes were wide open and his heart swelled in appreciation.

He quickly uttered the word *thank you* to her as she continued. " Lin is going to be my dad's companion in his room upstairs, the staff's living quarters. My dad loves to have Lin, and if Lin likes to learn to speak French, this is the opportunity to do so with the French professor." Mrs. Dong paused to gauge the response from her audience, especially from Lin who was ready to jump up and down at the opportunity to learn and to be around with the master. Lin now realized how fortunate he was at the time he thought the world was coming down against him. He could not fathom the twist of life he was experiencing at that moment. Minutes ago all he could think of was a dead end, no exit, nowhere to turn; everything was but a blanket of dark cloud on the horizon of his future, and now the blessing poured upon him. He felt loved and blessed and became speechless, for he did not find words to express his feelings but only his eyes could convey his feelings and gratitude to her.

And after a long moment, she continued, "I was told that, Lin, you have been thinking about finding a part-time job. Are you still pursuing it?" She smiled, which made her voice quickly echoed on the wall.

"Yes," he said with all enthusiasm.

"Then, I have found you a job. You will be tutoring my friend's son who is about a year or two younger than you. You will be going to his place, which is the coffee plantation outside of the city, on the weekends." She was looking at Lin, whose mouth dropped open for more surprises.

A thought flashed through his narrow mind, *This is great, but how can I get to the plantation? It would take hours if not half day to walk there.* As if reading his mind, and as a caring mother, she told him that she would give him her own bicycle so that he could ride to work.

"Mrs. Dong, I will never be able to thank you enough for your love and for all you have done for me."

Lin's voice quavered with emotion. He wanted to show her his deepest appreciation from his heart.

"Lin, you are welcome. I am just so glad I could help," she told Lin.

Everyone in the room was very happy for him. They congratulated him on his fortune for having a place to stay and a job to earn his living as a young student.

"Lin, it is Mrs. Nam who started on your behalf to talk to me. I would not have had a clue if she hadn't told me. Therefore, the credit belongs to her."

Just as she finished, Lin got down on his knees, saying, "Thank you, mamma, for saving my life again." It was quite a show, which made Mrs. Nam come down to help him up. She held him to her chest and gave him a nice squeeze to let him know that it was all about the love everyone gave to him, and he quite deserved.

It was such a happy hour with joy and laughter that Be could not help but tease her big brother.

"So, you are going to be tutoring or teaching. I should address you 'teacher' from now on, okay? My young teacher," she said with a big smile, and there was twinkle in her dark-brown eyes, full of cheers, joy, and playfulness, which brought the shy side of him come to surface.

"Oh, come on, sister, I am not a teacher, nor am I your teacher. Please, spare me," he told her sheepishly.

She did not stop there. Instead, she went on. "I want to be your student. Please teach me, tutor me."

Mrs. Nam jumped in to rescue him a gain from her daughter by saying, "Be, naughty girl. Leave your brother alone." That did it. But Be would not quit without giving him a look as if saying, "Brother, thanks to Mother, you got a break. But I am not done with you yet."

As the best wine was served last, Mrs. Dong looked at Lin and said, "Don't you want to know what your salary is going to be for tutoring?" She was looking at him, gazing his innocent eyes as if waiting for him, giving him a few seconds to get ready for another surprise, a knock his socks off one. "She is going to pay you five hundred piasters a month."

That drew a "wow" from the youngsters Be and Cu alike, and for Lin, it was a jolt, for he could never expect that kind of compensation at his age. It is like a whole week's worth of fishing in the village, provided that it was a good and lucky trip, for it was the only thing that came to his mind from which he could compare to. It was beyond his thinking of what he could have hoped for when he wanted to find a job to support himself and continue his schooling. This is the work of angels, and perhaps they are. They had been working behind the scene to bring about the result, which he saw at this moment. He wished he could identify his lucky star in the sky tonight, and at the same time, he also wished he could find words to express his feeling, his gratitude, his heartfelt appreciation to the two women from whom he had found the motherly love and care. He wanted to call them each mother but stood speechless and in awe from the revelation of the news.

Finally he was able to break himself loose from the shock, bowed his head, and softly said thank you to both of them. He let his eyes rest in theirs and convey in silent language more than his words.

Mrs. Dong was so happy that everything about her was smiling. Her big, round, brown eyes and her short haircut made her look in her early twenties, beautiful and generous. Her laughter was crisp and joyous, and her voice was soft and clear, an indication of a highly educated woman. Just before she went home, she said that Lin could stay in his new home any time the following day, the day before the school began its session after the holiday break.

Cu was thrilled that Lin could stay inside the school. It was not any different between the dorms and the teachers' quarters, the same distance. Lin assured Cu that he would see him often, every day perhaps.

Be, the quiet happiest person of all, came to Lin and said, "Brother, I am very happy for you and very glad that you are able to stay here with us." Her eyes slowly met his as if saying, "I would be very sad if you had to go elsewhere."

"Sis, you have no ideas how happy I am now. I would never want to leave you."

The new life began with Lin the following day at the new place with the professor, and next door was the principal's room.

It was obvious that the room was too big for one person. Lin was a perfect roommate to fill the space. An extra bed had been there already when he came over. He wondered if it had been there all along, as a guest bed, or was it now it just got set up? It does not matter, for he is so grateful that not only did he have a place to stay but also an educational environment for him to grow as a student and as a person as well.

The professor—slim, white-haired, kind-eyed behind the spectacles, and dressed up for the day—greeted him with a grandfatherly smile and said, "Welcome to our living quarters, my child." And without letting Lin say anything, he continued jovially, "So you are to stay to take care of your old grandpa, right?

Lin did not know what to appropriately respond to that except to bow of his head and utter, "Master, I thank you for letting me stay with you." He wanted to tell the professor that he could do a lot for him from cooking to cleaning and to laundering, but decided not to. He just wanted to let it take its natural course as the time comes and as the need arises.

There was not much for the professor to show him around. In the right hand corner of the entrance door was a tiny space for cooking. The space was sparkling clean, and he fell in love with it already. Pots and pans hung on the wall, shinning and spotless. The pinkish brick-colored clay charcoal burner would be a smoke-free cooking stove for him, what a novelty! No more "smoke gets in my eyes." Lin chuckled remembering the times in the house, in the boat cooking for his dad. Coming out of the wall was a bronze-colored faucet, running water! It's for all his needs for water. This is a royal life compared to where he came from. He controlled himself very well not to scream with his excitement ready to burst out like an overpumped balloon in his head.

In the corner of the room stood a bookcase full of thick books, most of them in foreign languages from French, English, to Chinese. Lin's eyes got fixed to the beautiful, hard-covered books in different colors. They must be very precious and expensive, he thought. Lin wished someday he could understand at least one of these languages.

"You seem to like books. That is a very good sign. Books will help you grow with knowledge and become a good person. You can look at, read, and use my books anytime you want to," the professor told Lin in a delightful tone of voice.

"Yes, master," Lin responded with gratitude felt in his voice. He chose to address the old man master, which he felt appropriate and to cultivate the closeness of the relationship between the master and disciples. He wanted to sponge off very whit of his wisdom, every bit of his knowledge from the master. And in order to achieve that, he must become a disciple, a good disciple.

After seeing everything in the room, which there wasn't much, the professor pointed to a brand-new sky-blue bicycle, which was standing on a stand by the wall and said, "Son, this is the bicycle my daughter gave to you so that you could go on about your businesses of tutoring." Lin was in shock! He could never dream of having such a nice brand-new bicycle. Is it a real thing, or is he dreaming, hallucinating from his imaginary world? Does he deserve it if it is real? Nonetheless, he was speechless! He was trying to convince himself that he was standing on the floor, barefooted, feeling the coolness of the floor, not somewhere in the ether. It seemed like an hour before he could say a simple "thank you, master" to the old man.

He wished he could say more. But he is who he is, simple like "sweet potatoes and corn" in the field. Field and river are where he grew up with, and countryside is where he came from. It would be impossible to peel the simplicity off him, and he would never wish to.

He then asked the professor if he could go over to say thank you to his daughter, Mrs. Dong, for letting him use the bicycle. As luck would have it, the principal and the angel all came out of their room, as if they had heard his conversation and wishes.

"Oh, hello, Lin, my child, I hope you like the place as much as my father does. As you can see, he likes to keep his place nice and clean, and I am very sure you like to keep it that way too?" said Mrs. Dong with her smile. She looked at him with much compassion in her eyes. "I hope you will like our gift to you to get you around and to go to our friend's place to help her son." She turned to her husband as she mentioned "our gift," which was well conveyed and nicely presented even to a child like him. "I will get you the schedule to your tutoring from my friend Michelle. It is all the weekends. However, it is just to be sure."

"Yes, Mrs. Dong, I do not know what to say. But I can say this: I will never be able to pay you back for all the things you have done for me." He then turned to the men and said, "Masters, I will serve you. I will do anything and everything you ask me to do. I promise."

The professor and the principal came over to get him up as he was knelling on the floor to show his respect and his appreciation, as a student would do to his master, beginning of his training. They both—no, actually, the three of them were pleased with the boy Lin, their student. They knew it was a very good thing and wise thing to do for Lin.

He was on the bicycle rolling to the plantation for his first encounter, first experience as a young tutor. He loves this two-wheeled vehicle; it was all in his dream, and here it is, he was riding on it. The late-morning breezes caressed his face, blowing his hair, and the sound of the pink-colored new tires rolling, rubbing the paved road could be heard. There were not many people on the road yet, maybe because of the weekend or maybe it is far from the city. Every now and then a few cars zoomed by him from both directions honking, as if telling him, "Do not cross the road." Last night, he let Be and Cu try it out, and he even let them each ride in the back behind him. He pedaled them out to the park, circling the soccer field, and what a great time they had together! Cu liked it so much that he even said, "This is much better than mine. It is much newer too."

Lin looked at him and jokingly said, "You want to trade, Cu?"

Shaking his head and with an innocent baby mile, he simply said, "It is your gift, brother. I know you are just teasing. Besides, the elders would be upset if we did."

What a wise little brother he has!

Teacher To Jean Pierre

According to the directions and hand-sketched map, he should not be too far from the site of his appointment. He gave it a last glance before he put it away into the pocket of his shirt. In fact, he could see the mass of green trees ahead of him, then the white fencing posts, holding barbwire, stretched miles almost to the horizon.

He suddenly felt nervous! He is going to meet the mother, the owner of the plantation, and her son, the one whom he will be doing the tutoring to. They all must be nice and kind people, for they are the friends of his masters. He was reminding himself that regardless who, what, how rich, how poor, how nice, how bad they treat him, he shall be doing his very best to perform his duty and to best represent his masters, who recommended him for the job. He was determined.

The gate in white, covered with red dust, was in front of him on the left hand side. He carefully crossed the road before he slowly turned in to see that it was closed, but unlocked. He got off his bike, hesitated for a moment to see if he should just push it open and roll in, or he should just wait outside, for he did not want to disturb or be considered intrusive. Besides, he did not have the exact time that he was expected to be there. "Afternoon hour" was all he was told to be here. Minutes went by; he decided to get on his bike after making sure that the gate closed behind him.

Far ahead of him appeared the thatched-roof, brown house, and he heard the dog barking. No sooner had he had time to think if he should stop and wait for the owner to receive him than the black and brown German shepherd, as big as himself, dashed out from the corner of the house behind the neatly trimmed hedge of white-and-fuchsia-colored hibiscus, only to be jerked back by a stretched leash. His heart stopped pumping, his limbs frozen; he was terrified at the size of the dog whose pink lips curled up, displaying his white sharp teeth, growling, and ready to tear him to pieces for his dinner. As stunned as he was, as frozen as he was, he found the owners, a young boy, almost his age, with dark complexion and sporty look in his white pull-over shirt. He wore a navy-blue short, on white shoes, and his mother, a middle-aged lady, beautifully well-dressed, leisurely walked out, cheerfully greeted him after she scolded her terrorist dog.

"Hello, Lin, my name is Michelle, and this Jean Pierre, my son. I am glad you have made it here." And turning to her dog, she said, "Please forgive my dog for making you scared. He is really friendly once he knows you, I am sorry."

Lin just had enough time to bow his head, greeting both of them, before she told her son, "Say hello to your teacher, Jean." It makes him feel quite uneasy at the given title.

"Hello, teacher," Jean Pierre said respectfully.

At that, Lin told him, "Please call me brother Lin; that would be just fine."

But before the boys could settle for the title, the mother showed her authority and got right in the business. She said, "No, no, that is not how it works, teacher Lin. Even one half of the word you teach, you are my teacher."

Lin could not argue with that even if he wanted to. It is said in the books. It is a well-known line, professed in schools and in society. This concept, this teaching, has been written in the stones for centuries, and it is a good thing to keep the society in check.

"Yes, Madame Michelle, I know what you mean. I listen to you."

Michelle was pleased with what Lin had said and gestured the boys to come to the living room after Lin had his bike stand on the cement court in front of the house. Lin was curious about the names she and her son have. Obviously they were not the Vietnamese names, and it dawned on him that she is the owner of the coffee plantation, who belongs to the affluent, the bourgeois class, who goes to French schools, speaks French to her friends and colleagues, and heavily influenced with French culture, and the French names naturally come in handy.

"This is our guest room," Michelle, with her smiley face, made the introduction. "This is where my son will do his study with you whenever you come, teacher Lin."

"Thank you, madame. I am delighted to help Jean, and thank you for your kindness and the opportunity."

Lin is still trying to get used to the word *teacher* imposed upon him. He knows that it is a beautiful practice and an ideal of the Vietnamese culture to regard teachers very highly in the society. In fact, it is next to the king in the social hierarchy. But he feels he is too young and has not earned the title yet. *Maybe someday*, a thought flashed to his mind.

"Teacher Lin, Jean needs your help mainly on his math but feel free to give him others if you feel needed. I now let you two get to know each other and get started so we do not waste our time, agree?"

"Yes, Madame Michelle," Lin said as she turned to Jean, who had been quiet all along, bent down, her hand on his shoulder, slightly moving, as if she were smoothing the wrinkles on his shirt.

In her motherly loving voice, almost whispering, she said, "Jean, listen to your teacher. Be a good student, all right?"

"Yes, Mom," the boy said obediently as he gave her a look of assurance as if saying, "I am a good boy, Mom."

As Michelle quietly sauntered out of the guest room into the front yard, Lin began his first conversation with Jean, his first student in life with a smile. " I like your name, Jean. It sounds like French. Would you mind tell me what grade you are in? And do you know that I am here to help you to improve your math?" Lin asked and sounded as being a teacher, a tutor, and a friend, all in one, as he could.

"My math is terrible, teacher. I just don't know how to explain it. I am just as dumb as a cow," admitted Jean, who now showed his openness and his weakness.

"No worries, Jean. I will help you to overcome that problem. You will understand it by learning it each step of the way, and you find it as easy as two plus two equals to four. That is math, right?" Jean, for the first time, laughed at the humor and now relaxed.

Lin gave him a simple math problem, and in just a few minutes, he could solve it all by himself. This gives Lin an idea that Jean was not really a buried stump that he was asked to come to unearth and to bring it to light. He chuckled at the thought and felt exhilarated at the task of doing the tutoring. Lin complimented Jean on his first success and gave him more assignments after explaining the basic concept of the math problems.

While his student, head down, focused on his work, writing, erasing, scribbling on a white sheet of paper, he, at the other side of dark-ebony oak table, was able to take a good look at Jean, a small-built, dark-haired, light-dark–skinned complexion boy on his cute almost-round face and big, brown eyes. His nose is high, that of a European descent. Lin wondered if he had a touch of French blood in him. Nonetheless, he is quite handsome young boy.

The room is large, furnished with dark wood furniture, solid, and they look expensive. At the end of the table, which he and Jean were sitting, is a smaller square table whose natural wood grains is beautifully displayed at the top and on its legs. On top of the table is a wicker basket filled with a variety of fresh fruits, from green-skinned oranges to a miniature golden papaya, and a couple of green and yellow mangoes. The aroma and the look of these fruits are very inviting. He is very sure these fruits come from the plantation as well. He felt the blessing at the moment that he is a part of the environment, and he was grateful for the opportunity serving the owner to tutor her son.

It was a full day work, but exhilarating. He was very happy that Jean had grasped the concept of math and solved all the problems very well. Jean was talkative and, of course, asked questions, and he got all the answers.

Inside the kitchen, Lin joined Michelle and Jean for lunch, which was prepared by a cook, the wife of the housekeeper and gardener. From the conversation, he learned that the couple, in their early fifties, had been with Michelle for many years, the wife as a cook and her husband, a gardener and manager for the coffee plantation. He is responsible for making arrangements to have extra hires to pick and to dry the coffee beans in time of harvest. He is also trusted with having coffee dealers to come to the barn, located next to the building, to negotiate the price of this hot commodity from the central highlands of Vietnam. Lin was able to meet with both of them and immediately built a good rapport among them.

He did not get back to the school until late in the evening. Despite a long first day at work and a long distance to bike home, Lin felt so good, so grateful for everything that seemed to begin to shape up his life and future. If he could continue, he thought, to do this during the weekend, he would have enough income to pay for his own expenses, including the food and rent. He could support himself without any money from his dad. He wanted to let his father know what he was up to and how fortunate he got into this tutoring job. It all came about in the name of loving care from those whose world he came into. He could think of how happy and proud his father would be when he received the news. But he would have to wait until he got his paycheck.

He knew Be and everyone in the family was waiting for him to get the firsthand report of the day at the job; he decided to stop by to see them first before he went to his place to see the professor and Mrs. Dong and her husband.

No sooner had he got off the bike and laid it flat on the ground than Be came out from behind the door, as if she had been waiting for him. She screamed out loud with all excitement, "Brother Lin, you are home. How come this late? Are you hungry? Are you tired?" She looked at him, and a series of questions flew out of her mouth, much of care, concern, and love.

Lin did not have time to answer because Cu and the mother all came out at the same time and happily said, "Oh, you are home, son."

"Brother, did you get paid for your teaching? We can go for some ice cream downtown, yes?" Cu teased him with a wide smile on his face only to be scolded by the mother.

"How come you are such a naughty boy? You both go get the food ready for your brother."

They both went inside after a simultaneous "yes, Mother" from their mouths. But Be did not forget to give him a squinting look from the corner of her eye as if saying, "Mom is always on your side. I will give you a break for now—but I will get to you later, brother."

While sitting at the dinner table enjoying his meal, he told the whole family how much fun he had at his work. He went into details of how scared he was at the big dog when he barely arrived at the plantation. In fact, he told them that his heart had almost stopped pumping, and his body was literally frozen with fear when the bear-sized German shepherd was only a few feet away from knocking him down, tearing him asunder for a doggy lunch. It was this close, he told them while showing the tiny gap between his thumb and index finger.

Be was sympathetic with another ordeal of his life, looking at him with her already-welled-up eyes and a soft heart for him as if saying, "I am glad that you are here at home in one piece and hadn't become doggy lunch so that you can enjoy the food I prepared for you, brother."

He continued to tell them the rest of the story of his day at the work, tutoring Jean Pierre, complimenting on how good and smart he was. J. Pierre did not have any hard time grasping the math concept that made his tutoring enjoyable.

"How was the lady owner of the plantation? The mother of the boy, was she nice to you, brother?" asked Be as she was listening to every bit of details he gave.

"Yes, sis, she was supernice to us, me and J. Pierre. She fed us lunch and gave us a tour of her coffee plantation. We did not have time go from corner to corner of the coffee farm. But it was a very large place. It would take hours to walk and see all the coffee trees. By the way, her name is "Michelle, a French name, and so is her son's, Jean Pierre. It is a little hard for me to pronounce it correctly. I like our names better."

"I am so glad it worked out quite well for you. I was anxious to see how it turned out, but I knew in my heart, you would not have any difficulties, son," said the mother at last.

Lin went back to his place after his dinner, thanking every one of the host family, especially his sister, Be, for saving his dinner, which not only did it touch his heart but also filled up his tummy from lots of pedaling on the road. He truly appreciated her special care for him. He silently thanked God for aligning his path to come to this household to be loved and to love it as his second family, where he found Be, his sister in life.

The professor, on his wooden chair, was doing his reading as usual at this time in the evening when Lin came in, who bowed and uttered his greeting while putting his bike in place against the wall. Looking up from his reading, adjusting his spectacle, he said with a smile, "You are home? It has been a long day for you. How did it go? Did you like it, son?"

And before he could answer the professor, the principal and his wife appeared at the door. excitedly said, "Oh, Lin, we have been anxious to know how it went at your tutoring. Did you like it? Did you like my friend Michelle and her son, your student?" Mrs. Dong asked in her soft loving voice.

He was confused at whom to answer first. Why do adults ask in a series of questions? Why can they ask one question at a time?

He thinks maybe because they have larger brains than the ones in their children. Lin did not want to be perceived as disrespectful to his elders and teachers but said,

"Oh yes, not only I liked it but loved it very much. I am truly enjoying Michelle, her son, and the husband and his wife working for them. They all were supernice to me. The boy J Pierre is fun to teach because he is a very smart boy." Lin told them everything from the beginning to the end, from the time he arrived when the giant ferocious dog almost tore him down if it were not for the leash that held it back, to the delicious lunch, and to the leisurely walk to see the coffee plantation. The tutoring was very enjoyable, he told them. Mrs. Dong was very pleased with his performance, his dedication, and especially to see that he was happy with what he was doing. She felt a surge of joy that she had done a great thing to help him out.

"I am so glad that you like to do what you did today. I am very sure that Michelle, my friend, is happy to have you help her son too. She wanted to see her son becoming a top student, and that is why she hired you to get him on the right path to getting there. You should get some rest so that you can do it again tomorrow, and I am very proud of you."

"Thank you," Lin said softly as she and her husband turned to walk back to their room. He wanted to tell her how grateful he was but did not know how to express it in front of others. He hoped that she would know it somehow.

Mr. Nguyen, the professor, reminded him that he had the food saved for him for dinner. Lin felt so bad that the professor had to cook for himself while he was gone. He told the professor that he had already had his dinner at Mr. Nam's earlier when he first got home. But he would have it in the morning before he went to work. Like a grandfather to his grandchild, the professor was very fond of him. He cares for Lin every step of the way, from food to his tummy, to the nourishment for his brain. Maybe because he has not had his grandchild of his own because Mrs. Dong is holding off on his hope of having one, or maybe because it was his natural grandfatherly love in him that he needed to express on Lin, or even from a kind heart of one human being to another. Nonetheless, he enjoys the loving care from the professor, who has begun passing on the wisdom of his life to him. He showed Lin his simple southern style cooking that he had learned from his parents and grandparents decades earlier. He had to learn to do the cooking, the washing, and going to school in the village as a young boy and worked his way up through high school, college, and went into teaching. His whole life reflects the simplicity and hard work. It was not easy in those days, in his younger years, and he could see Lin as his reflection of those tough times of his life. What he did then is what Lin is doing now in the very same pattern, no more, no less. That is probably why there is an instant connectedness between the elder and the youngster, and Lin felt the blessing bestowed on him from the above to have crossed this path with him. From what the professor told him, he could imagine his childhood over half of a century ago, tending livestock in the field, in the rice paddies of the Delta in the south, hot and humid most of the time except the winter when it is cold, and it is always colder when on your back is a thin, faded, patched shirt and a short that barely cover the dark, weathered, skinny legs. The hunger, more often than not, came somewhere in the middle of the night to make the night not only longer but also a lot colder, and the haystack by the thatched, mud-walled shed seemed never able to keep his body warm, despite layers and layers of hay on top his body. The professor's childhood was very much similar to his, poor and full of hard work, at the tender age which Lin thought of when the elder talked about his early years in life in the countryside. However, those years of hard work had molded and blossomed him into an educated man, a scholar, and a professor, as he was now. Lin felt inspired by the elder's success and realized that it would also be possible for him and others, regardless of circumstance, to be just as successful if he is willing to set a goal and work hard to reach it. He was thankful to the mothers, Mrs. Nam and Mrs. Dong and Ba Thong, to pave the way for him to reaching his life's greatest dream—that is, his education.

He then asked the professor how his day went while he was away at work at the plantation. He could not think of anything the elder would do besides grading his students' assignments and do his readings from among the stock of thick treasured, antique-looking books on the shelves in the back of the room. Perhaps, he might have had a walk to relax and enjoy the breeze, knowing that the professor is very health conscious from eating to keeping his mind and body a good fit.

The professor told him he had had a nice, quiet day and got things done. The elder then made a surprise comment and proposal to Lin that pleased him tremendously.

"Lin, since you have had French in grade school, I will help you become better with it when you are ready. I know Mr. Thong is teaching you English, but don't let go of it. French is important too."

Lin could not agree with the professor more, especially since he is in love with the sound of the language. It has a sound with such romance and elegance that could literally hypnotize the listeners.

"Thank you, master, for thinking of me. I will be ready once I have got everything situated, but it would not be long. I am very grateful that you are giving me everything to help me become a good student, a good citizen, and a good man, ultimately. I do appreciate your love, master." What Lin said pleased the master immensely. What was on his mind, his heart obviously showed on his face: the delightfulness!

The professor started his weekend nights teaching Lin not just French but also sharing his life stories and stories of others that had impacted his life. Lin enjoyed him as a master, who, for no reasons other than love, holds the key to open his heart and mind to shaping up his life. Conversely, the professor found Lin a poor student with an unloving childhood who deserves the gift of knowledge and love he wanted to share.

Summer comes and goes. Years had passed by, and Lin had become a more matured student physically and intellectually under the professor's wing. One day during a school break, the professor was on his way to his hometown in Saigon, and Lin was back to his home in the village visiting, which he had done a few times on his bicycle. Upon entering his home late in the morning, the sun was high, and the sky patched with white clouds; the neighborhood was quiet except a few dogs roaming in the streets. He found no one at home; front door was wide open, and chickens were roaming freely in and out as permanent guests at his place. Where were his dad and his stepmother? he wondered. Perhaps his dad was away on a fishing trip, but she should be home with his little brother. The dirty old clothes scattered on the dirt floor along with trash that make him sick to his stomach. Things had not changed, messy. The half-hung dark-maroon-colored mosquito net dangled lazily above the wooden bed with an old, stained straw mat spread unevenly on the bed. Spiderwebs here and there hung off the thatched ceiling and were noticeably dangling, slightly fluttering, moving about in the air, as the morning breeze seeped through the cracks of the bamboo walls. Lin felt sad as his eyes caught sight of the drinking glasses, which were murky, filthy, sitting on top of the dusty table in the middle of the house. He cannot help wondering when was the last time someone in his household used them and washed them. Until this day, many years had gone by, he's still unable to find her love for him. He could not figure out why his family had become so fragmented. Why is it that no one cared about the family anymore? It showed in this dwelling place, the carelessness as if it were an abandoned house—a haunted, disorderly house. While he was contemplating, wondering about his situation, about his family and how to improve it, his stepmother showed up at the door, showing no emotions, not welcoming. She gave him a stoic face even though it had been months since the last time he came home.

"Stepmother, I am home. How are you?" he bowed and said his greeting respectfully.

"Yes, I know you are home," she said perfunctorily. He sensed a dab of hostility in her tone of voice and felt that he needed to let her know that she has been utterly unreasonable in the way she had been treating him and that she had not been taking care of the house as she should. He pulled up his courage to speak his mind and told her.

"Stepmother, I don't know why you hated me so much while I have tried very hard to earn, to gain your love. When I was younger, you would not let me eat nor would you let me wear decent clothes. And just in case you forgot, you had even pushed me off the bed with your feet, not once but twice, in the middle of the nights, not long after the beginning of our relationship, stepmother and stepson, and I ended up plopping on the cold dirt floor. At first, I thought I had a walking dream, which caused me to land on the floor from my bed. However, when you pushed me off again, lying on the ground, I then realized that you never, ever, loved me, much less considered me your stepson. You did not want me in your life from the beginning when you came into our family. I try to forget the filthy words you dumped on me in the kitchen when I came home for lunch. Until today, you have not changed. I know you have been gambling for years and you have neglected to take care of the house. All I see is the mess."

"Shut up!" his stepmother screamed out loud, as if she wanted everyone in the neighborhood to hear her metallic voice. "I don't need you to teach me. You think you get your education, and you think you can come home to lecture me? This is my house. Go, go, and get out of my sight. Go, I don't want you here," she yelled at him as her hands gestured a sweeping move, pushing him out of the house.

"Now, my stepmother, be reasonable. I am not the little kid you used to treat me anymore. All I am asking you is to open your heart. You cannot hate me forever, and besides, I have not done anything wrong against you. I will go away as you wish. But, please, pay a little attention to the family. It is your family, and whether you want it or not, I am a part of it too. Please do not destroy it."

Lin saw her face turned from red to purple as her anger climbed up through the roof, to the sky. He quietly walked out of the door. He looked at his dilapidated house for a long moment, wondering what could be done to change her, to bring his family together, and to improve the home. He had come to a dead end, realizing that nothing he could do. He was very sad; his heart was heavy. He felt defeated as he got on his bike, paid a short visit to his uncle and Ba Thong, and headed back to the city. They were all surprised at his short visit but understood his circumstance, knowing that his dad was out on the river, fishing, and there was very little reason for him to stay. Ba Thong, with a woman's sense and motherly intuition, could tell something was not right but did not ask. She would know when the time was right.

In the meanwhile, his stepmother was frustrated with his words.

"This little kid, after a few years away in school, now came home and lectured me; it is something unthinkable and definitely unacceptable." She went into her rage against him. She wanted to hit something, to break something to help her release this madness in her.

"I hate him," she mumbled to herself. "If I could kill him, I would." She could feel the blood boiled in her heart to her head. Why she hated him so much from the day she came to his family, she did not know. She could not explain this devilish feeling she has had for him from the very beginning. He had not done anything against her, but she just hated him.

She then looked around the house. Yes, she has neglected to take care of the house because she had spent too much time outside on gambling here and there. She had won and had lost and had the thrill of the game. Her husband had told her to change her ways of living, to stop the addiction. Her parents had told her that they knew of her habits and that they were ashamed of her behaviors. All of these critiques and blames she could accept and hope someday soon she would change. But not from this skinny boy Lin, and who is he to teach her? Not now. Not tomorrow. Not in her lifetime. It is impossible. She finally said loudly, "I hate him. If I could kill him, I would. Oh, how do I hate him!" She angrily pulled the bamboo door, dragged it over the dirt floor to keep the chicken coming in, making the mess inside the house. She was hesitating where she would go between the gambling house at the end of the village where she had spent time and money or her parents' where her son had stayed while she was out doing her own business. She did not know why she came home in the first place, seeing Lin and to get upset by what he said. She should have just stayed there and played more. Unintentionally, she ended up at her parents' house. Did her conscience guide her?

On his bike, paddling uphill, downhill, back to the city, he was sad but glad that, after all for these years, he could pull up the courage to tell her what he did. He had tried very hard appealing for her love, but time after time, he utterly failed. He had come to a dead end; he did not know how or what to do to make it happen, to improve the relationship between the stepmother and son. Now he is far away from home, away from her, but he wants a loving home, where love and harmony reside so that he could come home and enjoy the family with his dad and his little brother. But it seems almost impossible to have it happen. He knows in his heart he does not hate her. He knows he has been terribly, miserably hurt by what she had done to him, by what she said to him, and the whole way she treated him. He prayed that someday, he could find the healing and peace for his soul.

The cool evening air caressed his face as he entered the city life. Street lights were on. The pedestrians, the honking of the cars, the motorcycles, and the shops made up the life of the city, which he got used to. He was thinking of going straight to his room, now empty, which he doesn't mind to be alone, by himself. He felt he needed some rest. The whole trip home, as it turned out, took a lot out of him. But he had already told Mr. and Mrs. Nam that he was going to the village for a visit, and all of a sudden, they saw the lights in his building, his room. What would they think? That must be a ghost that turned on the lights? No, not that nonsense! Robbery? Possibly, and they would be panic. They would come over with machete, baton, or perhaps with guns. No, not that kind of the hassles. He chuckled with the thought, and not before long, he was right in front of their place, and who spotted him and ran to welcome him first? It was Be, his little sister, and then Cu, and the parents. They were all surprised, for they had not expected to see him back that early. Be—with a bright smile on her face, with a caring, loving, sisterly, and motherly nature—said, "I thought you had gone to the village to visit your family? Did you ever go at all?" Be was full of concern in her voice. Her intuition lets her sense something that was not going right. Something must have happened that made his trip cut short, and he is here this soon. She will find out, she thought.

"Brother, you look tired; can I get you a glass of lemonade before I have dinner ready for you? Mom and Dad and Cu and I had dinner already. I don't think you had food on the way back here unless you had stopped by the tribes to get a taste of the tribal foods," she said with a smile on her face and a teasing look in her naughty, black eyes. Oh yes, tired and hungry he was. He had not thought of foods, nor was he thinking about or craving for anything in particular. He somehow lost his appetite. He was just emotionally and physically consumed with his own situation, dealing with his stepmother, who was absolutely unreasonable, which aggravated him immensely. But now, he is back to his second real family in which he found harmony, love, and care. He wanted to leave those unpleasant moments behind. He decided not to carry that which caused him anguish and heartache that may spoil the air in the loving family he was now in. Just like a good-natured kid, who has incredible ability to forgo and forget, he knows how to get to that magic switch to turn it on; he slipped right back to his being a youthful, playful, energetic boy. He dove right into the mood of the teasing game with his sister, Be.

"My dear, on the way back, guess what? I got lost."

"What, lost? You got lost?" Be, with her wide eyes open, half disbelieving asked him.

And then Cu joined in, "I don't believe you did."

"Yes, I was on my bicycle, chasing a big and very beautiful, colorful butterfly into a side road. No, no, actually the butterfly guided me off to the side road, a narrow dirt road, with bushes and vines on both sides. It was a quiet and a zigzag, winding road. I wanted to catch him, but every time I got closer to him, he flapped his wings faster, and then it widened our distance. I ended up having to paddle faster to catch up with him. Many kilometers of the road I paddled, I could not match his wings, and before I know it, I was inside the territory of a tribal village, by the hillside, with thatched-roof houses built on poles, which look like tall, skinny legs carrying the houses. The villagers, men and women and children, were celebrating, having the feast of their time. They were dancing around the campfire with white smoke floating up in the air, with the sounds of the gongs, the melodies of the flutes and drums and horns. The aroma of charcoal BBQ meats was thick in the air, inviting. It was such a lively inviting celebration. Since I was a lowlander, a good-looking boy, who entered into the village without an invitation, just a butterfly, I was an intruder and caught by two young bare-chested dark-skinned, loin-clothed guards who brought me to the village chief. Next thing I know he ordered me to be held inside the wooden shed next to the building so he could deal with me later. While in my confinement, distressed, thinking, contemplating, trying to figure out how to get out, a big brown-eyed, dark-skinned beautiful tribal girl whose hair was adorned with colorful feathers came over, unlatched the door, handed me a wooden bowl full of meat, beans, and brown rice. She told me to eat fast and get going before her father, the chief, came over. He would skin me or hang me to death because it is a law, the very strict law of her tribe. I did not want him to skin me or to throw me into the fire to become roasted meat; I listened to her. Quickly, I ate my food, and she helped me out onto my bike, and here, home I am."

"Wow, what a story and good storytelling too. But I don't buy it. I will tell you why—later. Now if you are not hungry, I am not going to bother getting you food. I guess you were well served by that tribal girl and no room for more food."

Be was not thrilled with the story and felt he should be left hungry. She did not know why. But that's how she felt. Cu, on the other hand, found it fascinating and wanted to know more. But before he could open his mouth to ask, Lin had told the sister that he had made up the story to tease her and apologized for making it up. That disappointed Cu too. However, he finally laughed, for he was fooled by the story or by his big brother's storytelling.

Up in his room after saying good night to the parents, Be, and Cu, the incident at home with his stepmother was like a movie on his mental screen playing forward and backward while he was lying in bed. He loves his dad, his brother, his family. But how could he make his stepmother love him? What could he do to make her a little kinder to him? Yes, just a bit kinder was all he ever asked of her. How could this prophecy, this very spell of "unless one finds bone, one never finds . ." be taken off from her? Does she really act on this mythical belief that the culture has had influence on her to blind herself from every flicker of love and compassion for a child who had lost his own mother? Or does she act on her own nature, her own personality of being mean and jealous? It is unimaginably possible, but is a reality, his reality. The image of her stoic face, the angry gaze in her eyes, the icy-cold cut of voice spewing unkind, filthy words outside the kitchen on that sunny afternoon kept haunting him. He wanted the healing, he wanted the harmony, and he was hungry for the togetherness of his family. But he was too small, too little, and his voice was too weak compared to hers, and he trembled at the gaze of her eyes to make it happen. He could never forget the feeling he had on that day. Terrified, yes, he was. Petrified, yes, he had felt. and there was also a feeling of loss, loss of hope of ever becoming a person deserved to live as a human being. Deep inside him was a flurry touch of hope, the hope to be free from her meanness and abusiveness. He noticed that whenever he was alone, all by himself, this very feeling always came back to him in the quiet of night, haunting him, or telling him to resolve it so that it would no longer be an uninvited ghost, unwelcomed visitor. He could have spent a night like this in his own house in the village or on the boat fishing with his dad. It would be a nice break for him to enjoy the family time of his life. But it was just something he had wished and continued to wish until one day, yes, one day, it would come true. He began to come to a sense that during a day, during the hours, between a sunrise and sunset, there is always a complication, a hurdle, a hardship that stands somewhere, and one must go through them, get over them, or crawl under them to find the meaning to his life. It was not easy for him. There were times he had hoped that it were. It is always a struggle, a tough fight for him, like rowing his boat upstream against the red, foamy current of the water on the river during the monsoon days. He knew now that he had to let go of it, the thing that troubles him, and let God come to make that possible. He would also have to ask the professor for his wisdom to lend him a hand to lift this heavy load off his shoulder. In this quiet of the night, he said his prayer to ask for God's hand to touch him for peace to permeate over him. The room became warmer in the night despite its seemingly huge emptiness, and he fell asleep.

Time of Trouble

"Brother Lin, someone is here to see you," Be called from the ground, projecting her voice up to the second floor to his room when the sun was climbing over the roof off the opposite school building, promising a beautiful day. Lin came out of his room, smiled, and waved to his sister, Be, and noticed a young boy whom he had never seen before. From a distance, the boy appeared to be a few years older and taller than Lin and showed some dark, weathered skin with toughness. Lin hollered down and told both of them that he would come down to meet with them right away. He was wondering who he is and why he was looking for him out there at this hour. He knew his friends within the school and a few outside, and none looked like him. Is he in trouble, or has someone sent him to start a trouble on him? Lin was thinking. With all curiosity he dashed out of his room, his feet skipped the stairs, down onto the ground, and there he faced the stranger.

"I am Tam, the son of Bac Sau," the boy introduced himself to Lin with a friendly smile. "My dad had mentioned that you were here at the school. So here I came."

Lin saw the resemblance between the two, the father and the son, and immediately liked Tam, for he saw Bac Sau in him.

"Oh, brother Tam. I heard Bac Sau had told me about you while I was staying at your house. Of course, it is no longer there. Did you know that it was burned down to ashes a while back?" Lin asked and saw the shock on his friend's face. Obviously, Tam did not know anything about the fire at his dad's place, for he had not come by for a very long time. Lin gave him some details of what had happened while he and Bac Sau were away for the New Year vacation. He could not give him much other than what he saw the day he came back, nor did he have any more information from his father when he came to see him at the school. Tam was saddened at the news of misfortune on both of them.

"Brother Tam, it is so nice of you to take your time to come for visiting me, and by the way, how is Bac Sau? Do you know where he stay now?" Lin was anxious to know more about the man whom he considered his second dad. Actually he would love to visit Bac Sau if he knew exactly know his whereabouts.

"Oh, my dad should be fine. I haven't seen him lately. But as unfortunate as it was that his house got burned down, you should find him at where he works and quite far from here." Lin was a bit disappointed, but before he could say anything about that, Tam continued. "You want to come with me? I take you downtown to meet with my friends if you have time."

Lin turned to Be, who was standing, still watching the two boys talking. She never saw Tam, but heard a bit about Bac Sau when Lin first came to her home, a homeless young boy. There is a connection among them. Be felt that she should encourage Lin to go with Tam for a change. After all, it is a break from school, no homework!

"Brother, if you want to go, I will let Mom and Dad know, and I will see you when you get home," Be told him with her usual caring and gentle way, which drew some curiosity in Tam's eyes.

"Yes, thanks, sister. Please tell them, and I will be home later in the evening," Lin reassured her as he turned and walked out with Tam.

"She is beautiful and nice to you, Lin. Is she your sister?" Tam asked with compliment and interest in his voice.

"She is the daughter of my teacher, but we are like brother and sister. Her parents are my parents as well," Lin told him.

Once they were out in the street, walking under the clear-blue sky and morning sun, Lin felt the connectedness between him and Tam; maybe he saw the younger version of Bac Sau in Tam. He felt that not only Tam was older than him, but Tam also has the maturity, the ruggedness, the machismo about him that Lin was immediately attracted to. His long, ruffled, black hair runs down, meeting the worn-out collar of his faded moss-green, long-sleeved shirt that matched the color of his knee-patched pants, which seems a few inches too long that sweeps the ground, and chokes off his black rubber shoes. He remembered that Tam had left Bac Sau and had been on his own for a long period of time, years perhaps; at least while he was staying with Bac Sau, he had never seen him. His mind began the search for clues as he was in a complete awe that how this young boy could manage to stay and grow up on his own, how this young man who did not want to have anything to do with his dad, denying to share the same roof with his father. What's really the conflict between the two of them that drove them apart? What school is he attending, or does he go to school at the moment? Where does he stay? With whom, or does he have job? All these questions competing for an answer were rushing in his mind, and he did not know how to start. He knew that in due time, he would know more about Tam. He wanted to hear from Tam rather than to question him, even though he was eager to know about this younger version of Bac Sau's. He certainly wanted to show some respect to his new acquaintance, his new friend.

Just before Lin could start a conversation, Tam had waved at a Lambretta, a mini passenger car, which was coming from the opposite direction. It made a quick U-turn and stopped at the curbside to wait for the two new passengers. It is a white, three-wheeled vehicle with a giant metal box in the back from which a wooden bench is mounted on each side to sit the passengers. The driver stayed at his single seat with both of his hands on the handles while the motor was still running, coughing out white smoke, permeating up in the air from a muffler underneath the passenger cabin. The two boys hopped on the back and found themselves plenty of room for just two of them. From where he was sitting, Tam told the driver where he wanted go: "downtown." The instruction was as short and simple as the jerk of the car when the driver released the brake with his left handle. He simultaneously turned the handle with his right hand to gas the engine, letting the white smoke whirl behind and fade into the air. Lin was glad that it started moving, for he felt he was going to get suffocated by the smoke trapped inside the box. It was the smoke from a two-cycle engine, which has a smell of the burned mixture of thick oil and gasoline that made Lin nauseated. Lin had not planned to have a ride with Tam on this mini passenger car. It just happened so fast that he did not even think it was happening. He could have used his bicycle to meet him wherever Tam wanted to meet. But all he did was to follow, as if he were being hypnotized by the older Tam. He wanted to tell Tam that he could save the fare by riding his bike together. But the noise from the muffler was so loud that discouraged him, and he did not want to bother. After a few minutes on the road, the tricycle made a stop to pick a young couple who share the seat with him. Lin thought of two more seats available and the driver would sure pick up a few more along the way to fill the space, making his trip a worthwhile. It wasn't a lucky day for the driver because that was all he had by the time he got to the bus station in the downtown area. Tam paid the fees for both of them, which Lin had no clue of the amount. All he did was to follow. It was the other side of downtown Tam was heading to. Lin had no idea about this area. He had never been to this side of the town, for he had no business, no needs coming here. He began to get curious, wondering if Tam would take him to his house, to the place where he lived, or somewhere else. He felt he should not ask any question in this regard because it might give Tam a feeling that Lin did not trust him, or perhaps think he was a nosy one.

Finally, Tam broke the silence with a smile and said, " I am hungry, let's go eat."

Lin felt the same way. He was hungry too. But where to eat? Lin was thinking they must be close by Tam's house so that he could cook some foods.

Before Lin could ask, he turned and headed to the direction of an open market, and there, at the other side of it, they both walked into a small restaurant, which was already crowded at lunchtime. The air was thickened with the smell of sizzling charcoal-BBQ'ed meats and other kinds of food that made his mouth watered. Lin was in shock, for he did not expect to have come to a restaurant for a lunch. Tam sure knows how to give his guest surprises, one after another. It wasn't a fancy high-class eating place. But the food must be good, for one could tell by looking at the happy faces of those who are enjoying their food here. It was a noisy little place. This must be a place where Tam frequented simply because a young girl—thirteen or fourteen years of age, a waitress, with an apron whose color had been changed from white to multicolor with grease and oil and food stains—cheerfully came over. She called him by name, grabbed his right hand, and led him to the corner far in the back where an only empty single table waiting as if he had made the reservation for the two of them. They both were talking very friendly as if they were brother and sister, or at least close friends that made him think of Be. He then introduced Lin to her, whom he called Be also. Lin smiled at her but a bit confused, amused at the name. She was cute all right, but it can't be that she had the same name as his sister. It took only a few seconds for him to figure it out that it was her nickname. Almost everyone in Vietnam has a nickname. The first born is called Hai (two), and the second born is Ba (three), and so on. It seems as if one was demoted one grade down in the hierarchy. How this business of nicknaming get started, he never had a chance to look into and never understood; there must be a book to talk about that nicknaming process. His thought was cut off by Tam's voice, giving her the order of his favorite, the rice noodles with skewered BBQ pork.

"Be, make it two, two bowls." Tam assumed that since it was his best choice, then it must be for Lin as well. Even Tam did not ask for his pick, but Lin would go for it anyway because he was hungry, and the smell of the foods, especially, the faint smoke and aroma of the pork BBQ in the air seemed to be tickling his nostrils and intensified his hunger. Anything would be just great and make him happy. He, besides, is known to be an easy-to-please person, for he never had many choices.

"Thanks brother, Tam," Lin said, looking at his friend, and kept his voice low, almost as a whisper in the busy place.

"You must have come here every often; that is why they know you by name and happy to see you." Lin continued with hope to learn some more about this new person in his life.

"I don't cook. This is my kitchen, where my lunches and dinners are, sometimes with friends, but most of the times, just me and myself. It is a part of my life, and I enjoy it." Lin sensed a mix feeling of what Tam just said. There is a bit of bitterness lying beneath a layer of icing on the cake of his life, which appeared to be aged, weathered, fully matured, and there is also a sense of pride in it as well. Lin noticed. He almost said, "You must be very rich in order to be able to eat out every day." But he held it on time. He will soon find out more about Tam, his work, and the place he lives.

While waiting for the order, Lin took a quick glance at the eating place with dark wooden tables, sided by benches lined up along the natural-colored wooden walls. It would be a nice U-shaped line of tables and benches if it were not for the table on which the two of them were sitting. This table seems to be out of the way that breaks the monotony. However, it must be the one the owner and helpers take their break and enjoy their meals. Lin felt privileged to be in the company with Tam whose influence sat him at this special reserved table, a special spot. He is inclined to explore more about this person.

One can talk and learn a lot from each other during a meal, a tea, a quiet park, or at any gathering. Over the giant bowls of food, at the reserved corner amid the noises of clanking plates, dishes, and people talking, Tam poured his heart out, telling Lin the story of his life.

"I was growing up with my dad"—Tam kept his voice low but audible between the two—"for my mom was left behind when we run away from the Communists in North Vietnam, the story of many Vietnamese in the country. About five years ago, I told my dad that I could not take school any more. I wanted to work to make money to help the family. Perhaps, I could save up some money to help my mom in the North even I hadn't a clue as to what village, what town she was living in. It was something I just wanted to share with my dad. But he was mad, very mad. He would not listen; all he did was to scream at me and told me that I had two choices. One is to continue with schooling. No negotiation, no compromise, and a must—yes, a must to show good grades in school. Two, to leave house, be on my own, no money, no foods, so support. As you see, I have chosen the latter. I love my dad, but I don't like his side of dictatorship. If he were not able fulfill his dreams of his life as man of letters, as a professional, a doctor, a dentist, why should he impose it on me to do it for him? Look around, you see many of them, I mean parents, they do the same as if they came out from the same school. If you failed, make your child, your son, your daughter, do it for you even it was against their will. I must admit that they all mean well, including my father; in his heart, he wanted the best for me, but he also should have considered what is my passion, my wants, and likes to make the best of me in life. I would like to create my own road map, chalk up my trails even he said it was wrong: 'Do it my way or no way.' Then I left. I try to come to visit him once in a while, but he is never happy when he sees me. I know why, but we never talk. He is a man with very few words, especially with his son. I then gradually cut my visiting him down to once a year, and that is why I came to see you this morning after I had learned from him about you, who is all for school and books. I had heard about you come to stay with him in his house and felt that it is good that you could take my place under his roof, perhaps in his heart too. You are me to keep him company. It was unfortunate that the fire burned down his house, and you two are separated." Tam turned out to be emotional and a good storyteller even though he does appear to be the opposite and on a gruff side. Lin was so far enjoying Tam and was very interested in listening to his life story. He could not wait to hear more about his real life, the life not being in school at his young tender age. What does he do for his living that he had chosen over the schooling, which to Lin was quite fascinating? All along he had believed that education is best for everyone who wants a better life until now.

"I never like books, much less the homework. I want to do something with my hands. I like the physical work. I'd rather be out in the world, working and making money. I love to eat good foods, and I have a passion for cooking, and because of that, a desire of becoming a chef was all over me and inside me. I could see myself in my white apron, white cap on my head, flipping the eggs, stir-frying the veggies, making soups and tons other dishes. I wanted to please my nostrils, to fill my lungs with aromas of Chinese, Vietnamese, Thai foods and more.

"I started out as a dishwasher. That is how you would have started in any field of endeavor. Take automobile, for example, if you wanted to be trained to be a mechanic, you would have to start with cooking, washing dishes, doing laundry for the mechanics who train you, cleaning tools after them for months before they actually teach you. Well, I got through the first stage of washing dishes, which was quite an experience. It was a hard work, especially on the day when the restaurant was packed with customers. I then became one of the helpers to the chef, cutting meats, chopping veggies, and of course, the cleanup after their messes. I felt great, for I actually had graduated from the class of dishwashing and elevated myself into a higher one, the level the culinary training to be a chef. Not too long I, however, realized that I had not gotten any pay for my work. I was promoted, and I actually worked with my sweat and blood! It was fine when I did the washing of dishes to learn the trade, just to have free meals, three times a day, seven days a week. I worked very hard for almost two years, ninety-eight weeks to be exact, for just the meager meals of the leftovers from the chefs and nothing else. I know it was brutal, but I figured that it was the price I had to pay, somehow. One day I asked the owner of the restaurant why I did not get paid for my new job, which he had told and promised me he would when I first started working for him. He told me he had never promised anything, and until I became a chef myself, then I could not collect my wage. He might have a dementia in his early age to forget what he had said, or he might have wanted to cheat me, for he had another helper, the old one besides me. But how could I forget what I was promised? I had worked so hard to earn the promotion, and now he denied rewarding me for it. I felt robbed and violated in the bright daylight in the city. This is injustice. This is very unfair. This is called robbery against the poor, the weak, and the meek, and I wanted to make him pay for it. Would the government listen to me, a young boy without a job, without money to file a complaint? Or would they give ear to a man with money and power, the owner of a prominent restaurant in town? They would probably laugh at me and say, 'Who the heck are you, young boy? Taking the owner to court? That is a joke, son. Don't you know chances are he could have you thrown in jail for daring to challenge his authority?' Or in this case, his cheating me. I then decided to get help from the other side of society, the world of the outlawed to punish him for robbing, abusing, and most of all, killing the hopes of others at their infantile, in the name of power, greed, and cheat. It is like a beautiful young bud from a flower bush, yearning to open, ready to greet the world, full of hope, full of enthusiasm, full of energy and potential; then, all of a sudden, the dark cloud of his wicked heart, the wind of his power-hunger mind, have formed a storm to his brutal hands, plucked it off from the tender greenish stem, threw it on the ground, and finished it off with a kick of his feet. That little young bud is me, got kicked off from the sidewalk of life, tried to bloom on his own on the muddy-soiled flat called or labeled the dark society. There are many youths about my ages and older out in the world of streets, not necessary of their choices, but the choices of those who imposed on them, the choices of the selfish and abusive from the ones that only care for themselves at the expense of the others."

Lin, while listening to his friend passionately telling his life's compelling story and eating his food, could not help see the parallelism between his own life and the life of his friend. The similarity of the two lives, one where his stepmother who has tried to choke off the yearning, the learning, the loving from his childhood with hatred, abusiveness, and selfishness, and the other whose tender life had gotten thrown off into a harsher world in the streets, robbed off his innocence, and chocked off his dreams, the dream of making contribution with his own hands at the early tender age. Lin felt the sympathy for this friend and wished that he could help, could do something to at least give hope for his future. Is there a future in the street life? He wouldn't know. Is there a bright future in the street of dark society of his? He doubted it. He felt that, despite all the ugliness, the unloving childhood he had experienced at home, he was blessed that he was still in school, nurtured with love and care from his teachers and friends. He still has a place he can call family where Cu and

Be are his brother and sister. It was a different world, and he wished he could share this intangible treasure with his friend.

The were still many questions in Lin's mind that he wanted to ask his friends, such as the place where he was staying. How did he make his living? How did he get his money to pay for his food and other expenses? But before he could ask all of these questions, Tam got up and walked toward Be, who was in and out of the cooking area, bringing food and collecting money from her customers. Lin did not see Tam pay for the food, which he must say was very delicious. Instead, they were talking, laughing, and next thing he saw was Tam's hand, waving, beckoning him to come forward and out of the door. Lin quickly followed Tam after whispering a thank you to Be with a smile, wondering if they had some sort of arrangements for the bills. He knows that in Vietnam, there are store owners who conduct their businesses with a handshake or based on a credit given to their friends and regular customers. In this case, payment is not expected till weeks, months later, or whenever money is available. Maybe Tam is in this category. Lin was still wondering and concerned.

He tried hard to catch up with Tam, weaving through the mass of human bodies in the open market under the hot sun. The mixture of smells from everything at the market ranging from aromas of fresh fruits, mangoes, bananas, pineapples, to foul odors of poops from chickens and ducks trapped inside the bamboo cages seemed to intensify under the heat of the afternoon sun that had quickly pushed away the savoring taste and smell of the food in the restaurant he just enjoyed. Outside of the marketplace, outside of the eating place, he was walking side by side next to Tam, thinking and wondering where he would take him next. On the dirt road to the west of the town they were walking and talking, Lin said thank you to Tam and told him that the food was excellent and he truly enjoyed the meal.

Tam Looked at Lin, and with a smile, he said, "I am glad that you enjoyed it. Don't you worry, now that I know where to find you, I will take you to many different places so that you could try more dishes that you have never had before. Do you still go back to the village to visit your family and friends?"

"Yes, I do. As matter of fact, I just came back from it yesterday." Lin told him about his unpleasant experience with his stepmother back in the village as if he were taking his friend on his fishing boat, on the river, back to the childhood past, revisiting each painful incident that he had had with his meaner-than-mean stepmother. Lin told him everything and wished that he could forget and forgive her. However, the way she kept on hating him, being unreasonable and mean to him, and pushing him out of his family, the pains in his heart increased and intensified, and forgiving, forgetting seemed impossible.

"I guess you and I were not at all lucky. We descended from not very bright stars," Tam, looking at the dark-red dusty road, counting his footsteps ahead of him, said resignedly and morbidly.

"I agree," Lin joined in the conversation, trying to catch up with his friend. "There were times I wished I had never been born. But the fact that I am here now in the city, in school, I am still a lot better off than many kids of my age, in the village, and even here in the city. I am surrounded by friends and loving and kind teachers in school. I just want to become a teacher. I want to teach the young children that love is possible, and that it should be practiced all the time regardless of ages; however, the earlier, the better. By doing so, there is no room for hatred to grow, no space for unkindness to expand. I want to be able to change what I have seen in my family, especially from what I saw in the way my stepmother has treated me. I want to eradicate the bewitched spell, which has run in our culture: 'Unless one finds bone in a rice muffin...' Do you think I am able to do that, brother Tam?"

"I hope so. It is not easy because it is the mentality that has been inscribed in our literature and culture for thousands of years. It will need thousands of you to do the job of changing it," Tam said with a matter-of-fact tone of voice. "I quite often feel sorry for any kid who has a woman coming into his or her life as a stepmother. I am very sure that person's life will be turned upside down; that person, mostly at a young tender age, will experience the hell on earth. I don't have to go very far to prove what I said. It is right here. It is you. You are the perfect example, and I am glad that you have a noble intention, a strong desire to change it. But remember, it isn't easy, or I could say, impossible!"

"My professor told me a Chinese proverb that I really liked and stayed with me. It says, 'For a thousand miles' journey, it all starts with the first step.' The important key here is to take that first step, and I do want to be the very first step of the journey," Lin told his friend with all conviction in his voice.

As the two amigos were approaching the corner of the street, Lin noticed that here stood at the right-hand corner a giant building—red, scallop-shaped brick roof, cement walls, and a facade, which had shown extensive weathered damages. There were lines of cracks from which green moss has grown out vertically, horizontally, crisscrossing each other like dark-green lines on a large map pasted on a giant wall under an open blue sky. There's not a sign saying what the building was, but there were people flocking, in front of if, and there were more sauntering slowly toward that direction. While Lin was wondering about the building, about the people, Tam told him that it was a playhouse. There also was a play that would be commencing very soon, and he wanted Lin to come to see. Lin had never had a chance to see one in his life and was eager to see it when Tam made an offer. He wanted to know what the play was all about; what's the name of the play? But before he could ask his friend more about it, Tam had left him to go over to the entrance of the building after he gave Lin his hand signal for him to stay put where he was standing. Lin saw Tam at the doors of the entrance and then quickly disappeared inside the building, as if he were the owner, the manager, or the worker of the facility.

Lin was really impressed and admired his friend's ability to do all what he has seen so far. Is it a part of his dark society that he had mentioned to him? Lin began to wonder. He seemed to have connections wherever he went. Minutes later from the crowd, which was getting bigger as minutes passed by, he walked over to Lin with a smile on his face and a red-orange-colored ticket to the show for him.

"Don't you have one for yourself? I am not going in there all by myself. Besides, this is going to be my first time ever to see a play, I mean the professional one like this," Lin said as he was curious that he did not see Tam's ticket.

"No, I do not need one. I know the manager and the staff here well. I can come anytime I want to. There are times I come to work with them to be a part of their team, especially whenever there is a big show, then I get involved to give them a hand," Tam said with a voice full of pride to Lin.

"This must be a world different from what we have in the village. You have probably seen them at some remote villages where a platform was erected with planks of wood in the open air. A colorful curtain, normally in red, is hung on a fine cable between the two poles. It is very primitive, very simple type of a stage for amateur performers, singers, and sometimes a short play to perform. It is a type of performance by volunteers to entertain the whole village during the holidays," Lin added his comment and was anxious to see the big play. But does he know what the play is all about? Not a clue! He wished there were some kinds of brochures, leaflets to let the viewers know ahead of time. Obviously, the crowd in front of his eyes tells him that none of those is needed. It's all about the word of mouth that gets the message out to the community. It is verbal bulletin that travels fast in every corner of the city.

"Do you know what's the name of the play, brother Tam?" Lin could not hold his curiosity and excitement.

"The title of the play is called *The Twelve Midwives*, and my friends who work in the playhouse told me that it is very good. Perhaps after seeing it, you might have some sorts of ideas or an answer to your own questions about your fate, your destiny, and why you have been treated the way you have been treated."

Lin had heard or read about the story in the Vietnamese literature, and it is a myth in which it is believed that each newborn, from the moment of conception, is assigned with twelve, yes, twelve gods, all female, perhaps you can call them angels, from heaven to tender the newborn. That is where the term *midwife* comes from because each of the twelve is specifically assigned to watch, to tender, and to care for specific organs of the infant from eyes, to nose, to mouth, and so on, and, therefore, influence the health, the intellect, and the future of the child. The comic, the amusing element about this heavens and earth intermingling affairs is that, despite the notion that they are sent from heavens on their mission to bring the best into a child's world, they do argue; yes, they enthusiastically use their voices with inflections! They do blame one another for not doing a good job, an excellent job, or plainly, an undesirable job on the appearance of a child. For example, a split-lip infant is the cause for the blame, which is squarely placed on the midwife who is believed to have neglected her job on bringing about a beautiful, healthy lip on the baby. Any defect at birth is a liability of the assigned midwife and therefore is responsible to the king of heavens.

The literature and the story of the twelve midwife-angels Lin had read now went flashing through his mind, and he could not wait to see the acting on the stage.

Lin told his friend about the play, which he had thumbed through the pages on the book and could not wait to go inside to see it begin.

At last the two of them got through the doors, immersed in the noisy crowd of about couple hundred people who mostly were already on their seats of the folding chairs or on the benches, while a few of them standing by the side of the walls talking, laughing, waiting for the show. The only two one hundred watts lightbulbs above their heads, roughly fifteen feet apart, oozing an amber-warm light for the whole room were dangling from the ceiling with the two thin black wires. The natural daylight seeped through the gap between the roof and the top of the cement walls of the building, like a long florescent light tube, which allowed him to see the heads of people, the viewers, and the dark-red curtain on the stage. Lin was trying to confine and suppress his excitement in this dim light, realizing that it was first time in his life to see the professional play with such a large audience. Standing in the back, squeezing in a corner, among others, Lin did not mind at all as long as he could see the play. He felt grateful and privileged already just to be inside the playhouse among the paid customers. While Lin was standing, observing, perhaps lost in the strange place, he noticed that his friend had left him and disappeared into the crowd. He did not say a word of where he was going, how long he would be going, which made him a little uneasy.

Lin had a series of questions in his mind that each was competing for an answer, but he was stuck and dumbfounded by his friend's behaviors. There is something of secrecy about this friend of his. Maybe he was a part of the team, a part of the organization that was putting up the show. Maybe he was a member of the "dark" society that he had mentioned earlier that requires of him to be absent temporarily for now. There are plenty of maybes inside his small head, none of which did he have any neither ways nor ability to find out. Instead, Lin felt a surge of admiration toward Tam for having these qualities. They are the qualities of strength and leadership.

Just as soon as the emcee—a young man, hard to guess his age, nicely groomed, in his black suit, white shirt, black bow that looks like a black dragonfly whose wings stretched and perched on his neck—made the announcement from the corner of stage, that the play was soon to begin, Tam showed up from the left side door, waved at him, and again disappeared. Lin did not know the meaning of the hand wave. Did he mean "Sorry, I have been gone. Stay put, I will come over" or "I'm alive, but too busy to come to get you" or "Enjoy the show." Obviously, Lin got the message. That is, he needs stay where he was standing and enjoy the show the best he could possibly can, without his friend.

The curtain, as if magically spit in halves from the middle, slowly spread to the sides of the stage, allowing the characters, dressed in gold garments, trimmed bright red at the end of the sleeves and collars. Those are the king and the queen of the heavens who were about to discuss the affairs on earth.

From his chair (throne) the king, with long white beard, rose up, walked slowly about the stage, deeply in thought, his head slightly dropped down, as if looking for ideas on the floor. He looked serious with his right hand slowly rubbing his chin for a few seconds and moving to his forehead, and then to his head, scratching. He was restless because of the complaints he had heard from his subjects on earth. At last, he spoke to the queen.

"My dear queen, you must agree with me that since the matter involved infants, children, and women, it is your responsibility to handle. I want to stay out of this." Not another word, he left the queen, jovially exited and disappeared into the behind of heaven.

"Is that it?" Lin was asking himself as he felt bored and cheated to spend time and energy and high expectation for the play. But wait a minute! The mood has been shifted and changed.

Surely, it is the matter of the queen. She was happy to be in charge, she smiled, waved the king off as he was leaving the scene. She ordered to call the midwives, a dozen of them, who cheerily entered the scene, talking noisily as if they were in the market, arguing and bargaining. It seems as if they did not know that the queen had ordered them to have her audience.

The queen clapped her hands to get their attention and raised her voice to get them go to their seats. Obediently, the midwives in their white garment like that of a nightgown, with light makeups on their faces, scurried to designated chairs. And all of a sudden, the lights went off as if the scene changes.

What happened? He felt odd. Was it really a part of the play? Question quickly flashed through his mind, but before he could find an answer, the side doors ahead of him and the front door behind him, all at the same time, banged open, as if they were wired on a timer. The uniform policemen and soldiers with rifles on their hands rushed in, and Lin could hear the footsteps pounding on the ground, running along the sides of the walls. The voice from someone in police uniform ordered, "Everyone should not move. Sit still. This is government troops and provincial police. We are raiding and searching for communist rebels. All must stay and sit still."

Streaks of light from the head and handheld flashlights, like star wars, crazily went flashing indiscriminately inside the small building along with the voices of the searching troops, hollering, creating quite a commotion. Lin did not know what to do. He wanted to get out of the building in order to find his friend. But he hadn't a clue where to find him; besides, everyone is ordered to stay put.

Minutes later, the lights were back on. One of the policemen said to the others, pointing his finger toward him, "He is one of them. Put a handcuff on him and lock him up."

"No, sir. I don't know anything. I am a student." Lin was shaken, and worse of all, he did not know what was going on.

"He is with the other guys. I saw him earlier," said the other, who must be an informant. Lin thinks this person might have seen him with Tam, whom he barely knew in a day.

"I think you made a mistake, sir. I don't know what you are talking about." Lin tried to explain and proved himself innocent from whatever was going on. He noticed leaflets were scattered on the floor, but could not make out what they were all about. He guesses that it was a reason for the raid, and he became scared.

"Take him away," the officer in-charge gave the order.

Outside of the playhouse, armed soldiers and uniformed police were seen around the building and across the street. Military vehicles and police cars scattered along the street creating a scene, an urgent and a scary one. Bystanders stood behind the barricade line to watch and to get a sense of what was going on. Lin now became scared as he saw a dozen young men, handcuffed, being led into a canvas-covered military truck. He tried to look for his friend, but he was nowhere to be seen, at least not among the youngsters being led away. Where is he? Is he one of the rebels or one of the leaders of the ring that the government troops and the police are after? If so, he could be in trouble, deep trouble even though he only knew Tam less than a day. He knew it was a mistake that they got him; the fact that he was separated and isolated from the ones on the truck is an indication of him being in a different category. But he had to prove himself innocent from this mess, somehow.

Now in the police car, which was plain silver color without signage, sitting in the back, feeling the cold metal of the silver handcuff on his wrists, Lin wondered where the police are going to take him. No one has asked him a question yet. Perhaps he is not a dangerous individual. Perhaps they already knew something about him, a poor and a homeless student! That is as simple as that. They should not have caught and put a handcuff on him in the first place. They should have just let him go, for they would not get anything out of him. He does not know anything.

He wanted to ask the young policeman who is at the driver's seat where he was going to take him, but was deterred to because the look on his face—stoic, unfriendly, and uninviting.

The driver started the car as the two policemen, the undercover, in civilian clothes, one on each side, got in the car, squeezing him in the middle. He felt smaller and helpless.

"Headquarters," ordered the man on his left behind the driver. He must be a high-ranking officer in disguise, giving the command.

"Yes, sir," said the driver respectfully.

The car rolled quietly on the paved road back to the provincial headquarters where he saw big buildings with high antennas, with communication cables, like spiderwebs, mounted on straight poles on top of their roofs.

The car at last came to a stop at the gate, and the uniform guard with rifle checked the driver and pushed the gate open.

Ushered into a ten-by-ten white-painted room inside one of the big buildings, Lin sat on a wooden chair by the table on which there is a stack of papers and a ballpoint pen. It is a well-lit room with a single florescent tube on the ceiling. This room is isolated far away from other offices. However, he could still hear the sounds from radio communication, beeping from somewhere in the building. He was told to sit still in the room and someone would come to work with him.

Within a few minutes, a tall young man in his late twenties, well dressed in white, walked in and gently closed the door behind him.

"Where are your parents? Are you in school?" the man asked him in a gentle voice as if he were an uncle talking to his nephew.

Lin told him everything about himself, where he came from, his parents and where they lived, and the school where he was attending. In fact, he told him that he was staying in with his teachers at school. He wanted to create an impression on this man that he is a good student and not a troublemaker. Indeed, the man, an interrogator, showed some interest in Lin's information and cooperation from his questioning.

"All right, tell me about the young man you were with this morning, the rebels; how did you get involved in this business? You are young and have a full future ahead of you." He paused, looking at him deep in the eyes, and then continued. "Your parents, your teachers, I am pretty sure they want you to focus on school so that you can be a good person, a contributor to society and to your country." The man continued in his soft voice.

Lin told the interrogator everything as it had happened. He only met Tam, who came to see him at the school this morning, whom he had never seen him in his life before. Lin only knew of him through his dad, Bac Sau, who mentioned about him a few times during his stay with him in his house.

"Very good. You seem to be an honest young person," the young interrogator showed satisfaction on his face and in his voice. "But I will have to keep you here until I can contact with your school, talk to you teacher, and to verify what you have just told me."

"Please, sir, let me go home, or else my teacher and his family will be very worried about me, about where I am." Lin begged the man. He could see in his mind how upset, how disappointed Mr. and Mrs. Nam would be when they heard about his. They might kick him out of the place he was now staying or possibly terminate him from the school because of his being accused of affiliating with the communist rebels. It would be devastating if it turned out that way. His imagination, his worries now got a hold of him. He just hoped that the truth to what has happened will save him from disgrace with his families.

"I will send you home as soon as I hear from your school. In the meantime, you will have to stay here. You will have some food for tonight. The guard will be taking you to the cell. Do not talk to anyone except to the guard if and when you need help." With that, the man took off without a word of comfort. He was helpless.

He knew he would be released sooner or later. But the idea of him staying in the police headquarters, being locked up in the cell like a criminal, an outlaw, and a hoodlum is too much for him to bear at this moment. His dad would be ashamed of him, for his dream and hope of him to become a good person, an educated man, would be crushed. Words of his troubles would travel quickly to his village, and someone would be happy and cheering at his misfortune. His worries were compounded and climbing up the roof, especially when his family does not know his whereabouts at this late hour in the day. They must be very worried about him. The only comfort thing is Be knew he had gone out with a friend. Would she be mad at him?

Lin could not tell the time of the evening when he was escorted by the guard to the cell, in the next building, not too far from the office. It was reinforced with black horizontal metal bars, topping it off with coiled barbwire. It was dark and late, for he could hear the crickets whining to his loneliness. The security structure somehow intensified the terrible feeling he had that he was treated like an outlawed; he would have felt much better if he had been kept right in the office.

Under the dim light from a single low-wattage lightbulb hanging from the ceiling in the middle of the room and free from the handcuff, which had been removed from his wrists by the guard, Lin spread the straw mat on the cement floor and reclined to it. But within only seconds, the decaying and mildew odors were so strong and became unbearable that made him decide to push it back in the corner of the cell. Now on the cold cement floor, Lin knew that it would be one of the longest nights in his life. The mosquitoes are welcoming him to his lot and are not in any way ready to say good night to him soon, or will they ever to? Everything happened so fast that he did not have a chance to register all events in his mind. A bright, sunny morning full of fun and a promise of new friendship now ended with a dismal situation, shattered and confused in the prison cell.

Why did Tam come to see him in the first place? How did he know where to find him when they never met? Did he come with a good intention for a new friend or merely to recruit a new member for his organization? Was the raid at the playhouse a coincidence, or was it a bad planning from his group. He asked himself with question after question, which he had no answers, and he was even more confused while trying to sort them out. He's made up his mind to never see Tam again. It is just more troubles to be associated with this young man. This reminds him what his dad and elders used to say: "Choose your friends carefully, or else they will break your heart." It is a lesson, indeed, to learn and to reflect on what his dad had told him.

Lin woke up to the sound of keys to unlock the door and the voice from the guard.

"Get up, son. Get ready to go home." The guard's voice sounded like a melody in the morning to Lin. He had been praying for that word *home* so that he could go home to his family. He sprung up from the cold floor where he had been napping throughout the night, fighting with mosquitoes, worrying about possible consequences from this incident.

"Since you have no records of running into laws, no connections with rebels, but is underage, young boy, one of your parents or your teachers whom you are staying with, as a guardian, has to sign for the release paper," the guard told him in a sympathetic tone of voice.

"Sir, I think I would have my teacher at school sign it for me," Lin said and silently prayed that the guard would accept his choice. He would be in the cell for two more days before his father could be here to sign him off, and worst of all, it would be an utter disappointment to his father if he found out that his son had been in jail for hanging around with the criminals while he should have spent time doing his school works. Yes, it would hurt his father immensely, and that would be the last thing on earth to do to his father. He was frightened with the thought and the consequences the mischievous event might bring.

"Now, get going. Someone will take you back to see your teacher at your school. He will have to sign the release paper," The guard said as he slammed the door close behind Lin as he walked out. "Don't you get in trouble any more. Do not waste your life.

You are very young, remember that!" The guard rendered his kind words of advice to Lin, at last.

"Yes, sir. I will remember what you said, and I thank you for your kindness," Lin said with all sincerity and felt such relief that he would be going home, soon. He promised himself that it would be the last time in his life to get into trouble with the law enforcement.

It was still early in the morning; the sun was still hiding behind the shade of a giant banyan tree, like a giant green mushroom, grown out in the middle of the red-dirt courtyard. The tree must have been over a hundred years old, giving shade to man and shelter to the birds that were chirping, flying in and out of the dense greenish canopy, greeting the new day.

He was now taken back to the office where he was twelve hours ago, waiting for the release paper, he supposed. He remembered he was handcuffed, apprehensive, and anxious when he was brought here for interrogation. Minutes passed by as he noticed people in and out of the offices, more men than women, some in civilian clothes, some in light-gray-blue uniform, but none came to his spot where he was standing, waiting, which seems eternity. His mind started playing tricks on him. Did they forget about him? He doubted. Did they change their mind on letting him go, instead, keeping him here for more questioning? Or, maybe, they have caught Tam and wanted him here for more information? His mind was like a wildcat, out from the cage, out of control, running aimlessly in the open field of imagination.

"Come with me," a voice came from a middle-aged man in uniform, approaching from an office behind him. Lin was not sure to where, but he followed the man.

"Uncle, are you taking me home? Am I free now, right?" With all sincerity and emotion in his voice, Lin asked the man. He wanted to let this uniformed officer know that it would be a waste of his time from the police department to keep him in jail, for he knew nothing about Tam and his rebellious organization. He was just a poor, innocent student.

"Yes, I am taking you back to your school." And like a father to his son, the man continued in his loving care voice, "Stay out of trouble, son. You are very young and have a good future ahead of you. Focus on your study at school, and you will be a good citizen."

"Thank you, Uncle."

Within minutes, they were entering the school on a jeep with no sign and a canvas top and clear vinyl windows in the back and the sides. From the entrance, Lin could see Mr. Nam and his family waiting at the administration building. How did they know? Lin began to wonder. The police must have already informed them about his troubles at the playhouse and the overnight stay at the police headquarters. He would have a lot to tell and explain to the family.

Just as soon as the car stopped at the side of the building, the officer grabbed the papers, got out of the car, and was greeted by Mr. Nam who, as a school official, dressed up in his dark-chocolate suit. They both shook hands, and they went into the office for their private conversation. Lin immediately got out of the car, walked over to Mrs. Nam, Cu, and Be, who were even more anxious to see him.

With a smile on her face, Mrs. Nam held him in her arms and said, "I am glad you are home. We were all really worried and missed you."

"I am sorry to have caused so much trouble for you, mama. I promise not to let it happen again."

Lin glanced at Be, standing next to Cu, to see her tears strolling on her cheeks. Her eyes caught his and quickly turned away as if saying, "You, bad boy, I don't want to see you anymore. I am sad."

Lin wanted to come to tell her that he was deeply sorry for the trouble. But he couldn't. Cu had already started to yell out loud from his lungs. "Brother, I am happy to see you home. I was worried about you sleeping in the street last night. Are you all right, now?"

"Me too. I am very happy to be home with you, brother. I won't go again, I promise."

From the office, Mr. Nam's voice was heard calling for Lin, "Lin, come inside the office."

"Yes, sir," Lin responded aloud and dashed on the steps and then into the office. He did not know what to expect. What will happen to him? He could not think of anything terrible that would be waiting for him.

Once he was in front of the two men who both have authority over him, one from the school, and the other from the government, they both looked at him, not threatening, not scolding, but with kind eyes.

"I want you to promise the officer not to ever have it happen again." Mr. Nam gestured to him and wanted him to make that solemn vow for the sake of his future. Lin knows in his heart that Mr. Nam loves him not only as his student but also as his son.

"Yes, I promise." Lin bowed his head before the man and to Mr. Nam. "I will never leave the school premise without your permission, master." He kept his head down for a long moment, deepening his respect and showing the gravity of his vow. He then turned over to the officer and said, "Thank you for taking me home. I promise to stay out of trouble."

The officer then left the building after he had the paper signed by Mr. Nam. They both seemed enjoying each other, shaking hands as Mr. Nam thanked him for bringing Lin back to the school.

Sitting on the chair by the dining table at Mr. Nam's, Lin was surrounded by everyone in the family, listening to what he had to say about his mischievous incident. He recounted every detail of what had happened to him the day before from the moment that Be hollered him down from his room to meet up with Tam, eating lunch with him in a restaurant, going to the playhouse, getting caught in the police raid, and, like at the end of series of bad luck, taken to be locked up in the police headquarters.

"It was just such a nonsense, bizarre, out-of-luck incident for me," Lin told his curious audience. "This Tammy boy, who came out from nowhere, whom I never knew from Adam, who, in less than half a day, had given me so much trouble is something I could never be able to figure out. I am truly sorry for making you all worried about me. I thought I would be back home here in the evening. But, as you can see, I was at the mercy of the police." And as if he had just discovered the odds stack up against him, he added, "And of my predestined eventful life too."

He turned over to Be, who sat quietly at the corner, and said, "Be, please do not be mad at me. It was out of my control. It was not even least of my intention to stay out with him all day, or to hang out with this guy all night. I never want to get in trouble with anyone, anywhere, let alone with you or with Mom and Dad. It was just my bad luck getting caught by the police for something I had never done. Do you think I am a bad boy, a bad brother to you?"

Be understood every word he said, sympathized his circumstance and situation, but did not know what to say. She could not sleep much last night, worrying about him because he had already had a tough and rough life. He needn't add any more misfortune into it.

"My son, go get yourself cleaned up and some rest," Mrs. told him as if relieving Be from answering his question. "It's already done and now a past. I am happy that you are home safe and sound."

"Yes, Mama," he said and bowed to everyone. "Thank you" he whispered.

He went to his room, washed up, went to bed, and fell asleep. He was dead tired.

The principal came back from the school break with his wife and Mr. Nguyen, his father-in-law, fresh and relaxed from the driving a long distance. After dinner, he went to his office to check on his mails and to catch up with his paperwork. Something caught his eyes.

There lay on his desk was a report from the national police headquarters of Banmethuot province with a red circle stamp over a black-inked signature of the authority at the right bottom of the paper. One can see a frown on this forehead when he read through the report. Is it really about the kid he loves? Did he really get involved with the guerrilla rebels that the government has been trying to wipe out?

Is he associated with or a sympathizer to this troublesome militant organization? This is a serious business even though the red stamps, one on top, one at the bottom of the paper, only say "Suspect." He wanted to believe in his heart that Lin is a nice, innocent young boy, a good student of his, the one his whole family fall in love with, from his wife, his father-in-law; even his youngest sister, who came for a short visit at the school, loved him. She did even mention about this young boy during this short break at home. He knows his limit. He knows very well the regulation and the rules governing this government-funded school, not just a public school, but also the school primarily and specifically for the tribal minority youths; students other than that are secondary.

The principal is now facing a very sensitive situation in which he could lose his job if he were not careful, if he stepped out of his boundary, if he broke that intangible fine line from the government. That is his reality. No matter how much he loves the boy, no matter how much he cares for him, he cannot keep him and let him stay inside the school compound. He asked for Mr.

Nam to come over to see him at his office to discuss the matter even though it was late in the evening.

The two men sat in the office, talked for hours into the night, but could not come up with any solution. They both loved the boy. Not only that, the two families had a heart for him. But a decision has to be made. The verdict was this: Lin had to go. Mr. Nam felt so bad because he had to deal with it firsthand. He is the one who signed the release paper from the police. He did have a feeling that would, at the end, become not so nice, not so pleasant. That is why he stayed silent, did not say a word when Lin sat at the dining table telling the story of how he got into trouble. He was debating whether or not to turn in the report to the principal. If he did not do it, he would lose the job. The whole family would have to move, to suffer. The consequence would be enormous and unimaginable. On the other hand, Lin would lose a place to stay or possibly get kicked out from the school, which would be the end of his future. His heart was aching at this thought, and he felt helpless. He did not know how to break the news to his family. They would be sick when he told them. It is like kicking his own son out of the house and into the street and becoming homeless again.

"Can you let him continue with his classes like any other kids?" asked Mr. Nam. "Should I let him know the situation and the decision that we just made?"

"I guess we can do that for now. I hope we won't have any audit or inspection, soon."

"I hope not," said Mr. Nam, his voice softened with care. "However, I will see Mr. Thong, his English teacher, in the morning. He always praises and talks highly of Lin and how good a student he is in his English class. I don't think there is any problems of having him stay at Mr. Thong's. I will talk to him."

The principal felt better at what Mr. Nam said. At least, Lin would have a place to stay and the cared for by his own master,

Mr. Thong, and the master's family. As far as his family, his wife and his father-in-law, is concerned, they would see that he did not kick him out into the street, but, rather, a transferred to a place of stay. He just hoped that Mr. Thong would welcome the idea of taking Lin as his own child into his family, even though he was much younger and single. At that, he asked Mr. Nam not to break the news to anyone, including his own family until he got the okay from Mr. Thong. He does not want to see any drama from the members of the two families, his and Mr. Nam's, upon hearing Lin's being kicked out. He knows very well how much the love and care they all have for Lin, and by doing so, he delays the shock.

The negotiation—no, the asking took place in the principal's office the following day after the morning session. Mr. Quang and Mr. Nam shared with Mr. Thong what had happened with young Lin during the recent school break. Every detail was retold from the beginning to the end, the jail cell at the police headquarters and finally the dilemma the two of them, the principal and the custodian, were facing against the school regulation. They both could lose their jobs and get possible jailtime if they allowed Lin stay and got caught. Mr. Nam asked Mr. Thong to consider having Lin stay with him.

The five-foot-four English teacher's face blossomed with a cheerful smile and said, "Mr. Principal and Mr. Nam, you both worry too much. Give him to me. I am single, staying with my mom and dad and my younger brother. For him staying with us, just add a bowl and a pair of chopsticks to our meal. I love the boy. He is one of my best students in class. It would be my pleasure to help him out. In fact, it works out perfectly for my brother because Lin would become his study companion at home. I must say thank you to both of you."

The two men had never dreamed of the outcome of the meeting, which turned out so beautifully the way it did. They told Mr. Thong that they were grateful for his generosity and kindness rendered for Lin's shake. They asked him when Lin could move in with his family.

He quickly said, "Anytime, he is more than welcome. My family would love to have him."

Everyone, including the principal's family, was present at Mr. Nam's house. Right after dinner, Mr. Quang broke the news telling everyone. He started with the report from the regional national police headquarters in which he was startled to see the incident unfold.

"It is an unfortunate thing that happened to innocent people," the principal's voice weighed down with compassion. "However, I have to follow the government 's guidelines and regulations, or else, I would be going home to the farm, chasing ducks." Mr. Quang tried to lighten up the situation. He went on to let everyone know that Lin would be staying with his English teacher, Mr. Thong, who loves him to pieces. He said there was nothing seriously changed. He still could go to school as he used to. The only difference is he would be staying with an English teacher instead of the French.

"I think it is a great trade-off. Perhaps a better deal for Lin because the French had left; the American now came. English is going to be the main foreign language in school. That is why I now am speaking English with my American friends, as you all know." Proudly, Mr. Quang smiled as he was trying to persuade his family audience, his wife, his father-in-law, and Mr. Nam's. The initial shock when Mr. Quang broke the news about Lin getting in trouble and the penalty that goes with now eased down as they looked at one another. They all felt that it was not as terrible as it first appeared. They were all now convinced that it would be a better opportunity for Lin anyway, even though they all felt the sacrifice in the trade-off, that is, his presence at dinners at one of the families. Lin would be still continuing with his job, tutoring at the coffee plantation to make his income.

"You are more than welcome to stay after school and have a dinner with us sometimes. We all will miss you, but it is a better move for you in the long run. Don't be so sad, son," said Mrs. Nam. And Mrs. Quang also joined in with her smile and a nodding of her head.

"Yes, Mama." Lin's voice soaked up with emotion. He had no clue there was a war going on, a debate, negotiating on his behalf. There, he sat nervously, quietly, listening to the principal's talk as he was pointing out facts and conjecture for his decision and suggestion. He knew he was in trouble or could be in trouble over the incident with Tam. However, he never knew he had been in such a mess that could alter his life to the worst, the life in the village with his stepmother, whose cold-hearted face kept flashing in his mind, giving him a feeling of being in a haunted house or a scary movie. He felt a knot, a twist in chest when the principal mentioned the incident that he was involved, a violation of the government's regulation bestowed on him. He was frozen at the conviction from the principal that he could no longer stay inside the school premise, a privilege of his lifetime. It was done; it was over.

Fortunately, as much as the fashion of his life, when one door shuts down on him, dark, painful, and hopeless, as it seemed to him, another one swings open with new opportunity, challenge, and hope for him. Oh, he did not know how to express his gratefulness to everyone for their love, care, and support. What his life would be without them? He felt love and loved.

"Brother, be sure to stop by after school to have a meal with us. I will cook good food for you," said Be at last. She had not talked to him ever since the day he took off with Tam. She was worried; she was sad and mad, for he had gone all day and all night. Where did he go with that friend of his? Did that boy get his brother in trouble? She blamed herself that she should not let Lin go with that stranger. She had a feeling something had gone wrong because Lin was never out late without permission from her parents. He has always been a responsible person, and for him not to come home late in the night, there must be some troubles. Now it's like his fate; things happened that he could not have any control. She felt sorry for him and for blaming him. She wanted to do something for him to make up for that.

"Yes, sis, but it will depend on my new place too," he told her and wanted to tell her that she should not be worried about feeding him, but he did not want to displease her for not acknowledging her care.

Another chapter of the history book of his life now just turned, not at his will but of heaven's will. Just within three years, he had gone from one place to another. Each time it seemed like a heartache but is better than another, and his life is blossoming like a flower, like a rose, rising atop of its thorny stem to admire the sky of the heavens.

Lin could definitely see the opportunity; being in Mr. Thong's family was truly a blessing. He could imagine being in an environment from which he cannot help learning and being better, academically and personally. He had seen Mr. Thong and his American friend, a combat pilot, one much taller than other, in their conversation, English, of course. How impressive it was! For the benefit of all students in his English class, Mr. Thong was able to ask his friend to come to his classroom, once or twice a week, to work on vocal drills. It was such a huge help, training the young students to pronounce English words correctly. His dream was to be able to speak this foreign language as fluent as Mr. Thong did at some point in the future. He felt the excitement running through his veins.

Moving In With English Teacher's Family

Lin was welcomed into Mr. Thong with nothing but love and care from his parents and his younger brother. Their joy, cheers, and laughter made his heart warm. His parents, who in their late fifties, came from farming background in the northern part of central Vietnam. They had survived the war between the Vietminh (Vietnamese communists) and the French, and they showed their kindness and love in their voices and the gestures they made.

They all lived in a very small house in the outskirt of the city whose street lined with a variety of tall, leafy trees from mahogany to eucalyptus. The elders have their own bed in a room next to the kitchen. A living room with a desk and a wooden bench on each side for study is a place for him to share with Mr. Thong and his brother, Dinh, at bedtime. There is a portable folding bed with a mosquito net for each one to sleep on for the teacher, his brother, and for Lin in a space more or less 350 square feet. Given the space, as narrow as it is, given the circumstance, as not luxurious as it is, they still are all happy to bring him to share, to care, and to love. If nothing else, this alone has made a big impact on and greatly influenced his life, that is, "love till it hurts" as he had heard from the elders.

The elders, especially, the mother, who is fond of cooking, would not let any of the boys venture into the kitchen. It is her territory. It is typical for Vietnamese moms who think time is more precious for their children to spend on studying and doing homework than anything else, including the work in the kitchen. It is the God-given motherly love that they find joy in feeding, clothing their youngsters, and sacrificing themselves for the sake of love so that their children would have a better chance in life to become officials, teachers, officers, and more. They are like mother birds patiently caring for their chicks until they are fully ready for their flights into the world.

Mr. Thong, a compassionate young man in his late twenties, five feet four, schooled and educated during the very tough time of war, a dedicated teacher, who taught English at other schools during the day, still finds time to teach Lin and Dinh at home. Once in a while, Mr. Thong would want the boys to practice. A conversation in English between the two in front of the elders brought so much fun, so much laughter to the whole house.

The mother would sometimes make a comment such as, "You boys sound very funny. You would have to scrap my tongue for me to sound like you. It is hard."

They would make fun of her whenever she made such a comment by telling her, "Mom, do you know why it is harder? It is because USA is fifty times bigger, so the language is also fifty times harder. We have to twist, turn, and curl our tongues fifty times to say it."

She would throw her hand halfway up in the air, shake her head, and said, "Oh, I would stick with what my mom and my grandparents taught me. It would take me another lifetime to learn what you kids are doing."

"But, Mom," Dinh would say, "when I say I am hungry. You would understand, right?"

She told him that because she had heard that sound a few times, specifically with the gesture with his hands rubbing on his tummy; she then understood.

"See, Mom, you can learn it too." Dinh would tease her.

And she would lovingly tell him, "You are just being so silly, son."

Mr. Thong's dad, Mr. Thanh—in his late fifties, an interesting and mostly quiet man who does not say much as if he traded his words for smiles—smiles for just about everything. He has a kind look on his dark, weathered face. The gazing kind of look in his eyes seems to invite you into his soul, trusting, loving. He had gone through a lot in his life as a farmer when he was a young boy and a soldier when he was only fifteen years of age.

"Wars and battlefields have taught me a lot," he would say to Lin as a close friend, a confidant even though they were decades apart in their time of life. "Lives are short and wasted in the battlefields. You are trained to kill, and you kill as you follow orders. However, in the end, when the dust in the battlefield settled, you cannot help wondering, pondering on what you have just done." Mr. Thanh became lost in his own world of the old days, the young years of his life. His voice softened, dropped to almost a whisper in the quiet evening with just the two of them home on a Sunday evening when the rest of the family was out at the Buddhist temple. With a deep sigh, he continued, "You actually killed your own brother whom you had been told your enemy, to hate, to destroy at all cost. I followed the pack, did what everyone's doing without questioning, and then one day, I woke up from this madness of killing. I dropped the gun, left the killing field, followed the Buddha whose teaching is nonviolence and honoring all lives, not just human lives but animal's and bug's lives as well."

The old man told him how hard it was to leave his unit with his buddies, with whom he shared countless life and death experiences in the field. And with whom he cared for, treated like his own brothers. But he had to turn away from them to follow his mind and heart on the journey of his life. He had to fight so hard to overcome the guilt of abandoning his comrades in arms. It was a double guilt that he had to deal with, one in which from his own conscience for taking the precious lives of other human beings so lightly at the squeeze of his finger on the trigger of his machine gun that brought down dozen of enemy soldiers at a time, like cut trees, crumbling down in a foggy day. Awards and medals upon his chest for his gallantry, his bravery, along with accolade after accolades from his commanding officers, were not able to suppress the quiet voice from his heart, which whispered louder and louder in the night.

He told himself, "This is insane, this is brutal, this is inhuman. I must stop. I must not continue this act of killing. How many lives have I destroyed on behalf of the party and a few on top? What made sense in the beginning is now senseless. And besides, I could be killed too."

The other is from his own reasoning, which was no less difficult for him to leave his unit. He knew in his heart that he wanted to get away from the blasting, deafening noise of weaponry, the explosion, and the screaming of human voices. But the bond he had glued the friendship among his buddies, the camaraderie throughout the years in the battlefield was so strong that seemed unbreakable. He did not know exactly how he did it. It had been many days and many nights in which he calculated not only the pros and cons for his decision making, to go or not to go, but also the risk of getting caught leaving, deserting his unit. He realized the danger of his intention and his action. It could be a bullet into his head as a penalty. He would be considered a "traitor" and treated as such, despite the shining medals, decorated from the killing field. But he would rather take that risk of dying than continue killing others. Then one day, a message came from his command that his mother was dying, and he was allowed to go home for her funeral. Shock and sad at the devastating news, he said good-bye to his buddies and quickly left the unit, leaving the jungle, knowing in his heart that this is the chance, this is the only God-given opportunity to say farewell to this bloody madness of the war. From the pains, the hurt, the loss to the burying his mom, died from a long-fought illness, which began with a cold, then turned pneumonia, sprung the opportunity for his life, a better life. It happened as if the mother died so the son could have a life. He quickly and quietly left the village pretending going back to his duty. Instead, he went south, hundreds of miles away, one city after another, on his bicycle, with a backpack half full with belongings on his back, looking for a place to start his new life. He finally came to stop and settled at a coastal village of the Khanh-Hoa province, where not only did he fall in love with the breezes, the waves, and the sand beaches, but also, at the first sight, he fell in love with a local girl and started his family. He changed his name, erased his identity for fear of being harmed by his military contact.

While fascinated and listening to the old man's story, Lin could not help relating it to the story of his own life, which had been nothing but a roller coaster, like riding his bicycle on the bumpy road of his life.

Curious at how his family grew and moved from the coastal city to this mountainous red-dirt province of the central highland, where red dust whirl in the air in place of fresh ocean breezes, where the cries of monkey in the evening in place of the sounds of waves breaking up out at the beach, Lin asked, "Uncle, why did you choose to move your family to this part of the country where it is isolated, not much to entertain, if not boring compared to the big city?"

"Well, we are not much of the city people. We are used to farm for a living. We sacrificed everything for our children to make sure they get their highest education, and when Thong graduated, he wanted to move here to teach; we followed him. It has been our joy to do that. As you can see, we do not have much, but we have our family together."

Lin was so touched with his story, his chosen life of simplicity in which love is the core, and kindness is a part of. Lin was so grateful that the old man had extended his hand to bring him into his loving family.

"Uncle, it will be another lifetime before I can repay for your loving kindness. I pray that God will compensate you and your family, abundantly," Lin said to him softly.

The two hearts of the young and old melted together in a mutual understanding and appreciation for each other in the quiet evening hours inside the house. Mosquitoes were out, landing on Lin's face, flying right at his ears, making the sound as if they were singing or saying, "Oh, oh, sorry."

Lin could not hold back the thought of telling the old man the story of his life when he was asked, "So, what about your life? Your parents? Where do they live?"

Lin poured his heart out, telling the man in detail the story of his life from the time his mom passed away to the time when his father remarried, which was the most painful time in his childhood life.

"I cried my heart out every evening asking my mom to come back to me or to take me away with her because my stepmother was brutally mean to me. I was not allowed a full meal when my father was away on a fishing trip, and he goes very often, most of time four to five days out of a week. I was not allowed to wear not even patched-mended clothes, much less the new ones. I got pushed off the bed with her foot in the middle of the night. She simply hated me, for I was not her own son. What the society, the culture says and I heard of now came true to me, that is, 'Until you find a bone in a rice muffin, you will never find love from your stepmother.'"

The old man sat still, listened to every word Lin said, and felt sorry for the boy. He stood up, like a father to his son, stepped over to hold Lin, squeezed him in his firm arms and softly said, "You have my love, our love, son."

"We are home, Dad, we are home." Dinh' cheerful voice was heard at the door as he announced his coming home with his mother from their visit to the temple. "Dad, how come you don't turn the light on?" Dinh continued as he noticed the living room was dark.

"Yes, son, we are here," answered the old man as Lin got up to the switch to get the light on. "We have been sitting here talking and forgot about the time, the light. Besides, I did not feel we need to. Saving, you know," explained the old man.

"Daddy," said his wife, Mrs. Thanh, who addressed him as daddy, must be for her kids, "we have some treats for you and Lin from the temple, a couple of cupcakes and fruits. It was crowded with lots of visitors today at the temple. You should have come with us." Her voice was soothing to him.

"Woman dear, thank you for the treats. That is very kind of you to think of us. We should join you next time," the old man said to his wife.

Lin was intrigued at the language the old man used to address his wife. There is a quality of intimacy in the words, the sounds and the voice when he said it, which was simply loving and romantic, even at his age. Maybe just because at this golden age he realized that it was the way, the only way to love and to express love to his lover, his soul mate? He also made an observation that the first name of all the wives never got mentioned as they submitted to their husbands. For example, Mrs. Thanh or Mrs. Nam or Mrs. Quang. There must be something sacred about their first names, one might wonder. Or they want to be attached to their husband's and melted in theirs, a sacred act of matrimony. Lin began to fall in love with this seemingly esoteric wisdom of the culture. No wonder why when a man and a woman, after taking their celebrated sacred vows, becoming husband and wife, they address each other lovingly as "minh" (body), as if other person was a part of his or her own self. It is an act of diluting oneself to become another, a transformation to union.

Just less than a week of his stay in the new place, Lin felt that his whole being filled with the blessing and the love again from this new family. Fortune and misfortune are taking turn to work on his life, helping him to see and to appreciate every moment of the human touch from all of those who have extended their hands to bring him close to their hearts so that he can feel their love and care.

Yesterday, after school, Lin spent some time and had a dinner with Mr. Nam's family. Everyone told him how much they had missed him, especially Cu and Be when they saw him as they were arriving home from school. They all screamed his name out loud as they stormed through the half-closed entrance door to greet him, for they had spotted his bicycle leaning against the wall by the doorsteps. Cu, with a big smile on his face, could not hold is excitement and ran right over to hold him tight after uttering his respectful "thua, Ma, con di hoc ve" (hi, Mom, I am home) to his mom, who sat across from Lin at the table. Be was somewhat more reserved in showing her enthusiasm after she said the greeting to her mom.

However, she held her gaze looking at him and softly said, "Brother, you did not stop to see us for the whole week after school." She wanted to say how much she had missed him but held back. "How are you? Do you like the new place with teacher Thong and his family?"

Before Lin could answer her, Mrs. Nam, as usual, intervened, protected him, and kept him from answering these "tough" questions from Be.

She told him, "Be, you can ask your brother later. Why don't you go in the kitchen to get the food ready for dinner?" Before she said an obedient *yes* to her mother, she got up, squinted her eyes, gave him a threatening look as if saying, "Brother Lin, you are just being lucky to have Mother cover you all the time. I am not done with you yet." As she was walking out into the kitchen, she was thinking, *Why does Mom love this boy so much? She obviously shows her favoritism over her own kids.*

The word *why* kept lingering in her head, yearning for an answer, while she was standing, tending the charcoal, glowing inside the terra-cotta grill oven, which was sitting on a four-legged stand in the corner of the kitchen. All of a sudden, Be felt her cheeks becoming blushingly hot. Maybe from the heat of the burning charcoal, glowing, crackling on top of the clay-baked oven, or maybe from the thought that her mom, in her motherly wisdom and love, molding her future with him. Mom has talked about him quite often lately. She mentioned the qualities of being caring, hardworking, and what a good nature he has. She talked about the poor and abusive childhood he has had with his stepmother. All of these qualities and his misfortune she had mentioned and talked about gave indication of her love for this brother Lin. Be had felt something missing in the air, something empty in the space that she could not pinpoint the day he had to move out from the school building. In fact, she silently wept in her room the evening she heard of the decision from the school principal that he could not stay in the building. She had never felt like this before. It's the feeling of something intangible, indefinable, indescribable tugging her heart like fresh morning air after a rain at night, like a fragrance of flowers in the garden at the temple she visited with her friends recently. Many of her friends at school always proudly talked about their big brothers who helped them with homework, protected them, and cared for them, and she had wished she had an older brother like one of theirs. One day long, long ago, she asked her mom why she did not have a big brother.

Mom said, "But you have a brother, don't you? Besides, would you rather be a boy?"

She thought it was funny for her mom to say that. It was as if she could change her into a boy. That was the end of it about the big brother.

She did hope that Lin could fill that role in becoming her big brother when he was staying in the school building next to her house. But things had been happening so fast, one thing after another. That hope, that dream of him becoming big brother for her never came true.

Be was standing in front of the oven for a long time, lost track of time, and forgot what to do first. She finally awakened to her reality and told herself, *Hey, dreamer, get the dinner ready or else...*

Meanwhile, Lin was in the room with the rest of the family, telling them about the new place and how loving and caring Mr. Thong and everyone in the family were to him. He told them the biggest boon was to be right next to the teacher to listen to and to learn from him. He made everyone laugh when he told them about the comment that Mr. Thong's mom had made during his practice on the pronunciation of an English word, the word *learn*. The "curling" of the tongue, the using of vocal cord, all of which she said, "Too hard! I don't want to be like a bird learning human language."

All of a sudden, Cu, like a little kid and a big smile on his face, jumped right in the conversation.

"Brother, I want to do it. I want to learn it. Can I come to stay with you?" Oopps, Cu did not know he got in trouble when he said that. Perhaps he was still a kid and said what he wanted to say without a second thought, and besides, kids do what kids do.

"You, my young man! You are such a naughty kid. Do you think you can just go and stay with him when he doesn't even have a place for himself? Are you ready to leave your dad, your sister, and me to stay somewhere else?" With a stern look, Mrs. Nam scolded her son as if he were about to leave the house any minute to go and stay with Lin. "Bad boy," she told him at last.

Lin felt bad. Because of him, Cu got into trouble with his mom. He looked sad. His chin was down on his chest. Upset? Maybe. Sorry for what he said that hurt mom's feeling? Maybe. At the very moment when Lin wanted to say something to comfort him and a few words to Mrs. Nam that Cu was just a kid, unaware of what he was saying, Cu got up, threw his arms around her neck, and whispered, "I am sorry, Mama. I did not mean to leave you. Love you, Mom." Lin had not expected that to happen from Cu. Obviously he was more mature than Lin could have thought.

Mrs. Nam was also pleased with her son. She smiled, held him tight, and said, "My little dog, I love you too."

Lin could not help sharing the joy of their expressing their love for each other and felt a tug in his heart, the longing, the yearning for the mother-son love, the very one he had been missing in his life.

"Why don't you go help your sister to get the food ready, Cu? She might need your help," Mrs. Nam asked Cu with her loving voice.

"Yes, Mama." Cu's voice was packed with joy and energy. He smiled as he sprung up from the floor, headed to the kitchen, knowing that he was off the hook. Mrs. Nam looked at Lin, shaking her head, smiling, as if saying, "My boy is still a baby, don't you see?"

Lin always felt like being a part of this family, and as such, he never wanted to be treated as a guest, but rather a son to the family.

He wanted to help Cu and Be set up and clean up after the dinner as he used to in the past, at home. He felt the love here, and it's the least contribution he could make with his hands and energy he had. Be was utterly happy with what Lin did and the time he shared with her and family.

Before Lin went home that evening, she told him how much she appreciated his time, and she asked him to come more often.

"Brother, you don't have to wait for a written invitation to come. Don't make us wait for you," Be said to him softly as he was leaving after he had said good night to everyone in the family.

"I promise not to make you wait, sis," Lin smiled and said to her, feeling what she meant with the word *invitation* she said. He felt as if she said, "I don't like the feeling that you just ignored us, after leaving here, to your new place.

It was indeed a beautiful evening as he was rolling on his bicycle home. The sun was setting behind the mountains, miles away from the city, painting the patch of clouds hung low in the sky with rays of amber and gray colors. The streetlights were on, casting a warm-yellowish light on the cement-paved street. It was a quiet evening except a few cars zooming by from either direction. Lin was taking his time pedaling, reliving the exquisite time he had had moments ago. What a lovely dinner he had with her family. He felt the love and care from everyone, especially from Mrs. Nam, who asked him constantly about his clothes, about his foods with such care and love from a mother.

"Bring your clothes home here so Be and I can wash them for you," she told him.

He was simply touched.

"What you two have been talking about all evening?" Mr. Thong's mom's voice bought Lin back to his sense of where he was at. He had gone off in time and space to let his heart and soul touched and filled with loving and care.

"Oh, I talked to Lin about my old-days' stories, just killed time while you were away," said the old man to his wife. "By the way, what did you pray to the Buddha while at the temple?" he continued, smiling as he was eyeing his wife.

"Do I have to tell you, my old man?" His wife smiled and teased him lovingly. "What I pray is always between me and the Buddha. It is a secret, but I did thank him for sending you off from the battlefield, many moons ago, and then to me. Is it enough for you, sir?"

"I guess so, my dear wife," with a grin on his face, the old man told his soul mate contentedly as she headed to her place for the evening, the kitchen.

Lin felt inebriated as if he were inhaling a mixture of fragrances of the colorful blossoms from the garden he was in and being a part of. He never thought that it could be possible in real in life, at least in his own life. The memory of his own turmoil of conflict and of toxicity in his family at the village has never left him completely at all. It is like a thief, waiting for a right moment, right time to sneak in and to steal his peace, his innocent. The verbal and physical fighting between his parents and the abusiveness and hatred that his stepmother has had for him for years all now came back to him in the midst of this loving family and caring environment. When it happened, he felt the hurt, the pains surging from the bottom of his being, like a storm taking on a young tree, ruffling its leaves, and snapping the branches. He had been pushing this painful sore deep down at the bottom of his soul, but every now and then, it seems, it had its own way to surface and visit him. He had tried not to let it bother him, not even want to think about it, and he was successful in doing that for some time, but he could never get rid of it for good. Most of the times, it crept in, at night in his quiet place for a few minutes or so, until he decided not to let this unwelcomed visitor entertain him anymore. It was always a challenge. This evening was somewhat different. It was such a nice, tender, loving moment with his new family where he's enjoying, soaking in the tenderness of it; but then his mind flashed right back to the village paying a visit to his little brother whom he had not seen for a very long time. He knows he loves his brother, and he always does, but he never had a chance to express his love for him because of his stepmother's giant shadow that stands between them, like a rock-solid wall, making his reach impossible. He wants to hold his little brother again to smell his sun-baked smell of his hair and skin. He wants to hold him tightly in his arms, as he remembers, and from the bank of the river, when the sun was high above in the blue sky and where the water is always clear that he could see the white-brown-colored sand at the bottom, jumps off into the water for a laugh-cracking dip, like a sizable tree trunk, holding its chopped-off branch, falls straight into the water, splashing, and the two of them, like dolphins, spitting water from their mouths, bobbing to the shore. They both screamed out loud with joy from the top of their lungs. Well, not true. The first time, it was a big cry from his brother, scared for his life. But after that very first and frightened experience, his little brother has learned to trust his life on him, and it has always been fun to do those tumbling jumps into the water again and again. Oh, how much he misses this little brother of his. His whole being is now flooded with memory after memories of his early years. He sure does miss his dad. Yes, he loves his old man who seems to shows his love by always being tough and rough on him, slapped him, beat him, punished him to the point that he thought his father was cruel, never loved him or cared for him. But he knows very well that his old man loves him, and that is the very reason he was able come here to the city to go to school to begin his new life, and to ultimately break the shackle that chains many generations of his family before him to poverty and illiteracy. Lin is so grateful to his dad's sacrifice to let him have a chance to break away from the vice of his evil, mean, ill-spirited stepmother who does not want to have anything to do with him, alive or dead. She would preferably go for the latter. Lin also realizes that this was being done with much tension and friction between his parents to free him up for the opportunity of education for a better life. His father had probably seen the same pattern that was a continuation from the many generations before him now being imposed on Lin to continue that very cycle. Therefore, he felt compelled to do something different for his own son; perhaps, at least, the very first step is education, in sending him to school, despite the economic hardship, despite the friction, and opposition from his wife.

"It's worth the fight," his father must have thought and believed in the cause for his fight, for his son' sake.

Why all of a sudden he felt this flood of emotion attacking him? Surely this loving atmosphere of the host family had something to do with it. He wished he could have been next to his dad, his little brother and breathe this quiet, loving air in this house. He fought very hard to keep his tears where they belonged for he had promised himself that he would never cry for his situation, for his circumstance anymore. He should never feel pity for himself again. As his mother had told him years ago when he was very young, "Boys are not supposed to be soft with tears."

He got up, decided not to stay in this maudlin mode. He felt he had been wasting his time and energy on the things he could not have any control of. He should enjoy this tender moment he has had in this house. He was thinking of what his mother actually had said and meant was, "My boy, you shall be strong. Be tough like a man."

He felt the need to contribute his time and energy to the host family. He just needs his common sense, in addition to his own judgment, to do what needs to be done in the house and for the house. It is simply because if he ever asked, the lady of the house would say, "Son, what a good boy you are. But if you want to help me, do your schoolwork because it is what you are here for. Everything is being handled. No need to worry."

The best thing he could do is to show his gratitude to the family, and he must have good attitude for himself so that he could be a great company to the host family.

> The Moving Finger writes; and, having writ,
> Moves on: nor all thy Piety nor Wit
> Shall lure it back to cancel half a line,
> Nor all thy Tears wash out a Word of it.
> Omar Khayyam

The school year was coming to an end with much apprehension in the air as a result of the war, escalating in the region and around the country. The sounds of gunfire could be heard from the outskirt of the city and neighboring villages. The students, as many years in the past, have gone home with their families. The dorms now became empty and vacant. The school yard, the soccer field have now returned to their summertime of quiet and loneliness. But the principal's family and Mr. Nam's have decided to stay behind inside the school, for they felt safer to stay than to travel. News of wartime full of uncertainty was on the air at any given time. All you have to do is to turn on the radio, and you will instantly get the feel of war right next to you. You could almost smell gun smoke in the air. There have been incidents of ambushes where cars and buses were blown up on the road, and bridges were sabotaged and collapsed into the water, making traveling hazardous because bullets and mines are blind to see who is the enemy and who is not. For that reason, Lin was glad and grateful to see them around. He spent time with both families, specially with Cu and Be who really wanted him to be around like a big brother, playing, reading, and telling stories. The three of them would go on their bikes to the park under the hot sun and blue sky, sitting on a marble-surfaced bench under the thick, green canopy of an aged, giant banyan tree, listening to the birds singing, talking, arguing above. They, too, filled their hearts with joy and laughter, particularly with Lin who challenged Cu and Be if they could figure out what the birds were talking about up in the canopy. It was fun and challenging, for they had to listen to the birds. And each had to come up with an answer based on his or her imagination, something like what Cu said while mimicking a chirping bird, "I don't like bird school. It 's too crowded."

Be would jump in and said, "No, no, the bird school is closed for summer vacation, haha!" Be's cute girly voice imitated another bird up in the air as she would look up to the top of the tree. What an imagination! They all had a great time with the game.

Besides this type of games, the trio would visit the flower patch displaying its beauty under the sunny, blue sky, with butterflies on their wings, landing on colorful flowers from crimson peonies to red roses, from yellow chrysanthemums to pink irises and many more that all seemed to be competing to show off their charms and splendors. With all things, Be was showing her most interest in flowers. She would take her time slowly touch each flower or caress and cup it in her dainty hands and bend down, closing her eyes for a kiss and to enjoy its fragrance. Lin, all of a sudden, noticed that Be had become much more quiet than she used to, and her eyes would gaze into far distance lands in the horizon, dreaming. He sometimes wondered what she had in her mind. What she was thinking of? A handsome prince in a castle of faraway lands, as children story or fairy tale goes and told? Whatever the change is taking place in her, he liked it too. He did not know why, but he did. Little did he know that he had become an observer of the changes, and sometimes, the observed and observer are the same.

"Brother Lin, would you like to go fishing with me?" asked Cu, cutting off his daydreaming thoughts. "I know a creek down the hill, at the other side of the park." Cu pointed his finger to the bottom of the hill where the creek snakes through the fallen trees and bushes. Lin then remembered that he had been to this beautiful green pasture once, with his art class from the school, to capture the scenery on the canvas, with landscape of the bluish-green hillside and its farming valley with cows and water buffaloes on their feeds. He remembered setting up an easel nearby the creek, and he could hear the running water like soft music of nature on the side. While working on the art project, he could occasionally hear the fish jumping off the water, playing or perhaps teasing him. He had completely forgotten not only about this place, but also the whole thing with fishing in general.

"Oh yes! I would love to. Besides, I know that spot, that creek. I was there with my art class working on an outdoors project not too long ago," Lin told him.

"We could go tomorrow if you wanted to." Cu looked at him, smiled, and continued, "I think Professor Nguyen and my dad would want go too. I heard them talk about going fishing a few days ago."

Hmm, Lin thought it was interesting, *the two old men get together for a fishing expedition?*

It took him a few seconds to figure it out how it all came about. They both grew up in the south where fish and rice were plenty. Rivers, swamps, and rice paddies are miles and miles alongside of the roads in the Mekong delta, which is known as the food depot for the South Vietnam. It is said that the fish in this region are so abundant that one can just easily scoop them up from the water with a basket. The farmers, men and women and their children, all know how to catch fish, from using bamboo traps to nylon nets or to pole fishing. Because of this living condition, which is far much easier than that of other parts of the country, and it is also said that the southerners are more generous and easygoing than those from other areas of the country, Lin could see some truth to it with those who have opened their hearts to him. Given the wartime circumstance as they were in, they must have felt they were all trapped to where they were, and perhaps they wanted to find ways to relax themselves and to find food and fun as they used to when they were much younger in the south.

"Are you kidding? Tomorrow? I can't wait," Lin told Cu with all excitement in his voice as if he were screaming. The fisherman in him had just come alive. His imagination immediately took him back to the village, the river, where he had had the fun of pulling a fish in with his pole, feeling the fight of the fish at the end of the line, and he had caught plenty.

As the three were heading home on their bikes, side by side, on the quiet road back to the school building, Lin noticed Be was very quiet, unlike Cu, who was excitedly talking about the fishing as if he were yanking one off the water. He turned to her and said, "Sis, you like fishing?"

"Boring!" she said, and it was in her voice too. Lin did not understand how in the world fishing could be boring. How can the excitement of reeling in the fish be boring? How can catching the food for the family to enjoy be boring? Maybe that is the difference between boy and girl, man and woman, husband and wife. Maybe that is why his parents were fighting most of the time because elements of mutual understanding and appreciation were absent at home.

He wanted to say something to bring her back to her happy old days, but did not know how. The reality is those days were gone, and she has changed too.

The fishing day came. He had been told to come early, and it was going to be a whole-day event, a whole day for just fishing, and there he came. He did not know he was in for a big surprise because the principal, Mr. Quang, was there too. He felt more like going on a picnic than a fishing trip even thought everyone was carrying a pole in his hand. The three elders—Mr. Nam, Mr. Quang, and Professor Nguyen—were on their white shorts, which made him feel like they were ready for a sports match, a tennis game, perhaps. Nonetheless, they were all happy to see Lin a part of the fishing team, for they all know his background, a fisher boy! Lin felt the pride to be among them, his teachers, whom he knows he could always learn from even outside of the classroom. At the same time, he could feel the pressure that he imposed on himself to produce results, that is, to catch fish. Just before they took off, Be handed him and Cu each a bag of fruits and snacks for the group. Lin looked at her with a grateful gaze and softly said a thank you to her before he paddled off to follow the crowd.

Lin was surprised or, to correctly put, amazed at the fact the elders were experts in preparing their lines and poles, and within minutes after arriving at the creek, they were able to get their lines into the water at separate spots, which tells him how good they are about the fishing. Lin left a big pot full of worms, which he and Cu had dug up the evening before, off the bank of the creek where everyone could get to it.

It is said that "in fishing, one can learn a lesson; the lesson of patience, and it is a virtue." Now the waiting game began as the sun was rising high up on the horizon. A few stretches of white clouds spread like thin cotton, floating in the clear-blue sky, promising a beautiful day and perhaps a good fishing day as well. It was quiet except a few birds chirping, buzzing from one bush to another. All eyes focused on the almost invisible thin lines, waiting. Every now and then a fish jumped off the water, splashing, making their presence known to the fishermen, teasing, not biting, as if saying, "You just have to wait—lunchtime."

The clear water, which streams off from the top of the mountains faraway, flows lazily between fallen trees and decaying logs, creating a perfect nesting place for fish of many kinds to hang around, playing, chasing on their prey. "The big fish feeds on the little ones," the saying goes, and how true too; it is in the world of human! The meek, the weak, and the helpless become victims and preys to the ones with power, bullied by the ones that are physically bigger, stronger. He realized he was, too, a disadvantaged one.

Lin, after a while with no bites on his line, left the spot where he was, left everyone at theirs; and with his pole, he walked upstream and gingerly, like a monkey, effortlessly leaped on the trunk of a tree that fell across the water. A strong current from the previous monsoon seasons must have pushed it to rest diagonally downward the stream. At the one end of the tree, where all the branches are under the water, he could see a school of baby fish, dark-pink colored, flocking, hiding behind the branches, and they were so many, so thick that it made the water look burgundy pink. That big chunk of colored water moved like a piece of deep-red, delicate, silk kerchief, twirling under the water every time the whole school of fish moved in unison, with a speed. It is quite fascinatingly beautiful, a feast to his eyes just to marvel at this phenomenon of the world of fish. Standing on the tree, his eyes were fixed at what he saw under the water as if he were being hypnotized by the school of fish. With the mind of a fisherman, he rushed to the thinking corner of his brain and asked this question: "Where is the mother of these millions of babies? She has to be here with her babies." He stood there in that spot for a long while, debating, whether or not to lower his line with a fresh worm on the hook to the mother fish. *A nice dinner with a big fish on the plate? A million baby fish without a mother?*

He quietly walked away back to the other end of the tree and jumped off to the bank of the creek. All of a sudden, he lost interest in catching fish. He saw himself as one of the baby ones that would be without a mother, if he lowered the bait.

Lin sauntered slowly to check on the elders to see if they had caught anything, had any luck. They all had moved and spread out farther from their spots, still standing, quietly focusing on their lines as if meditating on the fun or the boredom of the fishing, or they were imagining the fish that came, touched, sniffed at the worm and slowly shook his big head then swam away. Each nodded his head, smiled, and acknowledged his coming but stayed silent as if the creatures underwater would be scared if he said anything. However, as soon as Cu saw him, he excitedly told him that he had lost a big, black mud trout as he was pulling it in. He said, "It was a big one, brother." He showed the size of the lost fish with his hands and a big smile on his face. "I am going to get him this time," he continued enthusiastically.

At the end of the day when the five fishermen, seasoned and amateur ones, got on their two-wheelers peddling home, they had caught nothing. One said he had no bites, other a few nibbles, and one lost, a typical story of fishing games. Sometimes you gain; sometimes you lose. But the relaxation is indefinable. Despite everything else, no fish to take home to show Be, to prove his time out there was a worthwhile. Lin, however, felt that he had caught the biggest one in his lifetime.

It was during snack time, a break from the focusing on the fishing line, dreaming that it would, at any moment, be straightened, pulled, and bend the pole, or contemplating on life events, the teachers, the elders, all sat on a log on a patch of green grass, by the creek under the shade of a small mahogany tree, to enjoy some fruits of the day. They then talked about their concerns, the nervousness, and their anxiety because of the war, which had been escalating, spreading to many parts of the country. They talked about their childhood years, growing up in the south with many fond memories from the fields in the countryside to the schools in the city, and from the sweet memories of the younger days to their reality. Of course, the not-so-good reality of the day is that they were unable to catch one single fish, and they were disappointed.

"This is not a good day. It is pathetic! What should we tell our wives, our cooks?" Mr. Nam jokingly told his friends.

They then analyzed the possibility of different types of baits that were not attracted to the fish, the one for freshwater versus the saltwater one.

They all agreed based on their own experiences that worm is universal. It should work anywhere and everywhere there is a river, a pond or a lake, on the planet.

While listening to the conversation among the elders, Mr. Nguyen, the oldest of the three, whose observation of life events, whose insight and wisdom on his own life experiences were solidly rich, stood up, slowly walked on the grass away from the log, and as a teacher would do, he gave his lecture on the subject of the day.

"As I said earlier, worm is the universal bait. Not only is it a bait to catch fish, but also a guru that we, as human beings, must and need to learn from," explained Professor Nguyen. What a bold statement! Lin thought.

"How can this tiny, squirmy, slimy creature be a teacher for all of us when it is just as simple as a bait for fishing?" the professor posed a question to his friends in his conversational tone of voice, as if his audience were at the dinner table at his house. Perhaps, he was thinking of something of importance that he could not wait to share in a classroom? Gentle breezes coming in from the open grass field helped the open classroom stay focused on what's coming out of the professor's mouth. The sun was now high on the clear summer-blue sky. One or two sparrows exchanged their chirping on top of the tall tree nearby like soft music in the background.

"Think about this for a second," the professor continued with his insight. "Worm is the only creature that we know of when being cut in two halves, it becomes two whole worms. Did you ever notice that? Yes, two complete new whole worms. There, my friends, it is such a powerful transformational metaphor for us human beings to ponder." All became quiet. The birds stopped making any sounds. The time seemed to stand still. The professor's eyes are on his petite audience while other elders were slightly nodding their heads, thinking and absorbing the wisdom in silence. Lin felt like there's a thousand watts lightbulb that went glowing inside his head as the professor continued with his wisdom.

"I think the wisdom of the worm does not stop right there, but, rather, a long march into the hearts of mankind. Let me paraphrase what William Blake, the English poet, says in his poem. In fact, what I am telling you right now, my dear friends, is what I was inspired by this beautiful human being, a man, who was born in 1757 and grew up thousands miles from us, who had such a profound insight and observation on this tiny creature, a worm. He then wrote in one of the famous lines of his poetry as follows: 'The cut worm forgives the plow.'"

Lin felt the cool gentle breezes caressing his face as the six short words sank deep into his soul, like a glass of cool refreshing lemonade on the hot summer day.

"Let us explore a little farther, and let us stretch our imagination to the scene in which the worm utters those powerful words, shan't we?" The professor continued his lecture to his four students in the open-sky classroom. "Here is a worm, peacefully enjoying his life in his underground dwelling, moving about as freely as he wishes, safe from storms and hurricanes. One day, he felt, all of a sudden, his dwelling was rocking, rumbling like in a thunderstorm, getting turned upside down, sideway, and then tossed up in the air and down again. He tried with all of his strength to run, to get away from the shinning blade of a plow that was quickly approaching. But it was too late; the cold, senseless metal blade had caught him, cut him in halves, not equal in length. He turned, he twisted, he wiggled as his blood was oozing from his tubal bodies. Bloody he was, hurtful he was, devastated he was. However, in his brokenness, he looked at the shinning blade, the one that caused him so much pain, the one that wanted to destroy his life, and said, 'I forgive you!'"

As he uttered those three forgiving words without knowing their power, their magic, he immediately recognized the blessings and the healing for he had become two complete worms. The bleeding had stopped. The cutting had made him multiple, and most profoundly, he realized the very purpose of his existence: *I am the food for others, for the fish under the water, and for the birds above the ground.* Only in shattered and brokenness did he discover this amazingly beautiful paradox of life.

The professor's voice had trailed off to the end of his lecture. The auditorium stayed silent, no hand clapping, no standing ovation. Only the birds were flying, zooming by, singing, making their voices heard in the air as if they had been listening to it too.

Did Lin hear the triumphant music playing in his head? Did he hear the trumpet, the horn, and the singing? Yes, he heard them all, like an orchestra welcoming him home from the battlefield of pains and hurt for a long time. Chocked up with joy, Lin got up, with tears now welled up in his eyes, walked over to the professor, and said, "Thank you, master, for your powerful words of wisdom that have truly, at last, set me free." And as he said that, he felt something was not normal; he noticed something was out of ordinary. There is something about the way the elders looked at one another, something in their eyes that tells him, "A staged, a show, a setup to set him free."

Before the professor had a chance to response, Lin asked the elders, "Is it a planned fishing trip just for me, my teachers?"

"Son, yes, it is," answered Mr. Nam. "We all know you had a terrible, unloving childhood; you had been in pains for so long even though you tried to suppress or deny it. We had talked about you. We really wanted to help you out but did not know how. Knowing that you love fishing, and we did not have much to do to make our time worthwhile, Professor Nguyen felt that we could put a trip together, and he could use his wisdom and knowledge to lift you up and set you free from the bondage that your stepmother had chained you, shackled, and imprisoned you for a long time."

"Even though we did not catch even one little fish," Professor Nguyen joined in with his pinky up in the air to prove his point, "however, we landed the biggest one perhaps in our lifetime as teachers and educators. We had just fished our dearest Lin out of the river of his painful past, don't we all agree?"

The faces of all men, young and old, all brightened with smiles in unison, nodding their heads.

"I am so proud of you for, even at your age, have grasped the wisdom, the beauty from the slimy, squirmy worm," said the professor, as he turned to Lin, with his biggest smile for his accomplishment, of unveiling the light, of showing the beauty behind the shadow of Lin's life. Professor Nguyen was very pleased at the outcome of the whole fishing trip, in which, through a humble, yet a powerful metaphor, he was able to help Lin to penetrate and go beyond the darkness of his stormy past and to finally find the meaning of his eventful life. Just like the worm, not only does he forgive the plow, but he also appreciates the painful and bloody cut so that he has blossomed into meaningful lives.

The Epiphany

"Mom, I have found you at last," Lin said to his mom as he was lying in bed inside the white mosquito net, which was cascading down from the ceiling at the far corner of the room in the silence of the night. The tears of joy covered his face, strolling down to his neck, as he was talking to his mom, believing to be with him inside the net.

"I know now why you have left me, so that your will, your desire, and your mission of molding me, shaping me, making me a person you wanted me to become could be accomplished. For so long I have blamed you for dying on me; for so long I have blamed you for leaving me at my very tender age, and for so long I have blamed you for abandoning me to a painful and turbulent storm of my early life. I am so sorry, Mom. I now know why you have left me. Just like an iron alloy in the hands of a blacksmith, it gets to go through a series of the processing, from the softening it in the heat of an amber, glowing coal oven, to the hammering, bending, and the pounding before it gets molded into an useful tool, so too, you have used the iron hands of my stepmother to give me the experience of pains, to give me the taste of my own tears, and to let me feel my agony of abandonment before I could find the meaning of my life. Thank you, Mom, for guiding me to my awakening and, at last, my blessings."

"I love you, son." Lin could hear the soft voice of his mother whispering to his ears, and he felt her hands barely touch his cheeks as she kissed him good night.

Quick note of confession: The author, Lien Le, is Lin.
Spokane, November 18, 2012
Lien Le

Epilogue

"What makes the light light?" was one of the questions in the final exams in my high school year.

It seems so easy to the point that one may look at this very question and blurt out "What a question! Or, perhaps, it should not be a question at all for its plainness and simplicity."

Your answer might be, as our answers at that time, that it's the fuel, electricity, or the wick that makes the light light.

However, as it turned out, many of us flunked the test. The right answer should have been: "The darkness is what it makes the light light." In other words, light needs darkness to bring out light!

Why in the world did we miss such a profound wisdom?

Throughout my life, beginning with an unloving, abusive childhood, only until my adult years did I understand that the unloving, the abusiveness must have happened so that I could see the brightness, the blessings of my life.

There is a reason for it to have come in my life so that I can find the meaning of my life, and it allows me to see the beauty beyond the shadow, beyond the dark cloud.